THOMAS MERTON, BROTHER MONK

THOMAS MERTON
Brother Monk

The
Quest
for
True
Freedom

M. BASIL
PENNINGTON
O.C.S.O.

Continuum • New York

1998

The Continuum Publishing Company
370 Lexington Avenue
New York, NY 10017

Grateful acknowledgment is made to the Merton Legacy Trust
for permission to quote previously unpublished Merton material.

Printed in the United States of America

ISBN 0-8264-1012-X
Library of Congress Catalog Card Number 97-065115

To my brothers, THE MONKS OF GETHSEMANI, who have given to the Order and to the Church the gift of THOMAS MERTON, with deep gratitude, respect, and affection.

Contents

Introduction

A quiet, almost tentative knock sounded at the door. According to the practice of the Cistercians at the time, I gave a couple of sharp raps on the wooden side of the bed table. The conspirator entered. The room was Spartan in style. If I was to stand up and stretch my arms out, I would hit both side walls. Its length went only a couple of feet beyond the foot of my cotlike bed. The white stucco walls were bare save for a small crucifix; the window had only a blind, no drape or curtain. A small writing table and a straight back chair — and the picture was complete. This was Gethsemani, 1964 — the guesthouse, not the monastery itself. The monks did not yet have private rooms. The man probably most responsible for their getting them was standing before me, but he would be dead by the time they got them.

This was the first time I had laid eyes on Thomas Merton. He was all smile. Even his bald head seemed to make way for his smile; a big, broad, boyish, almost impish grin — the grin his friend Gene Meatyard would later capture when he gave Tom his first camera.

On this occasion it was also an apologetic smile. I was lying in bed with a fever, too sick to go downstairs to the sessions of the regional meeting that had brought me from my monastery at Spencer to Gethsemani Abbey. But the conspirator had an important document in hand that he wanted to place in my hands. I noticed that CONFIDENTIAL was printed prominently on the title page, but I also noted that the confidential document was mimeographed, and I wondered how many hundreds of others were in on the secret.

The scene was so typical of Tom. The matter was, indeed, weighty, but the situation was shot through with a certain humor. I will often use the name by which I knew my friend —'Tom.' He was known in the world as Thomas Merton. His name in the order was Father M. Louis. Or, to be more precise, Nonnus Ludovicus. A little plaque with that name inscribed on it hangs prominently on the wall of the main room of his heritage, by the entrance to the back rooms, his more private space. It had symbolic importance for Tom. The plaque was first made to hang over the entrance of his little cubicle in the common dormitory, the only private space the young monk had in all the world. Much of Tom's monastic life would be marked by the struggle to establish some truly private space in which to find the freedom to be to the rest of creation in the way that he wanted to be present, rather than in the way that someone or something or some circumstance demanded that he be present. The name Ludovicus is Latin for Louis—Tom had been given, probably because of his French background, Saint Louis, king of France, as his patron when he entered the Cistercian order in 1941.

I think that in many ways the name Tom best fits my friend and brother monk. Tom came across as a regular guy, one easy to be with, easy to talk to. When you were with him, you had his whole attention. He made you feel important and really worthy of his attention. At the same time he seemed to have little sense of how important he was.

As open and friendly as he was, Tom was at the same time a very private person. That might seem to be a strange thing to say about a person who has published an autobiography and several personal journals. Yet, as the monks of Gethsemani and any friend of Tom's would point out, there are dimensions of him that never seem to be sufficiently expressed in his writings: his wonderful humor, his humanity, his profound depth, and his almost infinite compassion. He was a warm, loving, joyful, present person.

Given the wealth of biographical material that is to be found in the Mertonian corpus, anyone who wants to get to know Thomas Merton has an immense amount of printed matter with which to work. Because Tom was such a rich personality, a man who never ceased to press the edges, to expand his vast field of interests, there is more to him as he appears in his writings than we can hope to grasp. Yet there is much about him that never got into the written word. His published works were all carefully edited, not only by him but by others, including censors of his order.

The Seven Storey Mountain is a good example of how selection and editing filter the image that comes through to us. This autobiography is one of the primary sources for getting to know Tom in his earlier years. However, his novel, *My Argument with the Gestapo*, adds much to it, as do some of his poems; they help us get in deeper touch with the feelings that are behind what we find recorded in the autobiography. The *Secular Journal,* which can be amplified by the unpublished journals from which he extracted it, also adds tone, as well as some additional information. Beyond these published materials, we have several manuscripts of *The Seven Storey Mountain.* The Boston manuscript, which Tom sent to his friend Francis Sweeney, an aspiring Jesuit poet, contains sections not found in the New York manuscript, which Merton gave to Sister Therese Lentfoehr. This latter in turn has material not found in the published volumes. Some of this unpublished material Sister Therese has made available in selective articles. There is to my knowledge, however, no extant manuscript that contains all the material suppressed by the censors of our order.

A case in point is the matter of Tom's son. Although there is much circumstantial evidence as to this child's existence, to the extent that many authors have asserted it, there is nothing extant from the pen of Merton to affirm it. It is a matter that was suppressed by a censor of the order. At the time Father Louis was writing *The Seven Storey Mountain,* after his first profession, he was sharing a room with one of his fellow novices, who was by then also professed. Father Anthony had been ordained a priest before he entered. Shortly after his profession he was put to work teaching theology to his fellow monks who were studying for the priesthood. As a teacher, Father Anthony needed work space, so he and Frater Louis were given a room where their desks stood side by side. Because of his theological competence and past experience, Father Anthony was named one of the censors of the order for the English (American) language. Hence it became his task to censor *The Seven Storey Mountain.* The guidelines for the censors of the order were not spelled out in detail. Although ecclesiastical censors, who also went over Merton's writings before they were published, were to examine the works only for doctrinal error, the censors of the order seemed to have a broader mandate, or at least they thought they did. Father Louis, through the years, suffered much from this vagueness. Censors attacked his work on many levels. One even declared him an incompetent writer who should take some courses in English before he attempted to publish anything. The question of propriety and the good image of the order constantly came up with the censors. Needless to say, this would have been an issue with regard to Tom's son.

As Frater Louis typed out the pages of *The Seven Storey Mountain,* he tossed them over onto Father Anthony's desk, so that Father could read them at his convenience and then send them on to the other censor, Father Gabriel, a monk of my community. When Tom's unfolding story told of the pregnancy, Father Anthony, a gentle, pastoral priest with much experience, was not particularly surprised. Tom would certainly not have been the first Cistercian who had fathered a child before he entered the monastery. It was something I always checked on as a vocation father, to be sure, if there was a child involved, that his or her needs were being met. Usually an adoption had secured the child's future and it was best or even required that the father be out of the picture. Father Anthony, without raising any objections, sent the material on to Father Gabriel. Gabriel's reaction was quite different from Anthony's. He felt that it would not be edifying for the faithful if they learned that a monk had at one time fathered a child. He wrote Frater Louis that he must delete the passage. Tom, fairly new at the censorship game, wrote back to Father that if it was all right for Saint Augustine to be known to have had a son out of wedlock, he didn't see why it was so scandalous in his case. Father Gabriel's response was terse: "You're no St. Augustine." I suspect the emphasis on the word *saint.* In any case, that bit of *The Seven Storey Mountain* disappeared, never to be seen again. Perhaps someday it will show up, as have some other things, on the back of something Tom typed later.

In his legacy Merton sealed certain of his writings for twenty-five years or longer. Expectations in regard to this reserved material seem to be extravagant. Those who have worked with it extensively say that it will, in fact, add little to what is already known.

Another limiting factor comes into play in getting to know Thomas Merton. Some of the deeper dimensions of his spirit, which are revealed in his poetry and prose, can be grasped only by those with a certain intuition or sensitivity or those who have had a similar experience. What one of the great Cistercian Fathers, Bernard of Clairvaux, once wrote, could have been said by Tom in regard to these shared insights: Those who have experienced these things know what I am talking about, and those who haven't—well, have the experience and then you will.

The need for a certain comparable experience to open the meaning of some of the material is in part the cause and justification of this book. *The Seven Mountains of Thomas Merton,* the authorized biography by Michael Mott, to which I owe a great debt, is especially good in describing the first part of Tom's life. Mott had some similar experiences in growing up. This is not the case, however, with regard to Tom's later experience as a monk and contemplative. Mott quotes a friend of Merton's to the effect that she was confused by Tom's many interests and activities in the last years of his life. I think that in quoting her, Mott was expressing something of his own feelings. How Tom perceived and experienced the unity of all through his contemplative experience of their one Source is not something that Mott seems to have grasped. Such unity of comprehension gives a person immense freedom in responding to all the varied aspects of his or her life and its complex context.

As one looking in from the outside, Michael Mott does an exceptionally good job of not misrepresenting the monastic way of life. Yet in weaving in the immense plethora of events in Tom's life, the woof of the fabric, the everyday life of the monk, seems to be almost lost. This is understandable. As Tom himself noted in the introduction to one of the last journalistic compilations he prepared for publication, his own journals concentrate on special events and say little about what took up most of his time, energy, and interest: the daily search for, and resting in, the experience of God, the way to true freedom. If many writers have found and portrayed Tom as a restless soul, it is because they have not seen his search in its context of an abiding contemplative experience. I think it takes one who has lived the monastic life to understand how this apparently restricted existence gives one the freedom to be and to be to all without fragmentation.

Father Louis's fellow monks have already shared a good bit about him. There is especially the excellent collection edited by his secretary, Brother Patrick Hart, *Thomas Merton/Monk: A Monastic Tribute.* But as the present abbot of Gethsemani, Timothy Kelly, wrote in *The Canadian Catholic Review,* it is not easy to write about a very personal relationship, especially when it was not experienced as something extraordinary, just as a rich, supportive friendship with a fellow monk. Tom was exceptional, very exceptional. And yet, on the whole, he was held and treated as just another member of the community, a very much loved member, loved more than he realized, but still just one of the monks. He had some colorful eccentricities—

good stories can be told about him—but was not seen as special. As a brother monk who lived the same Cistercian life at the same moment in history but a bit removed, I can fill in some of the lacunae, which will perhaps enable us to see Thomas Merton more integrally, more fully in context, more deeply.

Tom is a vast source of knowledge, wisdom, and life. No book can hope to bring forth all the riches of his gift to us. I would like to concentrate on a theme that has fundamental importance in his life and in the life of every person, above all every person baptized into Christ: the quest for true freedom. I want to set forth something of the richness of Tom's understanding of freedom and then trace the way he grew into it. I think this will not only give us some deep insight into Merton—as Abbot Timothy states so directly and simply in his article, "He was a free man,"—but also will enable us, monk or layperson, to get in touch with some of our own deeper aspirations, our own inner longings. It was because Merton was so in touch with his own life as being that of everyman (and everywoman—Tom lived and wrote in a time that was not yet sensitized to the sexism in the language we use; I am sure he would have quickly grasped the problem and have become sensitive to it in his writing) and was able to share that so well, that he has been one of the most significant spiritual masters of our time.

I had the privilege of serving my community as vocation father, the monk who interviews men who come with an interest in joining our community and then helps them prepare to enter if it seems the right life for them. In the course of three years I spoke with about 1300 candidates. Not one of them had not been touched by Thomas Merton.

As we all know, though, Tom does not speak only to men and women interested in monastic life, or only to Catholics. As I write this I think of Charles Clement, a doctor from Salinas, California. A young Quaker, he went to minister within the guerrilla-held territory in El Salvador. As he went he carried on his back seventy-five pounds of medical supplies and three books—one of them Merton's.

Tom's books continue to sell by the millions. The tapes we have of his talks are much appreciated. A television documentary on him was widely acclaimed. Conferences and seminars continue in a steady stream. Retreats and study weeks and university courses are constantly being offered across the United States and in other countries as well. Recently I received a letter pointing out that the case for the canonization of Padre Pio, who died in the same year as Merton, has been introduced at Rome. The writer wanted to know when we were going to introduce Tom's cause. I have little doubt that Tom is now a saint in the kingdom of heaven, but when it comes to the idea of canonization I think I can hear that wonderful hearty laugh we all liked so well. Unless that institution, which he loved with a very loyal love even while he did such a good job of taking it to task, begins to appreciate his insightful criticism, I do not think it will ever find him appropriate for canonization. Merton will never fill the bill as a plaster of paris saint. Rather, he is the kind of saint we can hope to be: a very human person with an ample share of the human's earthy flaws, yet a person who believes in one's own call to sanctity. Flawless saints somehow seem to shorten the mercy and wonderfulness of our God.

Each of us, as we listen to Thomas Merton, can come to realize how deep is our longing for true freedom, the freedom to be who we truly are and to do the things we are meant to do. This takes courage and openness. There is little value in reading about and admiring Thomas Merton's courageous quest, if we do not let it speak to our own lives. The quest for freedom is an unending one, and it is where we find our true selves. We images of God are more than we can ever comprehend. We want to live freely and powerfully out of the fullness we have so far found, using that as the source for finding even more. Sad would be the day when we latched onto some lesser image—lesser than all the fullness of God—and made that the perimeter of our ideal. It would inevitably be far short of the reality. We would be condemning ourselves to truncation. We are meant for more—always more.

Years have flowed by, time has marched on. Like any prophet, Merton was in many ways ahead of his time. Like any deep theologian, he belongs to all times. Like any true contemplative, his vision flows from the eternal now.

Yet Thomas Merton was a man. Much of his attractiveness lies in the fact that he was, indeed, a person of flesh and blood, body and feeling, time and place. And all these elements, though they touch the basic and perennial human, are of passing moment. Tom has passed on. He would be the first to proclaim it.

Many authors have emphasized and traced out Merton's remarkable development or evolution, especially during his monastic years. Everything validates our expectation that he would have continued to evolve. But in what way? Father Flavian ventured to speculate on one occasion that because of Father Louis' basic, romantic love of the monastic life he first found at Gethsemani, he would have evolved somewhat as did his friend Jacques Maritain, whose final book many wrote off as the fond reveries of an old man, a return to the past. If pressed, I do not think Father Flavian would hold too strongly to that opinion, given the fact of Father Louis' great openness, which flowed from an inner self constantly renewed at the Source of all life. But I have no desire here to speculate on what Merton might say today, where he might be, what he might be doing if he were still on the journey of life. I see him rather as a source and starting place. Our thoughts on the basics so coincide that it would not be surprising if our evolving thought ran on similar tracks. But I will make no claim to that. Tom never ceased to assert that all insight and all contemplative experience that sources our insight are gifts. And this gift comes from the God of surprises. All life, if this be true, is a response to him. There is a consistency in the way God leads us by his call and grace. And yet there is, to say the least, an imaginative creativity. To what would God have called Thomas Merton in these succeeding years? That is a secret happily hidden in the wondrous depths of the Divine.

Ultimately, what Father Louis was about was life, love, truth, being, a celebration of what is. In other words, God. That is what I want to underline in this book. His whole life was a quest for freedom—the freedom to be open to the wonderful reality that God has made, to God himself, to what is! To find that freedom, he entered upon or was led to enter upon what seems like one of the most restrictive lives possible, an enclosed monastic life based on a primitive ideal as interpreted by a post-Reformation Jansenist outlook. He chose not just the Cistercian life, but the Order of Cistercians of the Stricter Observance. We will look at this paradoxical—and successful—quest for freedom.

There is an immense litany of persons whom I must acknowledge. Father Louis' community of yesterday and today, especially the abbots and Tom's secretary, but so many more. The wonderful Naomi Burton Stone. If anyone can be called Tom's lifetime friend, it is she, the sister he never had. She enjoys quoting a remark Tom made about her "damned mothering way." And there is Tommie O'Callaghan—it is easy to see why Tom loved her so much. I was beneficiary of Bob Daggy's devotion to the Merton collection and to those who come to Louisville to use it, as well as the generous service of the custodians of the collections in Boston and New York. My own community's support has been important in this as in all I undertake. And the wonderful space to grow and experience Merton that was opened for me by my former abbot, Dom Thomas Keating, himself a great spiritual master and a true father and friend to me. The sharings with Tom's many friends have always been joyfully enriching. I recall the afternoon by the pool with Ping Ferry, the night in a Harlem shelter with Jim Forest, the annual ecumenical meetings with Douglas Steere (who wrote the introduction for Tom's last book), Jack Nelson, and Glenn Hinson, and the wonderful hospitality in the shadow of Canterbury Cathedral in the home of Canon Allchin. Father Flavian said of the friendship between Tom and Dom Jean Leclercq, "I never saw two persons so congenial." I, too, have benefited from that wonderful congeniality. There are so many others who have added their bit: Louis Bouyer, who lived with Tom in Strasbourg so many, many years ago, and Sergius Bolshakoff, the amiable Russian émigré and ecumenist—Tom wrote the introduction for his book *Russian Mystics*. I am conscious of bringing to these pages the gift of many, and I am grateful to each one of them. A special word of thanks to Father Flavian, Father John Eudes, and Brother Patrick, who have been kind enough to read the manuscript, offer valuable advice, and keep me from odd little inaccuracies. Whatever failures remain are fully my own.

And finally, I want to thank Tom for the most precious gift of his friendship and for all that he has given to us through his life and his sharing of that life in his writings. It is in communing with him in God that I think I have benefited the most.

M. Basil Pennington, o.c.s.o.

1. The Monk's Day

In the fall of 1967, having completed his editing of *A Vow of Conversation*, Tom began preparing an edition of his 1966 journal for publication. By this time he was using a tape recorder. He read from the journal, editing as he went along. To the edited journal he had prefixed a note:

On this tape I want to read some sections from a journal kept in 1966, a journal about what goes on in a hermitage, to a great extent. The best thing that goes on in a hermitage is nothing, and so you can't put nothing down. So therefore whatever is put down is usually the second best: that is to say, things about reading, things about work, things about messing around, and also occasional visits of people. One thing that this journal may give the impression of is that there are constant visitors, but in point of fact this is misleading because I have a tendency to put down visitors on account of the fact that that means something had happened and something is to be put down. But as I said, the best of the journal is not put down because it is what does not happen.

This passage refers specifically to life in the hermitage, but what it says is equally true of life within the community: monastic life "takes on two forms . . . some see it more in terms of a simple service in the cloister, liturgical prayer, and active work around the house. Others see it more in terms of solitary meditation and direct listening. But the contrast between these two should not be exaggerated; they're really doing pretty much the same thing."

"The best thing that goes on . . . is nothing." It is the spaces, when we simply are to God and he is to us. It is the daily routine, which becomes a transparent sacrament of God's presence and the connatural vehicle of our being present to him. This is what is important. It is the context for everything else. If the multitude of recorded happenings are not seen in this context, finding their fuller meaning in it and flowing out of it, then they are in danger of being misconstrued, at least insofar as to what they truly meant in the life of the monk Thomas Merton. Attentiveness to God is "not just a particular state or a peculiar kind of recollection, but it is part and parcel of love in everyday life."

Everyday life at Gethsemani when Tom entered in 1941 and for many years after that was very full indeed. A look at it in detail will shed much light on many of the things Tom has written, his feelings, his struggles, and his stresses, as well as what nourished his creativity.

Every schedule begins with going to bed. The night's sleep we get or do not get greatly colors the day. The possibility for a good night's sleep in a Cistercian dormitory in the 1940s for one who had had a long, hard day and was worn out by fasting and labor was good. Exhaustion could win out over all the obstacles. Tom at times did put in some hearty hours chopping wood, helping with the harvest, and so on. But early in his monastic career half his work time began to be devoted to writing of one sort or another, and some days all of his work time was. There was little to exhaust him physically. Sleep did not come easily.

The obstacles to sleep were many. His bed was four planks supporting a sack of straw. It seemed no matter how tightly the straw was originally packed — and I can remember fervent novices throwing their whole body weight into packing the mattresses — it rather quickly began to take on the contours of the monk's body with always a few extra odd bumps to make it more interesting. This "mattress" was covered with a sheet of material that might be any color or quality; durability and cheapness dictated the purchase of the cloth. Usually there was a sufficient allotment of blankets for the cooler Kentucky nights in the unheated dorm. The straw-filled pillow could be whacked and folded into some sort of comfortable shape.

Sleeping in one's clothing felt nice and snug on a cold winter's night — though the monk could get fairly well tied up in them if he tossed and turned in his sleep — but in the summer's heat, it was another story. The monastic wardrobe of the 1940s had hardly changed since the 1140s. There was a shirt without cuff or collar, drawers that tied at the waist and below the knees, leggings held up by the drawer strings and reaching down to cover the heel, and socks, all of the same sort of material used for the sheets. During World War II recycled flour sacks were sometimes used as material. Over this toe-to-neck covering was a full-length wool robe and a wool scapular, with a hood attached, that reached to below the knees. Both the robe and scapular were held tight about the waist by a leather (for the professed monks) or cloth belt. On top of all this the monk wore his ample, full-length wool cowl with its enormous sleeves. In all, he had enough clothing for at least three or four people; certainly ten times more clothing than any reasonable person would wear on a hot Kentucky night.

Mitigations were beginning to come in when Thomas Merton entered. There began to be an extra shirt for work, and then a work smock. Before that, for work the monk just fastened up the hems of his long robe with an intricate system of strings. He wore the same robe around the clock and slept in the day's sweat, adding the night's to it. Underclothing was changed once a week in summer, once every two weeks in winter; showers and baths were virtually unknown. In the early 1950s a new abbot general came from France to visit the American houses in the summertime. He spent his first night in the monastery in Conyers, Georgia. This rather ample monk later reported that he had tried sleeping on the bathroom floor—he had the bishop's suite—in his underclothing, with the shower going, in an effort to escape the heat. After that visit the American houses had no difficulty in getting permission to use cottons and synthetics, to lay aside the cowl at night, then the scapular, and then the robe, till finally the monks were free to sleep in whatever attire best suited them. But in the 1940s Frater Louis and his fellow monks had to try to sleep in their sweat-soaked clothes, enduring their prickly heat, with a hot Kentucky sun still beaming down upon them at 7:00 P.M.

Those fellow monks were very much present. Only a thin wooden partition about six feet high separated his seven-by-six cubicle from that of his neighbor. Not all the cubicles enjoyed the benefit of a window, but the air circulated over the partitions, as did the snores, snorts, night talk, and all the other moans and groans. Tom survived, just barely survived, this communal adventure in sleeping for about five years. We can see why he really enjoyed his few relatively brief stays in the infirmary. When I was a young monk my body used to run up a fever about every six months. It meant a few days in a private room, lots of sleep, and a few good meals. Eventually Tom did get a private room of sorts. Most monasteries had a few snorers' cells, little rooms or cubbyholes, somewhat apart, where the most

notorious snorers could saw their nightly woodpile without molest-
ing the whole brotherhood. Tom was given one of these, right over
the stairs, so that his sensitive ears got the benefit of anyone coming
in late or wandering around at night. After all, snorers didn't need
to be protected from noise. Tom tells us he learned to play a game
called insomnia: you toss and turn all night, counting off the hours,
and then you rise at 2:00 A.M., go to choir, and begin fighting sleep.
He was not the only one who played the game through many years.

His sleeping conditions alone would have been enough to justify
Tom's constant yearning for greater apartness and solitude. Of
course there were much deeper and more compelling motives also
at work.

Rising time for the monks was 2:00 A.M.–1:30 A.M. on Sundays and
1:00 A.M. on feast days. Because the monks had slept fully clothed,
little time was needed to get to choir. Traditionally the dormitory
was directly connected to the church by a night stair. Where the
large community spread the sleepers out, some had to make their
way along the dimly lit cloisters. At 2:07 A.M. the bell rang and the
monks began the Work of God. In those days, it was a work, indeed.

Saint Benedict had laid out an office, or course of liturgical
prayer services, based on the practices of the monks in Egypt,
reported by John Cassian, and on those of the Roman basilicas of
his time. It was quite moderate, calling for the 150 psalms to be
chanted in the course of the week, with some repetitions, along with
some hymns and responsories. In addition, certain lessons or passages from Scripture and the Fathers were to be read to the assem-
bly. Later centuries not only embellished Benedict's rather simple
office but added a number of "little offices"— abbreviated copies of
the canonical office required by his Rule. The Cistercian reform in
the eleventh century sought to return to the simplicity of the Rule.
It did not long succeed; embellishments again seeped in, including
a couple of little offices.

In the 1940s the day began with matins and lauds of a little office
in honor of the Blessed Virgin Mary, recited by heart in the dark. At
2:30 A.M. the monks settled down to thirty minutes of personal
prayer. Because at that time the monks could only kneel or stand in
their stalls for this prayer (and many had to stand, for knee trouble
was common), the situation was hardly conducive to that deep,
quiet prayer that Tom came to love. As one young monk told his

abbot, it was two minutes of prayer and twenty-eight minutes of spaghetti—if one succeeded in the struggle to stay awake. Then the lights went on and the monks set about reciting the canonical offices of matins and lauds: twenty psalms, some canticles; three or twelve lessons, ending on Sundays and feast days with the great hymn of thanksgiving, the *Te Deum*, a Gospel reading, and the abbot's blessing. At least, for parts of this, the monks could sit down. All, of course, was in Latin. This did not create the difficulty for Frater Louis that it did for many of his fellow novices. He was quite at home with Latin. If the lessons were difficult or the reader did a poor job, Tom had a small book, a breviary, in which he could follow the lesson as it was read at the lectern. For various periods during his first decade in the monastery he was one of the "cantors," with the additional duty to see that the choir recited all of this on a single sustained pitch. Only on Sundays and the greater feasts was the office sung with melodies—considerably increasing its duration. It is no wonder the young monk experienced fatigue, depression, and frustration after a workout like this each morning. And they called it prayer! These early hours of the morning were chosen for prayer by the monks of old because they have a certain depth and quietness to them—all creation is deeply at rest—so conducive to deep prayer. But this time of morning is certainly not conducive to this kind of prayer or to singing on pitch. It was always a struggle, always a beginning. I can remember on Thursday mornings—the office was longest on Thursday—after two hours in choir, coming upon the verse in Psalm 76: *Nunc coepi*—Now I begin! I would wonder what I had been doing the last two hours, two weeks, two months, two years, two decades. Yes, it was always a beginning, trying to hear the Lord and trying to find the words and the heart to praise him as he ought to be praised.

The night offices would finish after 4:00 A.M. On the ferial days, the days on which there was no feast, the canonical office was shorter, but a little office for the deceased was recited after it, so the time at which the services ended did not vary much. Then the monk-priests would each go to a small altar to celebrate mass. The nonpriest might be assigned to assist one of these priests. Actually, this was a blessing, for it gave him some active participation in the mass. The rest of the nonpriests would gather for a Communion mass. In those pre-Vatican II days the priest recited the whole of the mass himself (except for a few brief responses by the server) in Latin with his back to the congregation. For the rest of the congregation, participation was almost totally interior. The monks would rise shortly before the Communion rite, embrace each other in a sign of love and peace, and then receive the Host on their tongues. That was it for active participation. They would then settle down again for fifteen minutes of thanksgiving.

This time of mass and Communion could be a time of real contemplative prayer. But it was after this that the monk finally had some space for more personal prayer. In his first days in the monastery, Frater Louis found this early morning period, which often coincided with dawn, a creative time. He began to write some poetry—some of the best that he wrote—and some seeds of contemplation. But a wise spiritual father, his novice master, Father Robert, who would later succeeded Dom James Fox as abbot of Conyers, advised the young novice not to let his writing activity invade this precious time. It was advice Tom took to heart. This time became for him the most precious time in the day. When he finally moved into the hermitage and had more freedom, he even anticipated the office, praying it the previous evening, and spent these early morning hours in that deep, quiet prayer he so much loved.

This precious time for contemplative prayer did not last long. At 5:30 A.M. the monks would be back in church to chant the office of prime, both the canonical office and the office of the Blessed Virgin. Then there would be chapter. The community would go in single file behind the abbot to the chapter room. As the community at Gethsemani grew and grew, this moving from place to place began to take more and more time. The same general who opened the way for the use of cotton advised the monks of Gethsemani to move two by two. One by one or two by two, the time spent in walking in community was not lost. If one was perceptive, he would notice the rustle beneath the monk's cowl as he left church. He would be pulling his rosary from the pocket of his robe to begin praying his beads. Many a rosary was said as the monk went from church to chapter to refectory to work and back again.

In chapter, perhaps five days out of the seven, the abbot would give a commentary on the Rule of Saint Benedict, a portion of which would be read during the prayers that opened chapter. Even a speaker as gifted and fascinating as Tom would have been hard pressed to continue to deliver interesting talks on the same subject four or five times a week to the same audience for fifteen or twenty years. The abbot did, often enough, branch out to other related topics. Sometimes some news items would be shared. But for the most part it was pious exhortation in the direction of better observance. More rosaries were said. Some monks succumbed to sleep. Father Louis sometimes did some creative thinking on his own.

After the chapter the monks would return to the dormitory to make their beds and then, finally, they would go to the refectory for a cup of coffee and two ounces of dry bread. (It would be increased to six ounces during the summer labors and on Sundays and feast days.) After breaking their fast the monks would have about an hour for reading. Frater Louis's notebooks give us a fairly continuous record of what he read during this time. He liked to make notes and usually dated them. If the text he was reading was in Latin, much of his notes would be also. He was quite comfortable in the use of the language. His reading was quite eclectic. The Franciscan influence remained during his early years in the monastery, as well as his love for the scholasticism he first discovered through Etienne Gilson. But more and more he came to know and love the Cistercian Fathers. Little of them was available in English in those days but the large Latin tomes of Abbé Migne with their small print did not frighten Frater Louis. He found very compatible writers among them.

At 7:45 A.M. the monks would return to church for tierce of the little office, canonical tierce, and high mass, followed by sext of the two offices. Then the monks would begin a two-hour work period. It was in this period that Tom did much of his writing in his early days in the monastery. His first translation was done initially by hand, on the backs of used paper, sitting at his little desk in the common scriptorium or study hall. As time went on his work situation gradually improved until he was given some relatively private space in the rare-book room or vault next to the abbot's office. He was given an already well-used typewriter and it served him for the next twenty-five years. He used an electric typewriter for the first time in the bishop's office in Alaska in 1968. I have often wondered what Tom would have accomplished if he had had a word processor!

The morning work ended all too quickly if you were trying to get an article or chapter done, but it was long enough if you were out chopping wood in the freezing cold with a biting wind coming through the knobs. Almost as soon as the monks finished the morning work period they were back in choir for the office of none of the Blessed Virgin and of the day. There was then a few minutes to examine how the morning had gone or whatever practice one used for the particular examen, a procession to the refectory, lunch, and a procession back to the church.

Finally, there came a precious hour to be used as each monk deemed best. Usually one would be a bit groggy, full of potatoes and bread — dinner was the one meal where the monk could eat all he wanted; the other meals were carefully rationed. Thank God for good homemade bread, truly the staple of life. Vegetables did not fill too much of the void, nor did the salad, if there was any. Potatoes were a good filler too. Saint Benedict had benignly provided there should be two cooked portions at the main meal, so that if the monk could not eat one, he could partake of the other. The second portion was always soup. I can remember one monk saying, "You never know what is in the soup." And his listener responding, "You always know exactly what's in the soup." It was always whatever was served the day before, with some water added.

Tom especially loved the period after lunch. He would often take a book and find a corner behind the church near the community's cemetery, where even on chill days he could find some shelter. He could look out across the valley into the woods (where one day he would have his hermitage) and on through the knobs. Here many a poem came to birth and many a seed of contemplation was first formulated in his mind and even written in his notebook.

After singing the office of none, the monks worked again for two hours in the afternoon and then had a bit of time for reading before vespers at 4:30 P.M. If it was a ferial day, vespers would be earlier so that they could add the office of the dead to the other two offices. After vespers there was again a period of silent prayer in the stalls, this time for fifteen minutes. Then the monks went to the refectory for the evening "collation," a small amount of food with two ounces of bread and a cup of tea. In time there would be more flexibility about this evening meal, till finally the monks had a good bit of freedom as to what they would eat and how much. But in those early days a hungry man who had worked hard in the afternoon had little to satisfy his needs, and it would be a long time till the next day's dinner.

Hardly would the supper dishes be done than the community would gather for a period of reading, about twenty minutes, before returning to church for the final offices of the day, canonical compline and compline of Our Lady, and the famous Cistercian *Salve*. Tom admitted that the evening reading often found him sleeping. It would give him one more thing for which to repent as he made his examen after the *Salve*. Then he received the abbot's blessing and went off to bed.

Such full days pass very quickly. As we can see, even if Tom had been given all his work time for writing, it would have added up to only four hours a day, the time broken into two periods. He had little time to read, something that was very important to him. Fortunately, he was a good reader and a fast reader. He did cover a lot of basic material in his early days, along with what was necessary for his writing. He even found some time for poetry. But in all, he found precious little time and spaciousness for contemplation. No wonder there was a constant longing for a cell of his own with long hours for reading and prayer, what the Carthusians and Camadolese seemed to offer. Monks traditionally called their private rooms cells, for they believed that the Latin word *cella* was related to *caelum*, heaven. Such a place, such time and space, would be heavenly.

The schedule I have given is the weekday schedule during the winter season (September 14 till Lent). On Sundays and the major feast days there would be no work, allowing more time for personal prayer and reading. On such days Frater Louis would look out over the enclosure walls and wonder, especially as the community grew, why they were confined to such a small space, when they had a couple thousand acres of woodlands surrounding them. In 1951 he was finally given the use of a little shed for a bit more solitude during these free periods. When he became master of the scholastics the next year, he would lead the young monks out into the woods on Sunday afternoons, encouraging them to enjoy greater solitude. In time, but it would be years, his sensibleness would win out, and all the monks would have the freedom of the woods, and some of them would find their hermitages at Gethsemani itself and not have to cast envious eyes at the Carthusians and the Camadolese — indeed, they would enjoy even greater freedom and solitude than the members of these eremitical orders.

The monks' schedule did vary with the seasons of the year. During Lent there would be a bit less work time and more time for reading, but not much, for there would be more office and penitential processions. After Easter it would be just the reverse, more work and less time for reading as the summer work began. (The Cistercian schedule met a real challenge when the monks began to establish monasteries in the southern hemisphere and summer and winter were reversed.) The time of mass, and the accompanying offices and vespers would shift, but the balance of the day remained fairly uniform.

The Cistercians were not given to much in the way of artificial penances. There were enough real ones in the demands of the day, the work, the fasting, and fidelity to the quest for constant prayer and contemplation. There were two artificial penances in practice when Tom entered: the weekly discipline and the chapter of faults, with the public penances that flowed from it. I think for Frater Louis, as for many of us, the greatest part of the penance of the discipline was the ridiculousness of it. After the night office on Friday the monks would go to the dormitory, strip to the waist, and beat themselves for a couple minutes with a little rope whip. In the winter the chill of the dormitory was the greater penance and the whipping a good warming up exercise. I suppose we all tried, especially in our first fervor, to think some pious thoughts as we whipped ourselves, but the humor was bound to break through. I would love to have a record of the thoughts that went through Frater Louis's head as he performed this weekly event.

The chapter of faults was probably a useful means to keep observances up when they were so extensively regulated by many minute regulations. The chapter never touched on deeper matters and had the potential to engender a sort of police state mentality. Tom's good humor seemed to hold him in good stead here too. It took a while for him to settle into the Trappist mold. His high spirits would break out, especially at work. He would easily lead others into fun. And then he would have more fun in accusing himself and those whom he led on at the next chapter of faults. It was hard to take the more colorful penances seriously: eating lunch on the floor, kissing your brothers' feet, begging them for your meal. Dom James has said how edified he was to see this world-famous author humbly eating his dinner on the floor. I think that Thomas Merton was probably enjoying being the center of attraction, though he might have mustered up some pious reflections about it all, especially in his early days. The whole business, chapter and penances, slipped into history with the coming of the new era.

Tom did not live to see many of the changes that would come with renewal. But he saw some of them, and with his usual keen intuition he had a good bit of insight into where they would go and how far. Renewal had begun early in the Cistercian order. We tend to think of it as all coming out of the Second Vatican Council. But back in the 1920s a great Irish abbot in a Belgium abbey, Dom Columba Marmion, began to set a new tone in monastic spirituality, centering all on Christ, using the Scriptures, Liturgy, and tradition. A Cistercian neighbor, Dom Anselm le Bail, encouraged a gifted group of young monks at Scourmont to take a lead in exploring the sources of true renewal. In 1953 a new abbot general led the general chapter in voting in what seemed at that time like sweeping reforms. Because all the details of the monks' life were then spelled out in the constitutions of the order, the changes had to go to Rome for approval. In those days there was a general chapter every year. After nine months of waiting, the general pressed the Holy See for some response to the chapter's requests so that he could prepare for the next chapter. The esteemed cardinals, after ten months' deliberation, granted the monks fifteen minutes more sleep on working days (I think we laughed for fifteen minutes!), deeming the rest of the proposals too revolutionary and needing the consideration of a plenary chapter in 1955. Slowly the renewal went on: offices were simplified or eliminated, more time was allowed for contemplative prayer, studies were encouraged, adaptations to local and individual needs were more and more accepted. As the present abbot of Gethsemani wrote recently, "the Gethsemani of the 1940s was pretty grim . . . a system that had little respect for individuals." That has changed considerably, though there is certainly still room for growth in this matter.

Something of Merton's idealization of early Gethsemani never left him, and so he regretted some of the changes. He always loved the Latin, which he had the background to appreciate more fully than most. At the right time and in the right place he liked a certain amount of formality and ritual. At the same time he was rightly suspicious of the tendency to put all the emphasis on adapting the externals and little on renewing the deeper elements of the life. He saw the prevailing unwillingness of the institutions to truly respect and foster the individual. Shortly before his death he expressed the conviction that it might be necessary for a monk to leave the institution in order to keep growing. It fostered his growth only to a certain point and then tried to put a cap on it. It would be hard for the institution to sustain many Thomas Mertons, yet he wanted everyone to have not only the opportunity but to be encouraged to grow to his fullest potential. Such a specter is frightening to a superior who wants to stay on top of things, especially if he thinks he has to be the brightest star in the local firmament. Few superiors have the greatness of spirit to want their men to outshine them. Father Louis's last abbot was a man of such greatness.

The renewal of the Cistercian order has led to many adaptations in the life. Many of them now seem common sense to all of us. Father Louis saw the senselessness of much of what we were doing years before the adaptations came. Somehow he had the faith to live with it all, but to live with it in such a way that he helped the rest of us to see the need for change. He certainly was not alone in bringing about the renewal, but through the power of his pen he probably did more than any other to help us to move in the right direction.

The Cistercian order now sees as one of its greatest challenges the question of how to impart to men and women of today a true monastic formation. A profound shift has taken place. From the earliest times the way one became a monk or nun was to go in search of a spiritual father or mother or a community, and take up life with those who had the formation. By entering into the practice of the life one was formed. When a monk had bowed often enough to his abbot, something deep within him realized that the abbot held the place of Christ in the midst of the community. Bowing to the brethren each time we met one of them made us aware of the Christ within them. The prostrations at prayer brought realization of who our God is. Until recently, candidates accepted being brought into a life full of ritual, a ritual that they would be expected to observe to the full even though they did not understand the significance of much of it. In time, through experience, the ritual itself would reveal its meaning even as it formed the mind and heart. But a new generation has emerged, an authentic youth who does not want to do what he does not understand. He first wants to know the meaning of things, and then he can do them authentically. The problem with this is that some things can be really known and understood only through experience. The Fathers used to say, Those who have had the experience know, and those who have not had the experience, have it and then you will know. Merton, the existentialist, very much wanted to know the meaning of things and not waste time on the meaningless. Yet somehow he had the grace and the humor to be able to abide with things till they did reveal their meaning or fade away. In the face of an honest quest for truth, that is bound to be the outcome. This is perhaps one of the messages that Thomas Merton has for us all, not just the monk and nun, candidates and postulants of the Cistercian order, but for all who are living through the painful process of renewing a Christian community. To throw things out because they seem meaningless to us may be a great mistake. Maybe we need to risk letting them reveal their meaning, knowing that if they do not truly have meaning, in the face of such a challenge they will fade away. We can do this only if we do not take ourselves too seriously, but can grin at the apparent nonsense of some of the things we do together.

Tom lived for years through a daily schedule that now, even to the most obtuse of us, is seen as patently inimical to the proclaimed meaning and goal of the order he joined. But it certainly did not truncate his growth. If anything, it provided the discipline that fostered that growth, freeing him to grow even more. We will look at this fact more deeply in the coming chapters.

2. True Freedom

The Seven Storey Mountain: an unusual name for a runaway best-seller. I suspect that few of the hundreds of thousands who bought the book were aware of what the title alluded to, and even fewer understood the allusions as they applied to the life of the author.

Tom had first been introduced to Dante's *Divine Comedy* by his father. Later it was one of the electives at Cambridge, perhaps the one course that he did enjoy. And yet his drink-sodden mind prevented him at that time from drawing from it all that he might have. For Dante, heaven, hell, and purgatory were not only specific places. They were moral and anagogical allegories for states: hell for the damned, heaven for those who achieved the life of grace, and purgatory for those who suffer toward grace. When the Comedy is understood in the context of Dante's own life, and that is necessary to understand it fully, purgatory is seen as a monumental act of atonement. This sheds light on the meaning of the monastic life for Merton. The *Purgatorio*, with its seven mountains, was a good analogy for monastic life with its alternations of light and darkness, and yet its simple, regular, and serene development, so unlike the chaos of the hell that went before. Everyone in this purgatory was saved and wanted to do the will of God.

Tom would certainly not have been the first or the only one to have entered the monastic life with a view of making atonement for what had gone before. Rarely has this been the total motivation, but in more than one case it has been the dominant motivation that has led a young man or an older one to embrace the life of the cloister. Tom's irrepressible enthusiasm, however, could never have settled merely in the way of atonement. He would always be looking beyond to the goal, to the fulfillment that was to come. In the twenty-seventh Canto of the *Purgatorio*, Virgil, the guide, has finally led Dante to the summit of the seven-storey mountain of purgatory and is prepared to take his leave:

> Expect no more of me in word or deed:
> Here your will is upright, free, and whole.

This was the goal of the seven-storey mountain as it was expressed by Dante and as it was understood by Thomas Merton: a will upright, free, and whole; in a word, true freedom.

In a conference that he gave to the community at Gethsemani in December 1965, Father Louis pointed out how our culture generally induced people to think and act in a way that was bound to lead to frustration. The question it asked, Am I happy? was the wrong question. The search for happiness, for pleasure would always be frustrated. The real question, according to Tom, was, Am I free? Am I developing the freedom God gave me? This freedom is not a freedom of choice, always limited, which our consumer society is ever seeking to expand. Consumerism seeks to give us more and more choices in the way in which we can pursue happiness and pleasure, leaving us always subjected to the crying and ultimately frustrated need for happiness or pleasure. This freedom is a true freedom, which in this particular talk he spoke of as the "freedom of spontaneity." This is the freedom to respond with our whole being to reality. This is the freedom that is free from needing happiness and pleasure, from needing things and people; the freedom that is able to choose to take what it gets, to be delighted with the special things that come along, to respond to what is, with joy and thanksgiving. This is a freedom that frees us from predeterminations.

In the course of his last journey, Father Louis gave a series of talks to the Nuns of the Precious Blood in Alaska. He pointed out to the sisters how we are today living in a society that creates alienation. Many people do not realize this. We are offered many superficial choices, which engender the delusion that we are free. But actually we are pushed around a great deal by the media and by other people's expectations and demands. This produces the psychological condition of alienation, in which we are never allowed to be fully ourselves; we do not belong to ourselves. The real personal meaning of our lives is not allowed to emerge. We are dominated by someone else's ideas, tastes, desires: speak this way, act this way, see these things, do these things, have these things. And we are reaping the results of this lack of true freedom, this self-alienation, for deep down it breeds a profound resentment toward the persons and the society that does not allow us to be our true selves. This smoldering resentment suddenly erupts in terrible acts of hatred and violence. Tom went on to speak of the answer to this. It lies in coming to understand the full dignity of the person, above all in Christ, and attaining to that contemplative attitude that opens us to the true reality of ourselves, of others, and of everything in this creation.

In a talk he gave to his community in January 1966, Tom made a penetrating analysis of the concept of freedom in the work of Jean-Paul Sartre, the French atheist existentialist who certainly has had a great influence on the thinking of our times. For Sartre, we are free because we have chosen to be here, and we have to keep choosing, choosing ourselves. This is our very existence. If we would be truly free, we must choose to be our authentic self, but only for ourselves as the subject of this being. All others are to us objects, non-selves, not the self. Each person is enclosed within himself or herself and is willing himself or herself to be over and against all others—which is ultimately the morality of hell.

Tom considered himself an existentialist, but not in this dark, atheistic way. He rather drew his inspiration from Gabriel Marcel, the Catholic existentialist. Marcel saw that the only way to be free and to be authentically a person is to be wide open to what is, and therefore to be open to other persons as subjects and to be open to relationships. It is in relationships that each one discovers himself or herself more and more. In the mutual gift of respect and love, we come to know ourselves more fully, to enjoy ourselves more completely, and are able to be more totally and freely gifts to others.

The ultimate test of freedom is in the presence of death. Christian freedom appears not only when we choose life, but also when we freely embrace death, for death is not outside of life but a part of it. Our death is built into our life. Life and death are ultimately one. All the negative elements in our life are part of our death. Finally, in death we come to surrender all of our life. So death is the complete response of our life, a total surrender, a total openness to the Other.

In a total openness to God we remain totally open to everyone else. Tom related a touching story regarding the death of John Wu's wife, Teresa. Wu had been a close friend of Tom's, helping with his understanding of the Chinese tradition, its mystical writings, and its calligraphy. Wu's wife, Teresa, died a saintly death. As the family and the doctor gathered around her bed for the final hours of watching,

Teresa was completely present to them as well as to God. After a time, she turned to her husband and said, "Bring a chair for the doctor to sit. He has been standing too long."

This reminds me of a story Mother Teresa shared with me on one occasion. It is her practice when she is home in Calcutta to go out in the early morning with the sisters to gather up the abandoned dying from the train stations—a common place to leave them during the night among the sleepers. This particular day the sisters found an old woman, very ravaged. She would not live long. Mother claimed the privilege of caring for her. Mother did all she could to make this poor dying woman comfortable. She stayed close by, soothing her as best as possible. In her last moments, the woman opened her eyes, looked in Mother's eyes, and said simply, "Thank you." And she died. Mother remained prostrate on her knees and wept. Two women totally open to each other.

True freedom lies in being completely open, being a complete "yes" to God and to every manifestation of his love, his life, and his beauty. The presence in our lives of other persons, of many friends and loved ones, and of material riches, the many goods of this world, is never in itself an obstacle to true freedom, to contemplative existence, to a total being to God.

When he was novice master, Tom undertook to translate one of the small treatises of Thomas Aquinas, *De divinis moribus*. Tom never lost his appreciation for scholastic philosophy and theology, its clarity and order, and the help that these gave one in entering into a fuller understanding and assimilation of variety and revelation. In his translation Tom entitled the treatise *The Ways of God*. It is basically a study of the divine attributes with a consideration of how we who are made in the image of God can become like him by imitating in our own lives his attributes. Father Louis gave three talks to the novices about this work as he was translating it. The dominant theme that he emphasized in his talks was the inherent goodness and beauty and lovableness of every person and of everything, because each reveals God. Each person and thing shares in some way in God's being and in his beauty. Tom lamented the fact that we are more prone to see the faults in others, the lack of goodness and beauty brought on by sin and failure. It takes courage to see the good in others, because this challenges us and also calls forth from us the response of love and caring. For God's sake, because this is the way he sees things and we are called to be like him, to be lovers, we need constantly to see through whatever evil may be there disfiguring the divine beauty. There is not a single person whose goodness does not far outweigh his or her evil. Evil cannot be if goodness is not there as the ground that it disfigures. God never stops loving any one of us because of evil. He continues to endow each of us with the gift of life, being, and all that we need to attain the fullness of life unto eternal life. Therefore, Aquinas summons his reader to love and appreciate the good "always, everywhere and in every creature." This is indeed a contemplative attitude toward life, an openness that is completely free; in sum, it is consummate holiness. In the course of one of these talks, with his unusual humor and not without a bit of bite, the novice master related a story about an enthusiastic novice who was carried away with the power of an immense bulldozer and recklessly knocked over trees and gouged the earth. This was not the kind of freedom Tom was advocating.

More seriously, before concluding the text, Tom pointed out that our deep love and appreciation of all things created and our joy in them must be for God's sake. If we begin to do it for our own sake, soon enough we will become attached to having these things and enjoying them and we will lose our freedom. This is the juncture, the point, where relations with persons and things can become obstacles to our freedom. When we cease to be open to their being, who or what they are in themselves and in God, and begin to see them and value them insofar as they are beneficial to ourselves, then we have departed from the contemplative attitude and have begun to lose our freedom. Celibacy for the Kingdom is not a call to be loveless and unrelated. Rather it is a call to be wide open in love, appreciation, reverence, and respect for everyone, for who they truly are in God. It is call to universal love. Evangelical poverty is not a call to want and destitution. It is a call to freedom from the need to possess things so that we can truly reverence and enjoy them and use them in the way that is most life-giving. In this sense, as Tom says in *Thoughts in Solitude*, "Poverty is the door to freedom." As he wrote in *Contemplation in a World of Action*, God calls us "into existence and to freedom and love which is the fulfillment of that freedom."

Thomas Merton's one surviving novel, *My Argument with the Gestapo*, was written in the summer of 1941, when he had already accepted the basis for freedom that was afforded him in embracing the Catholic faith. He was still searching for a greater freedom from the enslavements that he had so keenly experienced in the secular world. The importance of this largely autobiographical novel for the insight that it gives us into the author can hardly be exaggerated. The novel, not having to be bound by purely factual information, gave Tom greater scope to use literary images and imaginary scenes and characters in order to convey more effectively the deeper meanings that were stirring in his searching soul. In the course of one of the novel's many interrogations seeking to discern the identity of "Thomas Merton," the central character, Merton himself, replies, "If you want to identify me, ask me not where I live, or what I like to eat, or how I comb my hair, but ask me what I think I am living for, in detail, and ask me what I think is keeping me from living fully the thing I want to live for. Between these two answers you can determine the identity of any person. The better answer he has, the more of a person he is."

Tom was a true existentialist, and the question is, Who is the subject right now? He is not yet what he is living for. He is rather the incomplete freedom that holds him back, not allowing him to be all he wants to be. The first step toward true freedom, toward being all who we want to be, to identifying completely with our transcendent self is the realization of who we are here and now. It is a humble realization, which recognizes all the obstacles to our freedom. As Tom writes in "Inner Experience," "The first step toward spiritual liberation is not so much the awareness of what lies at the end of the road — the experience of God — as a clear view of the great obstacles that block its very beginning, perceiving the tendencies, the habits, the attitudes within us which turn us against God and make us truly wretched. We begin to seek to be free of them." "There is a law in my members which sets me against God. Wretched man that I am, who can set me free?"

Merton spoke again and again in his talks and in his writings of these obstacles, usually in the first person singular or the collective we. He knew them well. But he knew, also, that they can bind us only to the extent to which we allow them. If we free ourselves from them by acknowledging them, we can then cut through them and go on to love. "To serve the God of love, one must be free, one must face the terrible responsibility of the decision to love *in spite of all unworthiness* whether in oneself or in one's neighbor." The struggle for freedom is a long one, it is a lifelong one, breaking through, unshackling oneself from any number of unfreedoms.

It is not just a question of physical freedom, of being able to go about as one wills, to meet people, to get information and books and music, to come in contact with culture and life. In his novel, Tom writes, "It does no good to be free in this city [world]. This freedom to move around is not the freedom I was looking for. I admit that for many people it would be enough to gain that freedom, and a terrible thing to lose." Merton goes on to bring out that the freedom to move about in this world is usually purchased at a price. In the story the Germans gave him this freedom because they thought that what he had written was smut, that he had bowed to the values of the world as the world sees them. This kind of freedom Tom freely gave up upon becoming a monk. Although he appreciated the contacts he had with people and had a great desire for information and books and music and for contact with culture and peoples and what was going on, nonetheless he always accepted the fact that he had given all this up and that his access to these things was controlled by religious authority.

Unlike the monk who voluntarily gives it up, some people have this freedom taken away from them. Yet such persons can remain eminently free. Merton, who wrote with such power, poignancy, and compassion on the death camps of Nazi Germany, points out how in these very camps many found a profound freedom. When all was taken away from them, they were forced to find that their true self-worth and dignity, their true freedom, came from faith and love of God. They found that God had not abandoned them, that he was near, within, protecting them, not allowing their ultimate destruction. It was no longer some powerful extrinsic God who came from afar to liberate, but it was a God who dwelt within, and they were free to go to their center and be with him in fullest freedom.

Never was man freer than when Jesus hung nailed to a cross.

The quest, then, for true freedom is not a quest for physical freedom, but rather for spiritual freedom. Indeed, as we walk through the world we need to find some way to free our lives from the clutter of the world. A life that is constantly filled with bustling activity, with the demands of others, with the distractions of the latest news, leaves no space for us to find ourselves, to live, to be, and to act out of our own inner self. One of the purposes of the monastic cloister and the hermit's solitude is to be free from the clutter of the world. To some extent everyone needs to find some of this freedom. We all need time to listen to the sounds of silence, to the deeper yearnings of our own human hearts. In this regard some decry the constant blare of stereos with which young people so frequently fill their lives. Tom was a great defender of the young and had a wonderful rapport with them. I think he might say, in fact this blare of music that some surround themselves with is, in a way, their cloister. It creates for them a space, a solitude. This was why Tom played Duke Ellington records at top volume on his portable phonograph in his study at Oakham. It blocked out other sounds and gave him the space to think and to read and to study.

The secular world not only can clutter a life, it tends through its media and through its peer pressures to fill our lives with induced needs. Madison Avenue, through newspapers and magazines, through billboards and subway posters, and above all through television, seeks constantly to convince us that happiness and fullness of life can be found only if we gobble up the products of a consumer society and indulge ourselves in innumerable pleasures. Christian faith has the power to free us from the world's particular myths and idolatries and confusions. Tom saw that the Christian's first mission was to live Christian freedom in whatever way God gives us to live it, whether it be in the secular world or in the cloister. The Christ to be preached, whether by word or by silence, is the Christ of Christian freedom, of Christian autonomy, of Christian independence from the arrogant demands and claims of an illusory world. It is not a freedom from the world as nature or as creation, or a freedom from human society. The Christian is free, or should be, from the psychic determinisms and obsessions and myths of a mendacious, greedy, lustful worldly society. The secular world pretends to exalt liberty, but it actually enslaves us, making us dependent on artificial needs, which it then pretends to satisfy. In fact, it subjugates us to what is lower than ourselves. In and of itself, however, the world does not have any real power over us. It succeeds in inducing these false needs and these false values only because of our inner needs to feel superior to, or at least be accepted by, others. The real masters who rule us and rob us of our freedom are indeed within us. They are our own aspirations, feelings, emotions, habits, and passions. As Merton wrote in *New Seeds of Contemplation:*

No man who simply eats or drinks when he feels like eating or drinking or smokes whenever he feels the urge to light a cigarette, or gratifies his curiosity and sensuality whenever they are stimulated, can consider himself a free person. He has renounced his spiritual freedom and become the servant of bodily impulse. Therefore his mind and his will are not fully his own. They are under the power of his appetites, and through the medium of his appetites they are under the control of those who gratify his appetites.

We can perhaps easily see how important it is to break free from the demands of lust—it can grind us and drag us about and get us to do the most stupid of things. We can see how gluttony can destroy our health and drain our lives of vitality and energy. Or love of comfort and laziness can keep us from accomplishing so many good things we want to do. Uncontrolled anger can drive us to acts that will destroy our lives and the lives of those we love. We may readily see the need for striving to free ourselves of the domination of many of our passions. But some passions are subtle, such as ambition and the drive for success. In the "Inner Experience," Tom notes that "He who needs to be exalted and for whom mysticism is the peak of his ambition, will never be able to feel the liberation that is granted only to those who have renounced success." We can be driven by passion in pursuit of even the holiest and most sublime things—the object will not make the difference. If we are driven and unfree we can never open the space in our lives for that for which we strive and find the enjoyment in it that we want and are meant to find. So long as we are not free from the subjugation of our passions and emotions, our desires and aspirations, we will never be free from division. We will never have the freedom to bring the whole of our being into unity. We will always be pulled this way and that.

We tend to be dominated not only by our passions and emotions, but also by our own ideas. We tend to become rigid, attached to our ideas, convinced of our own wisdom, proud of our capacities, and committed to our personal ambition. This enclosure within our own ideas prevents us from being open to see reality, prevents us from growing through change, from being called forth by the constantly greater revelation of reality in our lives. Close akin to this domination of our own ideas is the way in which we are dominated by our prejudices. We get fixed impressions of people and we put these persons in little boxes with no possibility of their ever escaping to reveal their true beauty to us. We close them off from all possibility that they might develop and grow and change. We also develop prejudices in regard to ideas, programs, and projects and refuse to see them in any other light. On the eve of the Second Vatican Council, Tom reflected on the challenge that lay before the Church, and as was almost always the case with him, he then brought it home to himself. Using biblical imagery he wrote that it was a "a matter of coming up out of Egypt into my own country. I am nearly forty-eight. I have work to do; to get free within myself, to work my way out of the conditions and habits of thought, the garments of skin (as if I could do it by myself). But one must want to begin." He did want to begin; in fact he had long been working at it. The 1960s, concomitant with the time of the Council, were, indeed, years of tremendous expansion in the thinking and the concerns of Thomas Merton. Shortly after the close of the Council, in the first days of 1966, Tom was reading Bultmann and he wrote, "How many of my own old ideas I can now abandon and revise. . . . He [Bultmann] has made clear to me the full limitations of all my early work which is too naive, insufficient except in what concerns my own experience." This advocate of intellectual freedom, though, saw the dangers on the other side. Although he had a certain sympathy for situation ethics as a reaction to the exaggeratedly formal and legalistic emphasis on the objective demands of authority, he saw that it departed from true existentialism. It was not a true response to reality because it reduced everything to personal and subjective choice. To move everything into this area of total indetermination does not liberate the person. It sees no truth or reality other than the arbitrariness of feeling. A freedom that lies in following the whims of one's feelings is no freedom at all. True freedom is the freedom to see and to respond to reality.

Tom also points out that "modern man needs *liberation* from his inordinate self-consciousness, his monumental self-awareness, his obsession with self-affirmation." We can be so completely taken up with ourselves that there is no freedom left to be to others, to be to God, and, indeed, to be to our true self, for our true self is one who is in relation with others, our true self is that self which is within God. One idea that we most need to be liberated from is the concept we have of ourselves or the ideal that we construct for ourselves and to which we seek to force ourselves to conform. On his fiftieth birthday Tom wrote with some exaggeration: "What I find most in my whole life is illusion, wanting to be something of what I have formed a concept."

Father Louis may have seemed singularly free from the temptation of playing the role of the ideal monk, and yet he was an idealistic person and he did constantly struggle with the ideals he set up for himself and the realities he had to live with within himself. And so do we all. If we have any vision that calls us forth, we have an ideal. But we need to know how not to let the ideal become solidified and in itself set limits and confine the full vitality and growth of our lives. We need an ideal and we need to know how not to take the ideal too seriously. We need an ideal but we need also to know how to be detached from it so that it can constantly grow and call us forth to ever fuller life and growth. In the "Inner Experience" Tom extols "the full sense of liberation experienced by one who recognizes with immense relief that he is not his false self after all and that he has all along been nothing but his real and homely self and nothing more, without glory, without self-aggrandizement, without self-righteousness, without self-concern." With this "yes" to what really is, not only does the false self, the ego, disappear, but one is open to infinite possibilities. Who we truly can be in God is without limit. This can be frightening. "The dread of being oneself is the great obstacle to freedom, for freedom equals being oneself and acting accordingly."

We are called to stand on our own two feet. In his last talk, the one given at the Pan-Asian Monastic Conference in Bangkok, Merton related a story about Chogyam Trungpa Rimpoche. At the critical moment when the Rimpoche had to make his decision about leaving Tibet, he found himself isolated in a mountain hut. He did not know what to do. So he sent to a neighboring abbot friend, saying, "What do we do?" The answer came back: "From now on, Brother, everybody stands on his own feet." Tom commented that that was an extremely important statement. We all do need some external supports and structures to grow. Who could begin life without a mother and father? What child does not need a family in order to grow? And we all need interaction and relationships with others to keep growing. Tom entered a monastery in order to find structures that would help him in his struggle for true freedom and to find a community of brothers who would support him in that struggle. And yet, true freedom demands that we be free even from the communities and the structures that support us. Ultimately there is no friend who can fully understand us, who can walk with us all the way. We must go forward and walk on our own in response to who we are and who we are called to be in God. Tom, being true to himself, courageously stepped out of the normal support system that the Cistercian community gives a monk and moved toward an ever more solitary life. One of the concerns of his final voyage was to see if there was not a still better solitude to support him in his quest for true and perfect freedom.

When Tom was preparing an article on the Georgian letters of Boris Pasternak, he spoke to the community at Gethsemani about them. He pointed out and commented at length on a particular statement in the last of the letters, written shortly before Pasternak's death: "Everywhere in the world one has to pay for the right to live on one's naked spiritual reserves." It costs to come to this point of complete freedom. Thomas Merton was willing to pay the price.

Years before, Tom wrote about his perhaps greatest struggle when he wrote in *New Seeds of Contemplation* that resentment is the "last-ditch stand of freedom." He probably did not then suspect how much he would have to continue to struggle with resentment. Resentment is not a real exercise of freedom. It is rather the "mute animal protection of a mistreated psychophysical organ." Resentment is a false statement of freedom. But the problem is to learn how to renounce resentment without selling out to the organization people. Tom saw the answer in renouncing the shadow or false self that sees itself menaced. The true self can never be menaced. Whatever claims the organizational people make, they can never touch the true self.

There is yet further growth for freedom. It can go beyond freedom from our passions and emotions, from phony needs and mind sets, from the false self, and from supports and structures. We can even free ourselves in regard to the real needs of our life. Tom had a good experience of this in December 1959. From the day when, as a retreatant, he stood on the back road, almost precisely in the place where one day a road would lead up to his hermitage, but stood facing not in the direction of the future hermitage but toward the immense abbey on the escarpment before him, he wondered if his need for solitude could be fulfilled in that place. In the years that followed he struggled with the question. He cast longing eyes to other forms of monastic life that seemed to offer more solitude. Finally, in 1959 he came to what he thought was the resolution. He made an appeal to Rome to leave Gethsemani to find a place of greater solitude in Latin America. On December 17 a response came from Rome. It seemed to be a definitive no. In accepting the dictates of his superiors in this matter that was vital to him he found a new freedom. He wrote that day to his abbot: "The decisions made have left me very free and empty. I can say they have enabled me to taste an utterly new kind of joy." In his journal he wrote, "I shall certainly have solitude. . . . Where? Here or there makes no difference. Somewhere. Nowhere. Beyond all where. Solitude outside geography or in it. No matter."

Ultimately, we seek the openness of evangelical freedom, the freedom that comes from complete trust in the Father. This is the freedom of which Jesus spoke in the sermon on the mount: "Your heavenly Father knows all your needs. Seek first the Kingdom of Heaven and his justice and all these other things will be provided."

It may seem curious to some that a man in quest of true freedom should have entered one of the strictest monasteries in the world. But self-discipline, freedom from ourselves, is one of the first and most fundamental steps toward freedom. Tom, in some way, had the insight to realize how much he needed help to discipline himself. Even after his conversion to the Catholic faith his life was in some ways still quite undisciplined. It is not easy to wipe out the habits of years and replace them with new and stronger habits. Perhaps some of this insight came to Tom from his Indian friend, Bramachari, of Columbia days. Later Tom would write that yoga makes use of a variety of disciplines and ascetic techniques for the liberation of the human spirit from the limitations imposed upon it by material worldly existence. Tom saw Paul's "servitude of corruption" (Romans 8:19–21) as the karma that the yogis seek to free themselves from to come into that liberty which the Christian knows to be the glory of the children of God. It is only by renunciation of passion and detachment, through the crucifixion of the exterior self that we can liberate the inner person, the new one in Christ. Inner freedom is purchased at a price. We have to renounce other forms of freedom in order to have this kind of freedom. Tom would write in *Contemplation in a World of Action:*

> It is necessary to accept restrictions, restraints, self-denial, sacrifice, and so forth. To people of our times so intent on human fulfillment this can indeed seem scandalous. It takes a particular kind of insight to see what in so many respects is an unfulfillment is in truth a way to the highest kind of fulfillment. . . . Basically there is only one kind of freedom which is the freedom of the Cross. It is the freedom that comes for one who has completely given himself with Christ on the Cross, has risen with Christ, and has Christ's freedom—not simply in ordinary human spontaneity but in the spontaneity of the Spirit of God.

True freedom then, the freedom of the children of God, is something that always reaches beyond, is not something that is sought in itself for its own sake. It is part of our quest for God. In *New Seeds of Contemplation* Merton writes, "This then is what it means to seek God perfectly: to keep my mind free from confusion in order that my liberty may always be at the disposal of his will to cultivate an intellectual freedom from the image of created things in order to receive the secret contact of God in obscure love." We seek freedom then on every level of our being in order to be able to be free to return to our source—the Source of all freedom and Freedom himself—through the fullest possible communion and union in love. And we are willing to pay the price that is necessary for that, that is the meaning of *ascesis*, self-discipline and penance.

There is no contradiction between freedom and the ascent of faith. "To believe is *to be free to trust in God quite alone*" and to be free from every other form of dependence and reliance. This is true freedom. Faith itself is a matter of freedom and self-determination, a free receiving of a freely given gift of grace. We cannot assent to the message of God if our minds and hearts are enslaved. The person of faith is free to listen to the Word of God in his or her heart, is free to obey the Lord and to obey others in the Lord without fearing the truncation of the true self: "The highest freedom is found in obedience to God." Christian faith frees us from the world's myths, idolatries, and confusions. There is then an obvious interaction between faith and freedom. They grow together. If we need freedom for faith, it is faith that leads us into true freedom. Ultimately, it was the Christian faith, first intimated to him by Gilson's *Spirit of Medieval Philosophy*, that led Tom into an understanding of true freedom and guided him in his pursuit of it. In his commentary on Albert Camus's *Plague* (which is in itself a short of myth of freedom), Merton writes that "Christianity introduces a higher dimension of liberty, the gift of divine freedom which is called grace." Christ saved us freely using his freedom, he brought us to freedom through the use of his human freedom.

As early as the 1940s, in an article published in an obscure journal, *The Tiger's Eye,* Tom speaks about the experience of the freedom of God:

In a placid and breathless contact the summit of your own soul opens out into the huge freedom of God . . . it becomes suddenly clear to you that you never knew anything until this moment. That all the experience that has ever gone before this is nothing but the scattering of fragments. Up until now you have never possessed truth: you have only seen partial limited aspects of it, isolated sections without much ultimate meaning.

It is in the experience of God, the God who is freedom, that we discover our own deepest freedom. As Tom writes in *Contemplation in a World of Action*: "If we never encounter him, our freedom never fully develops." Our encounter with him, our response to his Word, is the drawing forth, the calling out of our deepest freedom, our true identity. In *The New Man*, Tom brings out that our perfect self-realization lies in "our anguished freedom, coming into contact with the life-giving freedom of him who is Holy and Unknown."

The way God rules us is by liberating us and raising us to union with himself from within. The Christian should be able to reassure modern humanity that God is the source and guarantee of our freedom and not some sort of force standing over us to limit it. As Tom dares to say, "God is freedom." For this reason our true freedom, our true liberty, is something we must never sacrifice, for if we sacrifice it we are renouncing God himself.

If our true identity lies in freedom and if God is freedom, then to understand prayer properly we must see it as our freedom emerging from the depths of our nothingness at the call of God, responding to God. Prayer is the flowering of our inmost freedom in response to the Word of God. Prayer is not only a dialogue with God, it is the communion of our freedom with ultimate Freedom, his infinite Spirit. It is the elevation of our limited freedom into the freedom of the Divine Spirit, the Divine Love. Prayer occurs when our freedom encounters the all-embracing Charity that knows no limits and knows no obstacles. Prayer is an emergence into this area of infinite freedom.

In this communion of freedom we come to discover the creative energy of love—not love as a sentimental or sensual thing, but as a profound, self-giving expression of freedom. All the powers of our soul reach out in freedom in knowledge and love and they all converge again. They all gather together in one supreme act of love that is radiant with peace. This total giving of the self in love in the freedom that is love has two aspects to it. On one side it is a sort of mystical death that completely separates us from created things. Without such there is no perfect freedom and there is no passing to the other side, which is the promised land of mystical union. We have to have the courage to go beyond all our thoughts and images and concepts and even our very selves, all that is created, and open to and enter into the complete emptiness if we want to find the perfect freedom of the children of God. The Spirit will guide us and teach us the meaning and role of this abyss of freedom that opens out within us, which is meant to draw us utterly out of our own selfhood into the immensity of the Divine Freedom. "What happens is that the separate entity that is you apparently disappears and nothing seems to be left but the pure freedom indistinguishable from infinite freedom, love identified with love. Not two loves, one waiting for the other, striving for the other, seeking for the other, but love loving in freedom."

In *New Seeds of Contemplation* Merton asks himself if there are twenty persons alive in the world now who see things as they really are. If there are such, they are truly free. They are not dominated by attachment to any created thing, to themselves, or even to the gifts of God, no matter how supernatural or how special. Undoubtedly such an experience of freedom is had by few and even by them perhaps rarely enjoyed in this transient life. Tom believed that there were not twenty such persons alive in the world but he felt that there must be one or two and that they were the ones who would be holding everything together and keeping the universe from falling apart.

Merton saw in the first Christian generation an example of the freedom given in Christ by the Spirit: "They experienced the new life of liberation 'in the Spirit' in the perfect freedom of men who received all from God as pure gift in Christ, with no further responsibility to this 'world' other than to announce the glad tidings, the imminent 'establishment of all things in Christ.'" That generation believed that the kingdom was at hand and they stood prepared to immediately enter into it. They detached themselves from everything and joined fully into the life of the community, caring for each other in a unity of mind and heart. When the Parousia did not arrive, this same freedom became embodied in the martyrs and those who embraced the faith with the spirit of martyrs, ready to give all in order to enter into the kingdom. When the age of the martyrs ended — if indeed it has ever ended: is it not more truly present today than ever before? — the torch was handed on to the monks, who embodied this ideal of Christian freedom in the Spirit, ready to renounce all in order to enter into the fullness of the Kingdom of Love.

We are created by God in freedom in order that we may exercise the options and the self-dedication that is implied in the highest kind of love. We discover and develop our freedom precisely by making those decisions that take us out of ourselves to meet reality as it truly is. We cannot see or experience this reality adequately unless we see all in the light of him who is all being and ultimate reality. As Christ promised at the Last Supper, the Spirit, the Paraclete, comes into us to enlighten us. She teaches us the ways of freedom by which we open ourselves to experience reality as it truly is and to come into true relationship with those around us and all that surrounds us. In this contact we become aware of our own autonomy, our own freedom, and our own self-identity. We find out who we truly are. When we are secure in this self-identity, we are ready to give ourselves completely in love to God and to others.

At the end of the book *Contemplation in a World of Action*, which was published after Merton's death, is the transcript of the taped talk "Is the Contemplative Life Finished?" Reading this, it is evident that Tom's faith in the contemplative life never diminished. He saw it as a life dependent directly on God to guide, form, and purify in silence, prayer, solitude, detachment, and freedom. The contemplative life is capable of leading a person to the fullest possible realization. Although Tom had many contacts in the world at this time, he did not see these contacts as necessary, making him in some way dependent and less free. Instead he saw them as something good that he could freely enjoy and use as opportunities of helping others as long as they did not impinge on his true freedom. At the time Father Louis gave this talk, Dom Jean Leclercq was urging him to move out, to be more present to the world, to travel about and bring his gifts of wisdom and understanding to others. But Tom made it clear to his abbot that in accepting the invitation—originally inspired by Dom Jean Leclercq—to go to the Orient, he was planning one trip only, with the hope of finding at the end of it a place of even greater solitude. Tom did write in "Inner Experience" that "solitude is necessary for spiritual freedom but once that freedom is acquired it demands to be put to work in the service of love." That is absolutely true. It is of the very nature of participating in the freedom of God, that freedom which is Love and which impels him to expansive love of all creation. But it is the responsibility of each one of us to exercise that service of love in complete freedom according to our own proper vocation or place within the community of the Church and the human family. As Tom writes in "Elias—Variations on a Theme":

> The free man is not alone as busy men are
> But as birds are. The free man sings
> alone as the universes do. Built
> Upon his own inscrutable pattern
> Clean, unmistakable, not invented by himself alone
> Or for himself, but for the universe also.

No one can doubt the depth of the concern that Father Louis brought to the world and to his brothers and sisters in the world in their struggles for peace, justice, and freedom. Tom felt that monks should follow world events and be concerned about them. He often prefixed his talks to his novices and later to the community as a whole with comments on current events. He saw one of the roles that the monastery was to fulfill was to be a place where those who were actively engaged in the struggles of our times could come for understanding, support, and renewal. Unfortunately, few of those who are called contemplatives have really heard this word of Thomas Merton. Many of them still remain aloof from the struggles taking place in the human community and are content to pray about them in a sort of detached way. On the other hand, contemplatives who have opened their minds and hearts to hear the terrible needs of their sisters and brothers in the world have all too often been tempted to become directly involved in that struggle, rather than continue in their contemplative path. Father Louis's way was the middle way, the contemplative way, and a difficult way: to be truly concerned, involved in mind and heart, and yet to remain to the struggle as a contemplative presence. This is why his contribution was unique and powerful. Some activists, with less depth of vision, urged him to come out and join them. But others, such as Dan Berrigan, Jim Forest, and Ping Ferry, knew the importance of going to Gethsemani to be with Tom, of keeping in touch with him as a vitalizing source, and of supporting him in his singular and largely very lonely, as well as solitary, contribution.

There is no truly free society except in heaven. But that heavenly society is to be reflected as much as possible on earth. It is the responsibility of the Christian person to seek to bring this about. It needs to be reflected on earth by a society that is united by self-sacrifice and love, mercy and compassion, selflessness and a participation in the Divine Pity. The free person, liberated from his or her own need for pleasure and immediate satisfactions, is free to reach out to help relieve the needs of others and in turn to help them to become free and to find their own inner truth.

It lies within the power of the truly free person to choose to be nondestructive and to cooperate freely in the creation. The power to destroy is an illusory power. It is something that we fall back on when we doubt our freedom and our power to create. It is only an appearance of power. True power lies in our freedom to align ourselves with God's will and love to be true creators of life and hope and freedom. It is only if we can free ourselves from the fears and prejudices that presently entrap us in a world that is set upon mass destruction that we can hope to find the way to a new world society that is ordered to peace and justice and the well-being of every member of the human family. Tom wrote to Ping Ferry, one of his close friends in the peace movement, "What we all have to do is to get as free as possible from pre-judgments in order to try to do the immense pioneering job of thinking that is demanded if we are going to come to grips with this problem at all." As he wrote in *Conjectures of a Guilty Bystander*, "The only thing that is stopping us from living humanly is our own deeply ingrained habit of illusion." The most important thing that the truly free person can bring to the world is a shift of consciousness. When we come to know our true freedom, which is our true dignity, then we can work together in a noncompetitive way for the well-being and dignity of all.

When Father Louis was novice master he had four conferences a week with the novices. These touched on the basic matters necessary to form the minds and hearts of these young men who were aspiring to understand monastic life and decide if this was the way they were called to embrace. Tom prepared these conferences well and we have in his taped talks a good basic treatment of monastic history and Cistercian spirituality. Tom had a wonderful way in the course of these more scholastic talks of making their matter relevant to contemporary concerns. (In a letter Tom tells Catherine Doherty, with some exaggeration, "I prepare conferences, then tell them something entirely different. If I gave them what I had prepared, then that would really be folly.") In the course of one of his talks on Peter Abelard, a twelfth-century representative of the emerging scholastic theology who clashed with Bernard of Clairvaux and received summary judgment, Tom launched into a discussion about freedom. He saw it to be "the most characteristic of modern problems—a very important problem," central to the questions of war and race relations. As was frequently the case with this man of words, he saw that there was involved here also a problem of meaning: "What do people mean when they talk about freedom?" He went on to say, if you want to talk about something as big as the topic of freedom you have to divide it up. Then he outlined the different kinds of freedom that might be considered. First is moral freedom, the one about which we tend to be most concerned, the freedom of choice involved in virtue and sin. And then there is spiritual freedom, about which most of what we have already written in this chapter concerns itself. Then there are others: freedom of conscience or religious freedom, freedom in relation to law, and freedom in relation to the authority in the Church—this was the freedom that came into play in the case of Peter Abelard. And finally he spoke of political freedom. I will share a few of Tom's thoughts on each of these last three. And then I will say something about Merton's freedom in relation to his writing, something central to his life.

In regard to the interrelation of freedom and law, there is a delightful passage in Tom's novel, *My Argument with the Gestapo*. It opens with his statement, "There are two orders, the order of law and the order of freedom, and I'll give you two guesses which one I think is more important." (In a talk later in his life, Tom says unequivocally, "God is on the side of freedom.") In the discussion that ensues with the interrogators, who seek to establish the need to live under law, Merton's responses are filled with biblical allusions: "Ask the lilies of the field concerning the first law of nature, they toil not neither do they spin. . . . Foxes have holes and birds of the air have nests, and I will lie down among the beds of flowers in Casa." He concludes with his statement of principle: "The things I owe Caesar can best be said negatively: that is I owe him whatever he asks that does not conflict with what I owe on another level of loves and debts."

In his talks to his novices, Father Louis constantly tried to make them fully aware of the fact that law, all law, even the Holy Rule, is for people. He warned them of the danger of making law or the Rule an end in itself, as though perfection could lie in fulfilling all the precepts of the Holy Rule. Law is based on the common good. There is, of course, the assumption that the common good is the good of each and every member of the community. This assumption must be ready to give way to reality when reality is contrary. He warned against the danger of taking refuge in the law as a means of avoiding coming face to face with the demands of true charity.

The question of freedom and Church authority is indeed a complex one. In the case of Father Louis himself, in some ways the complexity is simplified and in some ways it is made more complex by the fact that he freely made a vow of obedience to obey his abbot in accordance with the Rule of Saint Benedict, which gives the abbot almost unlimited control over the lives of his monks. Sometimes in exasperation Tom lashed out at this authority, as when he wrote to his abbot:

Do you not have an inordinate tendency to interfere in the workings of conscience and to suppress by violence those desires and ideals which run counter to your policies? Do you not tend to assume that your policy represents the last word in the spiritual perfection of every one of your subjects, and that anyone who is drawn to another way is leaving the path of perfection simply because he is not following your ideas?

But in the end that same abbot was able to give testimony that Father Louis was one of the most obedient of all his monks. Tom found the freedom to obey because he knew by faith and by experience that through obedience he found even greater freedom and grace.

He was conscious of the great temptation of the institutions of the Church, including monasteries, in their quest for security and control, to hamper the freedom of the Spirit and the true growth of the individual. On the feast of the Epiphany in 1965 he wrote:

One of the great temptations of an over institutionalized religion is precisely this: to keep man under constraint of his own and the society's past so that this safety appears to be freedom. He is "free" to return to familiar constraint but this interferes with his freedom to respond to the new gift of grace in Christ . . . a great truth that must be brought into our view of the Church. Otherwise, where is the Holy Spirit? Where is the soul of this Body?

In a paper that was published only a few weeks before his death, "Final Integration," Tom looked at this question in detail in regards to the monastic institution. He came to the sad conclusion that it was often necessary for a man to leave his institutionalized monastery in order to have the freedom to continue to grow in the way that God was calling him. It can be said to the credit of the community of Gethsemani and their superiors, who were blessed with such an extraordinary confrere as Thomas Merton, that they not only tolerated but in many ways supported his extraordinary growth into freedom and his unique expression of the Cistercian contemplative life.

Merton wrote a great deal about political freedom. He was concerned about the racial problems that were so close to home in his Southern monastery. Yet his concerns went far beyond the local. He reached out to many parts of the world, to slums and ghettos and to political prisons. He had a special concern for his fellow writers, with whom he sensed he formed a true community. The most important contribution he felt he could make and which he ceaselessly did try to make was to help people realize that even in enslavement and oppression they need not lose their true freedom as long as they remained in touch with their true self and their dignity as a child of God. On the other hand, he saw clearly that it was often the case that persons who enjoyed the greatest political freedom were, because of their lack of inner freedom, enslaved to the whims of others.

The area in which Father Louis perhaps most immediately and most keenly experienced the struggle for freedom was in regard to his writing. As a young writer he had had an overwhelming desire to be published. Naomi Burton Stone, Tom's literary agent, speaks of this and it is revealed in the course of *My Argument with the Gestapo*. At one point, the hero—who is Merton himself—expresses his disappointment that his manuscript was not read into the records of the court so that it could at least have that publication. This novel was written in the summer of 1941, when Tom was struggling with the question of a religious vocation, which necessarily involved his freedom to write and publish. He seems to have resolved the question of publication when he says in the closing lines of the novel, "I think suddenly of Blake, filling paper with words, so that the words flew about the room for the angels to read, and after that, what if the paper was destroyed? That is the only reason for wanting to write, Blake's reason." So his resolution is that it will be enough if he writes for only the angels to read. It is good that he did attain a certain freedom in regards to publication, for in the years to come he would see censors rip his writings to shreds, leave them sitting on the shelf for months and even years, and in some cases forbid publication. In the end it was his own freedom, expressed in his literary legacy, that held back certain pieces from publication.

If he freed himself from the compulsion to publish, there was still the compulsion to write. In the last days of his vocational discernment in 1941 he was still asking whether the one or the other alternative would provide him with the opportunity to continue writing. Finally, he was able to let that go, knowing that when he chose the Cistercians, there was a real possibility that he might never be able to write again. In the monastery, not only did he find the opportunity to write but he found that he was actually commanded to write. This, perhaps, demanded even greater detachment from his writing. The first books that he published were the ones that were written in obedience on topics that were chosen by others. He considered them among the worst of his writings.

When he wrote his novel in the summer of 1941, he was concerned about his integrity as a writer: "If there exists a kind of freedom that can be advanced by bad writing, I don't want any part of it." But years later he would find himself not only writing a script for the audiovisual presentation at the Vatican Pavilion in the World's Fair at the request of Cardinal Spellman but rewriting it according to the prelate's prescriptions. And he would find himself writing a message of contemplatives at the request of Pope Paul VI in a way that would respond to the expectations of others. Fortunately, he was able to hold these demands lightly, and continue to do the writing his own creative spirit demanded of him. In his "Answers on Art and Freedom" Merton wrote, "The artist who expends all his efforts in convincing himself that he is not a non-artist cannot justify his vexations by appealing to an ideal freedom. What he needs is not an ideal freedom, but at least a minimum of practical and subjective autonomy—freedom from the pressures by which society holds him down. I mean freedom of conscience." This Tom was always able to maintain, no matter how great the pressures and restrictions placed upon him. He kept writing and usually he found some distribution, even if only through the media of the mimeograph.

The place where I think Tom's freedom as a writer was most compromised was in his succumbing to the claims of fame. Tom saw himself first of all as a poet. He was attracted to the freedom of the poet. When critics reviewed his poetry according to "accepted" expectations, categories, or canons, Tom took the further step into antipoetry, where no authority could be marshaled in reviewing it. But in many ways his life became too busy, too productive, trying to keep up with the fame and claim of *The Seven Storey Mountain*—a claim his earlier published poetry never made—to have the space and the freedom for poetry. He wrote his best verse in his earliest days in the monastery, when he was in some ways most free. His horizons, though, were still quite enclosed, so the poetry tends, with some significant exceptions, toward the pious, lacking the depth of humanity that mark his later writings.

In an essay on freedom and the artist, Merton states that "In the last analysis the only valid witness to the artist's creative freedom is his work itself. The artist builds his own freedom and forms his own artistic conscience by the work of his hands. Only when the work is finished can he tell whether it was done 'freely.'" According to his own scale, few of Tom's writings measured up to his standards, and the standard of freedom was one of the standards by which he judged his works. Tom had a great admiration for the Russian novelist, Boris Pasternak, and reached out to him in friendship. He summed up his esteem for Pasternak in this terse way: "What does he see? Freedom."

In *The New Man* Tom stated that a person is alive "not only when he exists and acts as a man (that is to say freely) but above all when he is conscious of the reality and the inviolability of his own free-dom and aware at the same time of his capacity to consecrate that freedom entirely to the purpose for which it was given him." This realization does not come into being until our freedom is actually devoted to its right purpose. We truly find ourselves and are happy when we know that our freedom is functioning to orientate us toward the goal that we seek in our deepest spiritual center to achieve. I believe this sums up the quest of Thomas Merton's life.

In this chapter I have spoken of the quest for freedom rather abstractly. It will be, perhaps, more instructive and more interesting to see it as it was lived out in the various stages of Thomas Merton's life. Returning to the image of the seven-storey mountain, I think we can see seven stages in Tom's quest for freedom. First was the quest for basic human freedom, which he exploited and abused. Then came his quest for the freedom of faith and the fuller freedom of the monastic life. Within that life he continued to seek, finding a freedom to be open to all reality. He went on to seek the freedom of the eremitical life. In all of this he was seeking the freedom of final integration, which prepared him to enter into the ultimate freedom of the Kingdom of Heaven.

3. "Free by Nature"

In the first sentence of his autobiography, Thomas Merton tells of his birth. In the second he goes on to state, "Free by nature, in the image of God, I was nevertheless the prisoner of my own violence and my own selfishness, in the image of the world into which I was born." We are all born free, but we often do not realize it. We need to come to know our freedom—with its attendant responsibility—and then use that freedom in a lifelong struggle to become truly free.

Tom's statement is a theological one as well as an existential one. In our freedom lies our greatest dignity; therein we image God. This is so because in our freedom lies our power to love, and God is love. This is a creation-centered theology, recognizing that our call to divinity comes from our very creation. It is a traditionally Cistercian theological outlook. The Cistercian Fathers dwelt often on the human person as the image of God, an image that has lost its likeness: "prisoner of my own violence and selfishness." Tom would later speak of this defaced image, perhaps more accurately, as the false self. It is the self that has gone forth from God, its true image, into the "land of unlikeness"—a prodigal son. Following the typology he has drawn from Dante, he sees "this world" as "the picture of hell," a land of unlikeness where one can, indeed, stray far from God. Tom's ascent through the seven mountains of purgatory toward the goal of true freedom has not yet begun. First, he must pass through the "hell" of this world "in fear and hopeless self-contradictory hungers." Fear, because the false self, which is made up of what we have and what we can do and what others think of us, is so very fragile. At every moment we fear someone will break through and discover how hollow we are, that is, who we think we are. Hunger is a good, graphic, concrete word for the insatiable desires that enslave and consume us even as we seek to consume the things for which we hunger, "to grab everything and see everything and investigate every experience and then talk about it."

Merton entitles the first chapter of his autobiography "Prisoner's Base." The game is perhaps not as well known in these days of television-induced passivity as it once was. It is an exciting game, with its alternations of running free and waiting to be set free. It is a good image for Tom's earlier years, with their periods of institutional discipline followed by liberation, usually brought about by the act of a father figure. Perhaps one of the things Tom resented in Dom James Fox, so long his father abbot, was the latter's unwillingness or inability to liberate the monk from the institutional discipline. Dom James, too, had his superiors. When he finally allowed Father Louis to have a hermitage on Mount Olivet, Tom awaited the visit of the abbot general with trepidation, fearing the general might command that the little cinder-block house be torn down.

The death of Tom's mother in 1921 was, in a sense, Tom's first liberation, when he came fully into the hands of his father, who had far less inclination to discipline his son. The two of them were soon off for the summer to Provincetown at the end of Cape Cod, where his father so dominated the scene that Tom never mentions the presence of his aunt. After a short stay in the school on Long Island, which Tom found quite foul and evil-smelling, Tom was again off with his father to the freedom of Bermuda. He gave the school there a few days' trial and then he was allowed to escape and, in the rough-and-tumble existence of a boardinghouse, do pretty much whatever he wanted. He was even left free to fend for himself in this adult environment, eight-year-old though he was, while his father went to New York to sell some paintings. Tom's return in 1923 to a more disciplined situation in his grandparent's home did not last long. At ten he was off to bachelor existence with his father in France as they created a home in Saint Antonin. Then came his unhappiest period of imprisonment, his two years at the Lycée Ingres at Montauban, which were relieved only by Sunday visits to his father and vacations with him. Perhaps the stresses of this imprisonment, more than anything else, brought on a tubercular condition, as imprisonment well might, which won for Tom some months of freedom in the country at Murat with the Privats. In June 1928 his father came to Montauban to take Tom off to England. As they rode away from the Lycée everything echoed for the twelve-year-old with the cry of "Liberty!" It is one of the more graphic moments in *The Seven Storey Mountain*. Then there were the schools of England, more gentlemanly than those of the French, but perhaps more galling at times for the young man, who saw through their trappings and detested their pretense. The young player continued to experience new breaks into freedom, one coming in the painful form of his father's death, another in the impressive liberality of his grandfather, and still another in the acculturation passed on to him by his godfather. The game was fairly over by then, for Tom had arrived at the stage where no one need any longer give him physical freedom. It was time for him to begin the struggle for the freedom that only he, with the grace of God, could give himself, inner freedom, the freedom that truly counts.

Father Louis's life is, rather interestingly and neatly, divided into two distinct halves of equal length: twenty-seven years outside the monastery and twenty-seven years within. Most of the first period was spent in the exercise of a false freedom; the latter was wholly devoted to finding a true freedom. Both might be said to have been largely successful in what they sought to do. This was so because his life was grounded on a solid foundation of basic human freedom. Most of us will never be great saints or great sinners because we do not have enough freedom, enough sense of self, to give ourselves fully to anything, good or bad. Tom did have that sense of freedom and self, thanks in good part to his earliest training at the strongly disciplining hands of his mother.

There is an interesting parallelism between the two halves of Merton's life. Both parts enjoyed or profited from, at the beginning, a strong discipline administered by a loving disciplinarian for about seven years: in the one case, his mother, in the other, Dom Frederic Dunne, his first abbot. They both encouraged him in his writing and put him through paces he did not wholly enjoy but that bore good fruit. After their passing he was much more on his own, especially in regard to the development of his writing abilities. Because after each one's passing there was no one there who really understood and walked consistently with him, someone whom he could fully trust, he did some wild and stupid things. In each case, toward the end of the period there was a friendship with a very special woman, moments of particular enlightenment, and finally, a breakthrough to another life.

Ruth Merton wanted her son to be independent, to have his own ideas, not to run with the crowd. "I was to be original, individual, I was to have a definite character and ideals of my own," he wrote later. She started his education at an early age and pushed him along. Discipline and persistence as well as pride went into the task. She was a bit chagrined when her son's independence expressed itself in headstrong stubbornness. On the whole Tom judged her successful, though for him, her dedication was remembered as "worried, precise, quick, critical of me, her son." He did develop a strong attachment to his own will and his own judgment, ever reaching for freedom, not realizing, as he rejected subjection to others, he was enslaving himself to his own subjectivity. When he later turned to monastic discipline to achieve his true freedom from this subjection, he saw it as "the ultimate paradoxical fulfillment of my mother's ideas for me." I think in the end his parents must be proud of the way their son excelled in the highest of all arts—the spiritual art—and used what art he had as a writer, poet, and graphic artist to share that spiritual art, with an impact on the lives of millions.

Tom gave some of the credit for his training in freedom to his father, who early read to him from *Greek Heroes*. The ideals of the early Greek state were somehow grasped and stored in a precocious and thirsting mind. It was more, though, by example that Ruth's husband, Owen, formed his son to freedom. The young couple might be called Bohemian: their lives certainly expressed courage and freedom in the way they struck out in search of what they wanted and then decided to create it together in a foreign country. Only the outbreak of a world war brought Ruth home; Owen never returned home. Nor did he ever stop traveling. He wanted to be a good painter and he always welcomed an opportunity to advance his art, if not his artistic career. Only death finally stopped him. His religious search was not so obvious, but in the end the two came together as he sketched icons while he lay on his deathbed.

His son, too, enjoyed and took advantage of a remarkable freedom to move around. After all the journeys with his father, shortly before Owen's death he began to travel on his own. His first trip was from England to Strasbourg during the Christmas holidays in 1930. He was then only fifteen. A couple of months after his father's passing in January 1931, the sixteen-year-old went off to Florence and Rome and then to the United States for the summer. The year 1932 saw him again making his way through Germany at the time of Hitler's first national electoral campaign. In 1933 he enjoyed a long tour in southern Europe and then visited America for the summer. Before he was twenty he had crossed the Atlantic at least nine times. If World War II had not erupted he would surely have returned at least once more in fact, rather than solely in fiction. But as he said in his novel, freedom to move around was, by the time of his writing, 1941, not the freedom for which he searched.

By the time he was engaged in writing his novel, he had begun his quest for true freedom, but at fourteen he was seeking another kind of pseudofreedom, an independence that allowed him to follow his own whims. That summer, 1929, he was taken to Scotland by his father and then left there when his father fell ill and had to go to a London hospital. A stern hostess tried to get Tom to conform and stay with the crowd. The youngster listened and then went off to read his French books, hiding in the branches of a tree, and to trek across the fens and do his own thinking. In the following months at school, like many an adolescent, he systematically broke rules to establish his independence. He said later he was "rapidly building up a hard core of resistance against everything that displeased me: whether it was the opinions of desires of others, or their commands, or their very persons." He had begun to learn how to manipulate authority.

His sense, as well as his state, of independence took an immense leap in June 1930, when at fifteen he learned that his magnanimous grandfather had made him financially independent. He now had investments, stocks, and even an island. He would, of course, be under a guardian and on an allowance till he came of age. But as he was fully aware and later asserted when his guardian reprimanded his extravagance, it was his money to spend. When he felt down or wanted to celebrate, he would spend it on all sorts of luxuries, from silk ties to good liquor. Although such independence was heady enough for a high school lad, the way his grandfather went about informing Tom of it did even more to give the young man a sense of himself and his freedom. Pop, as his grandfather was affection-ately called, sat the fifteen-year-old down and went over with him all the details of the current, worldwide financial crisis and then explained the provisions he had made to secure Tom and his broth-er's futures, doing all this as though he were explaining it to a knowl-edgeable adult. To add to the "man-to-man" camaraderie of the occasion, Pop presented Tom with a pipe and encouraged him to smoke—even though it was against the rules of the school. Tom later wrote, "It was the first time in my life I was ever treated completely grown up." Tom's parents, in the spirit of the freedom that they passed on to him, had sought to avoid any financial dependence on the Jenkins family. Pop's munificence was now given to Tom in a very different way. It was easy for the lad to see only the freedom it permitted and not the dependence it involved.

Pop, so eager to provide, gave the boy too much credit for maturity. And the man he appointed Tom's guardian did the same. Dr. Tom Bennett, Tom's godfather, became a model for Tom. Bennett was a man of considerable sophistication as well as affluence. His fashionable London apartment became Tom's home, until the young man's rowdiness and carousing became too obstreperous for the doctor's wife to endure. But that would come only during his disastrous Cambridge year. During his last years at Oakham, the public school he attended from 1929 to 1932, Tom learned from his godfather and from the books, especially the novels, they shared, a whole new set of values, which he gradually began to apply with the unbalance and enthusiasm of his youth. Pleasure and self-indulgence became the norm. Looking good was paramount. At Oakham Tom could not get into too much trouble; rules were strict and opportunities few. At Cambridge, rules were strict by current standards, but opportunities abounded, and then there were always the trips to London.

Tom's well-established independence opened the way for him to indulge his passions freely. As he put it, after his father's death he felt "completely stripped of everything that impeded the movement of my own will to do as it pleased. . . . I would think what I wanted and do what I wanted, and go my own way." On the voyage back to England on the eve of his entry into Cambridge, Tom spent a good deal of time with some American girls on their way to fashionable European finishing schools. In a section left out of the published autobiography Tom says, "Two of them had some of that crazy intentness on getting drunk which everybody seemed to have in the nineteen-twenties and which I was about to acquire myself." In fact, he soon spent most evenings in the bars of Cambridge or London, and it was a habit that was to carry over to Columbia. There were even shadows of the habit in Colombo in the last week of his life, when as a lonely traveler he sought out a bar with a good jazz band.

On the previous Atlantic crossing he had learned something about the potential enslavement of another passion. In an omitted section of his autobiography he describes the voyage "as if I walked up the gangplank saying to myself: 'Now I am going to fall in love.'" And he did that. He paid the consequences at the end of the voyage when the infatuation was abruptly ended. He wrote about the experience fifteen years later: "I'd rather spend two years in a hospital than go through that again! The devouring, emotional, passionate love of adolescence, the love that sinks its claws into you and devours your insides day and night and eats into the vitals of your soul." The young man who prided himself on being so free to do whatever he wanted was in bondage to his feelings and emotions. Passionate love is enslaving, and Tom continued to seek it out: "For some ten years I was constantly torn to pieces."

We do need to get free from the domination of such emotions. But that does not mean we are to become passionless, that we do not want to continue to feel and feel deeply. Tom, writing to Catherine de Hueck in 1966, asks her to pray that they will "grow in hope and freedom" and do so precisely in and by deep feelings that are really a great good, though we may prefer any other at the time they are with us. In the same letter he warns about the danger of worldly feelings getting hold of us: "One must weep with the world . . . but also we must gradually get so that the world and its rule of terror does not reach in to try to dominate our inner soul."

If a certain enslavement to liquor and tobacco did take hold of the young student—though he was never an alcoholic—something more pervasive was at work. Tom Merton fell very strongly under the influence of Tom Bennett. Tom B. was always on the "in" of things. He knew his way around and people knew he knew his way around. Translated by Tom M. to campus life, this meant being with the most sophisticated of freshmen, in on all the drinking parties and in on all the other forms of carousing. "I had learned in novels that the questions of right and wrong didn't exist." In that year Tom became acquainted with the writings of Sigmund Freud and embraced his teaching about the evils of sexual repression. He was a young man who needed to be free and fulfilled and to prove he was a real man—the pipe and the clothes didn't prove everything, though he used them to fullest advantage and at considerable expense—and this meant he needed to be a big man with the ladies, especially with the one known as the freshmen's delight.

All of this led naturally enough to disaster. As far as scholarship went, the need to carouse overcame the previous imperious need for books. Not the possession of them—Tom still bought prodigious amounts of them, further increasing his financial difficulties, but his love of actually devouring them and drinking in the knowledge he craved. The low grades and the overspending and even the "lurid reputation" flowing from his misconduct probably would not have brought things to a head, at least not so soon, if it had not been for the pregnancy. This profoundly embarrassing "ineptitude" was the decisive impropriety that turned his very proper godfather and guardian against him and terminated his Cambridge career. It challenged Thomas Merton to take another look at the way he was seeking and exercising freedom.

The experience led to a shift in models. Tom was hurt and hurt deeply by the rejection on the part of his godfather. Tom couldn't even bring himself to say a decent good-bye when he was leaving England definitively. Bennett's castigations seemed immensely unfair to Tom. After all, he was only trying, in his own way, to live according to the values and standards set for him by his guardian and the books his guardian had encouraged him to read—at least, that was the way he saw it. Yes, he had made mistakes in his interpretation of what that meant. He had gone too far. But a young man should be entitled to make some mistakes. As he says in his novel in a macaronic telegram to his uncle, "*Purqoi no comprenni ke se apladen tanto les plaisirs en los Romans, mientras en la vita vienen condannat.*" All right, he had misjudged. He repented. He was ready to face the consequences. The deeper hurt and the real rift came from the fact that his model was not willing to face the consequences. For Tom Bennett there should be no consequences. There was something in the young Cambridge existentialist, who was both an idealist and a realist, that felt strongly that this nonacceptance of consequences was wrong. Years later Father Louis would tell his novices that the difference between childish autonomy and a real autonomy was that the person who was really autonomous acted according to conscience and was ready to answer for the consequences. Not that there could not be factors that might excuse one. When he arrived back at Cambridge late from his aunt's funeral and was "gated" (confined to his quarters) for being out late he was quite grieved. There was a justifying excuse. Yet, in the case of the pregnancy he did succumb to his guardian's decision to take care of things quietly, and he moved on. It was something of which he would never be proud. "Taking care of things" was perhaps, even probably, the best way to handle the situation for all concerned, including the young woman and their son. But accepting the way out, without examining if it truly was the right thing to do, was not accepting the consequences. There was a certain naive immaturity in the way the young Cambridge student gave himself uninhibitedly to the satisfaction of his desires in the name of freedom, but there was also a certain integrity that wanted to remain intact, a fidelity to reality, to what was, that would undergird his whole life and search. For ultimately it was a search for truth, which revealed itself in time to be a search for him who said, "I am the Truth."

This question of fidelity to consequences reminds me of a humorous incident from Father Louis's early days in the monastery. As I mentioned in Chapter One, in those times we had a practice called the chapter of faults. It was supposed to be a forum for fraternal correction. But first the "criminal" got a chance to correct himself. It went something like this: When the community was gathered in the chapter house, the superior would say, "Let us speak of our order." The monks who had some fault of which to accuse themselves would immediately prostrate themselves full length on the floor. At the superior's command they would all arise, and then the superior would call them out, one at a time, to tell everyone of their fault. If there were a great number who had prostrated, the superior would call forth only a few of them. The faults to be brought to the chapter were the external infractions against the Rule and the usages—there were plenty of them, as the book of usages was more than three hundred pages—not the interior failings that one would bring to his spiritual father in sacramental confession or spiritual colloquy. The superior would respond to the self-accusation with some advice and penance. After the monks had had an opportunity to accuse themselves, the brethren were given the opportunity to accuse each other. "Are there any proclamations?" the superior would ask. Those who had something against Tom would say: "I proclaim Frater Louis." And the accused would fall to the floor in a full prostration until all the "proclamations" were made and the superior told the proclaimed to arise. Then one by one the proclaimed would come before the superior, hear what his accuser had to say, and receive whatever admonition and penance the superior cared to give. It was permissible for a monk to accuse himself and another together. Tom's high spirits, of course, didn't die the day he entered Gethsemani. He was forever cutting up in one way or another. One of his fellow novices tells of Tom and Frater Odo doing towel dances in the washroom, or grand parlor, as they still call it at Gethsemani—the name must have invited such antics as towel dances. Tom's independence would break through the overlay of regulations and ritual that tended to make Trappist life a rather solemn thing. Often enough he was accusing himself—and not infrequently including another whom he had drawn into his fun— for their carrying on, for he felt the consequences of their actions should be readily accepted. The ones who felt aggrieved were those whom Tom had drawn into his horseplay, willing or unwilling, and whom he then drew, also, into his accusations. Father Augustine told me of one such incident from their novitiate days. Tom and he were working on the rocks in the creek. Tom soon drew him into a game that involved a certain amount of useless signs and nonsense. The monks were then still limited to a primitive sign language for basic necessary communication, but more inventive souls found ways of communicating just about everything through creative signs. This kind of play, of course, was forbidden and deserved a proclamation at the next chapter of faults. Tom duly proclaimed himself and Frater Augustine. Dom Frederic gave the two of them a good lecture on sacrifice and penance. After chapter, Augustine advised Frater Louis that for the future the good frater could leave him out of the proclamations. (I don't know just how he said that in signs!) When Tom became father master of the novices he himself entered fully into the game of the chapter of faults and had novices prostrating at the usual places and performing all the other traditional penances.

Tom learned something from his disaster at Cambridge. In order to do the more important things he wanted to do—though it is questionable just how much he really wanted to graduate Cambridge and go into the diplomatic corps—he had to sacrifice and discipline some of his desires. At Columbia his drinking and womanizing did not cease, but he was able to curtail them sufficiently so that they did not prevent him from pursuing the education and the liter-

ary career that he wanted. To some degree he integrated his experience into his work. If some of Father Louis's admirers were shocked
when his friend Ed Rice later published some of Tom's unseemly
cartoons from Columbia days, Tom himself was later disgusted by
them—both for their moral content and because they were such
poor art, slavish imitations of what others were doing. And, as he
said, even the authorities seemed "to take it for granted that it was
the normal and healthy thing for an undergraduate to be completely filthy." It would be a time before he would come to see that
in still pursuing these conforming pleasures he was undermining
his real happiness: "Nothing so completely blinds a man, morally
and spiritually, as slavery to the appetites of his own flesh.... It
would take five or six years to discover what a frightful captivity I
had gotten myself into."

Michael Mott in his authorized biography makes much of the
recurring mention of suicide in Tom's journals in these difficult
years. I think perhaps he makes too much of this. There is, however,
a passage in the manuscript of *The Seven Storey Mountain* where Tom
says that in giving in to lust "we start out on the way to an unhappi-
ness and misery which will eventually make us desire to seek liberation from the horror of what we have done, by suicide." I don't think
Tom ever truly contemplated this course to pseudoliberation; there
is certainly no account of it in his writings.

As Tom recovered from the depths of his Cambridge experience,
that which was most pernicious still lay uncovered below the surface. He had seen it for a moment in Rome. It was a moment of special visitation, when it seemed his father came to him. In the light
of that moment he saw his own misery and pride and his "soul
desired escape and liberation and freedom from all this with an
intensity and an urgency unlike anything ever known before." He
prayed—"praying out of the very roots of my life and of my being . . .
to get free of the thousand terrible things that held my will in their
slavery." But Rome soon enough got lost and he was swept up into
the value system of his godfather. A few years later he would identify
in his journal that which most deprived him of his freedom: "The
hard yoke we are yoked under is the yoke of our own pride and self-
love"—the illusion of the false self that is served at such cost to freedom and happiness. As he moved ahead to find the freedom of the
faith and of the cloister, he would come to uncover, little by little,

this gripping illusion and, freeing himself from it, move into true freedom.

Curiously, one of the things that would give Tom a push in the direction of freedom from his self-centeredness and self-serving desires was communism. During his year at Cambridge he was so taken up with his pleasures that he was virtually oblivious to the important social movements that surrounded him. The depression, or slump, as they more graphically called it in England, was on, and there were rumblings of war on the continent. There was a huge peace march in Cambridge in late 1933 and a hunger march in February of 1934, yet Tom makes no mention of these events in his autobiography. He had kept the *Communist Manifesto* of Karl Marx in evidence in his study at Oakham and was highly interested in Gandhi's visit, but that was before he began to lose control. As he was sailing back to England in 1934 to get his permanent resident visa for the United States, he listened at length to a steward who was a covert communist. When he was settled at Columbia he gave communism more of a hearing. With this, there began to be a shift away from his dominating and enslaving self-centeredness and an opening toward concern for the social justice that communism professedly but ineffectually sought. This was a concern that would grow in genuineness and absorption the rest of Tom's life as he grew into the discovery and freedom of his true self. It would take a strong faith to enable him to truly recenter himself.

Naomi Burton Stone in the preface to Merton's novel, *My Argument with the Gestapo*, remarks on how many scenes from Tom's early life are found in his imaginary return to England and France. The literary form of the novel has an advantage over the straight autobiography, for it enables the author to employ fictional elements to bring out more strongly his or her experience of events and places. There are often several levels of meaning in Tom's challenging novel. The character named B. undoubtedly represents a particular young woman who caught Merton's fancy in his Oakham days amid his dreary Scotch exile. But she also represents all women and, in particular, the mother of his son. There is an interesting and important shift in the presentation of B. in her successive appearances in the novel. At first she appears as an air raid warden, dressed in military attire replete with helmet, her skin darkened by smoke. She is very much a part of the grim and grit of England being destroyed by the blitz, symbolic of the inner corruption that is eating at that society's vitals. In this role she is cast as an easy lover, available for one-night stands. In her last appearance in the novel, though, she comes out of uniform. At this time she looks to Merton, the hero of the book, as her friend and says how important it is that he go away because "for the sake of my own self-respect, I would be happy to have a friend somewhere where there isn't so much of the war, as if there were part of myself, off, somewhere, in a reasonable place." Merton, who cast himself as a "crazy poet" and "as a person who has no place in wars," affirms he is as responsible for the war as any of those fighting it, because of his sins, and confesses his youthful lust toward B. But now there is a theological dimension to his love for her, and a respect. In some way thus does Tom express his justification for where he is in relation to this woman; it seems best for her, according to her wishes, that he be "off somewhere, in a reasonable place." The one thing that is sure in the novel is that there has been a change in the relation: "And all I am saying is that you are my friend because I like you, and I cannot talk about it much, and I only found it out today when I changed into these clothes." More than clothes are surely changed; the symbolism is deep.

In the novel Merton vents his spleen about Cambridge. These are probably the bitterest passages in all of Tom's writings, including those about the Holocaust and the bomb: "Oh, peering Cambridge, I taste you in the broken skin of my lips like the bloody leather of twelve-ounce boxing glove. [Tom was a boxer at Oakham, a good one.] I constantly hear the dried scraps of putty falling from your windows onto the linoleum floor, I smell the awful cleanness of soap in the dank showers underneath the College Buttery, where the soccer player hanged himself. . . . The thought of you empties like old gin out of a glass that has been standing several days, among the clean plates. . . . Cambridge, you are as restrained as postmarks on a letter, but you are as disquieting as syphilis or cancer." And much more. We all do tend to blame places, more than environment deserves. There was no reason in itself why Cambridge could not have been a good environment for the young scholar. Clare is a gracious classical building set between the great schools of Kings and Trinity on the river, across the way from Caius. The master's Garden in The Backs is one of the most beautiful I have ever seen — no wonder Tom had chosen rooms overlooking it for his second year's lodging, in spite of the proximity of the master's own. As one comes in from The Backs, on the key of the entryway arch is a most interesting head, with piercing eyes, open mouth, all inquiry and inviting dialogue. I could not help wonder what interesting dialogues it might have had with a very drunk student sneaking in the back way.

The last pages of Merton's novel contain a parable on the physical freedom that Tom had earlier said was not his interest—that free run of the world granted his fictional counterpart by the Nazis because they were convinced he was just as smutty as they. The parable is the story of a soldier who had suffered tremendously in the war and was taken prisoner. Escape was all but forced upon him, only to release him to even more terrible agonies. In the end he finds himself in a certain peace, yet "I cannot be sure whether I am waiting for something, because there isn't anything to wait for. . . . I might as well be dead, but it just happens that I am not." He is on the brink of "hell." The passage to purgatory is not yet certain.

It is in this novel that Tom first adopts the theme from Dante that he would later use in his autobiography: "I make this journey for the reason Dante made his." And what was that? "He goes to win his freedom." (*Purgatorio*, Canto 1.) It is at mass Merton learns "If I remember I am nothing, I will know the danger can take nothing from me. . . . If I remember that I have nothing called my own that will not be lost anyway, that only what is not mine but God's will ever live, then I would not fear so many false fears. . . . You who fear the words and ideas and opinions of men, you only fear these because you love them too much. . . . You lived in a world where pride had long been burning underground like a fire smoldering for a hundred years in a caved-in coal mine." Only when the underground fires of pride have been extinguished by the full realization that of ourselves we are indeed nothing, but we have all in God, that we are in God, then will we finally be free, free from all fear, free to be our true selves.

4. The Freedom of Faith

When Tom Merton received Tom Bennett's letter advising him to forget Cambridge and a diplomatic career he was too hurt and too adolescent, in spite of all his "maturing experiences," to admit to it with any forthrightness, but his life of licentious freedom had led to a dead end, to the destruction of life and opportunity. He lost some of that false freedom, but he found a new freedom. The hold that Tom Bennett and his sophistication had on Tom were definitely broken. The shackles of British propriety and class system fell away. In spite of his adolescence, through this experience he gained enough insight to see that the life lost was not in itself a true and satisfying life. Tom would one day tell the novices at Gethsemani to thank God even for their past faults, for they are past and they are, in God's wondrous providence, occasions for moving us forward on our journey. He added that he did not want to make a general confession but if it had not been for some of the sins of his youth he might well have ended up a second-rate diplomat off in some corner of the British empire rather than a monk at Gethsemani.

And so yet another subject of the king was to find freedom on the other side of the Atlantic. Tom quickly sensed something of his new freedom and, after an initial letdown, with his characteristic buoyancy, he was able to enter into life at Columbia with enthusiasm. It was a new scene, an opportunity to try again. The desire he had so timidly expressed to Aunt Maude so many years before on top of a double-decker bus in London — to be a journalist — was now a real possibility, encouraged by his loving and supportive Pop. And, what was important, the young man now realized that he had to exercise some restraint on his animal passions if he was to retain the freedom to pursue the kind of life he wanted. He had his first inkling that self-discipline is one of the components of true human freedom.

In the novel he would write six years later, he has B. ask him, "What have you been doing?" "Trying to find something, I don't quite know what" is Merton's response. Happiness, of course, would have been one way of putting the answer. But what is happiness, where is it to be found? Happiness is never found when it is sought in itself. Happiness is always found in something else. I think one way to say it is: happiness consists in knowing what you want, and then knowing you have it or are on the way to finding it. Tom knew keenly the "want," but he was confused as to the "what." Not totally though. One thing was clearly emerging: he wanted to be a writer. Writing would be part of the final answer, whatever it was. But there was something more. Something that came from his very nature and from his baptism — though he would hardly have thought of that at this moment in his life — as well as from many of the persons and events that had touched his life thus far.

"What we want" — that is not a wholly arbitrary choice. As human beings, with minds and hearts fashioned in the image of the One who is ever creating us through the sharing of his own being of knowledge and love, we have an infinite thirst to know and love. We can know happiness only when we discover the way in which this insatiable thirst can be slaked. We must come to discover the infinite source and fountain of knowledge and love, or at least some promising way thereto, or we will constantly be experiencing, and running away from, the dryness of that thirst which cracks and burns the human spirit.

Merton went on in his novel to say to B., "There must be other meanings on another level and I have come to look for them."

Returning to his grandparents' household at Douglaston, from which he had departed abruptly and tearfully nine years before, Tom came again under an influence that did inhibit his freedom. Pop was a magnificent, generous, loving, and garrulous man, a man few could not love. Even when Tom was a child, Pop had treated him as if he were an equal. Tom was always welcome and made to feel truly at home in Pop's office, be it downtown or in the study at Douglaston. When Tom was but fifteen, Pop had established his grandson financially in a most adult fashion. But in all this manly openness there was one prejudice that stood out in Pop, and this he passed on to the impressionable youth. Pop was strongly and outspokenly anti-Catholic. True, the outspokenness virtually ceased when Elsie, Mrs. Jenkins's Catholic companion, entered the household as virtual housekeeper. The wall of prejudice was breached by her presence. In time she would marry into the family, becoming Tom's aunt. But long before that her devout parents would become the young man's friends, and there is nothing like friendship to break through prejudice. As Abraham Lincoln once said, "I don't like that man. I have to get to know him better."

If his mother's father bred into him a certain prejudice—a prejudice he would have to shake himself free of if he were ever to be truly free, for there is no freedom in prejudice—Tom's father bred into him an openness toward the freedom of the Catholic faith, and he did this in many ways.

We might say Owen began by bringing his son into the world in a Catholic country. Tom expatiates on the radically Catholic culture of France in the opening paragraph of the second chapter of his autobiography, listing such elements as chants, monasteries, cathedrals, the poetry of Prudentius, Augustine's *City of God* and his *Trinity*, the *Moralia* of Gregory the Great, the ecclesiastical history of Bede, the theology of Anselm of Bec, the sermons of Bernard of Clairvaux on the *Canticle of Canticles*, the poetry of Caedmon and Cynewulf, of Langland and Dante, Aquinas's *Summa*, and Scotus's *Oxoniense*. I dare say, that the *Summa Theologiae* of Saint Thomas Aquinas would be far more familiar to most than the *Oxoniense* or theological corpus of Duns Scotus—and both would have been unknown to the young Merton when he was in France—but they were to have a great impact on Merton's life, as would Dante's immortal canticle, *The Divine Comedy*, and the sermons of the Father of the Cistercian School of Spirituality, Bernard of Clairvaux. During some of his most formative years, this vagabond youth would be immersed in Catholic culture.

When Tom was ten his father took him back to live in Saint Antonin in the Aveyron Valley. A medieval shrine town, Saint Antonin centered on its church; most of the streets led to it. As Tom later wrote, "Here, everywhere I went, I was forced by the dispositions of everything around me, to be always at least virtually conscious of the church." All of Tom's friends were Catholics, at least nominally. Catholicism was in their bones and showed itself in their mores.

Coming into this Christian atmosphere, his father, for the first time as far as Tom could remember, exhorted his son to pray. His father's religious spirit was now very much in evidence. A hallway conversation might spontaneously and without embarrassment turn to words from Scripture and deeply religious exhortation. Daily mundane occurrences, such as the crow of the cock, were associated with Gospel realities in a way that remained with Tom as long as he lived. Tom's steps, however, were never directed to the small Protestant church in the town. At this time Owen Merton was moving towards openly embracing the Catholic faith. In actual fact, he never did. The son reasoned later that Owen was held back because of the disruption his conversion would have caused in the family in view of Pop's prejudice. Owen's sons still needed their grandparents and he needed his sons. It was all a bit complicated. And time was to make it more so.

Perhaps one of the most important things that Owen did for Tom during these years of intimacy was to share Tom with the Privats. A doctor judged it a matter of life and death that Tom get away to the country and get built up, for the eleven-year-old was in danger of becoming tubercular. The wholesomeness of the Privats's farm in Murat and its produce that enriched his diet were life-giving. But the Privats brought something else into the life of their young guest: the sureness and freedom of their faith. His cockiness wanted argument. But they would have none of it. Rather, in the fullness of their ancestral faith, they felt and quietly expressed a loving concern for this child whose life was not grounded on the solid foundation of the Catholic faith. This was the first intimate glimpse that Tom had of what the faith could mean. After a good bit of wandering, he would, ten years later, with anguish of soul, find himself groping toward such sureness and freedom.

The years of intimacy between father and son would be few and they would be often interrupted. Three years after that autumn on the Privats's farm, Tom would seek out his father in a ward in a London hospital. On the occasion of one of these visits, he found the dying man sketching. But the sketches were unlike any Tom had ever before seen, certainly very different from anything one would expect from a painter of landscapes. His father explained that the hieratic figures were icons, the traditional and powerful representations of the divine coming from the Christian East. They would come to have a great deal more meaning for Tom a couple of years later, when they would turn a tourist into a pilgrim. His father would be there then, too, although already more than two years dead.

Tom won a scholarship to Cambridge at the end of 1932. He would have ten months before classes would begin. As a reward, his guardian gave him, for his eighteenth birthday, a wallet full of tickets and money for a grand tour of the Continent. It was in Rome, in that spring of 1933, that Tom finally saw icons in their full glory as they adorned the apses and walls of the oldest of the Roman basilicas. The majestic, sometimes terrifying, Christ, drew him. The deeper meaning was revealed to him, not by the poetry of D. H. Lawrence, which he first sought to use and then hurled across the room in disgust, but by a moving experience of his father's presence. This moment of grace, perhaps the first real mystical touch in Tom's life, opened his soul to a flood of repentance, a desire for a new kind of freedom, freedom from his sins. It was in many ways a confusing experience for the young man. He began to pray in depth and to search the Scriptures. But when it became too confusing for him, he went out and indulged in meaningless extravagance. He was not yet ready for a real conversion.

His freedom was also still bound very much by human respect. It would be many years before he would be completely free of this, if ever. But the insecure adolescent couldn't even conceive of being free of it. He still lived very much in the image of what others thought of him. When he returned to Douglaston for the intervening months before school, he hid his Bible for fear of ridicule and his prayer was limited to attendance at dissatisfying services in various Protestant churches. Finally, he settled for Zion Episcopal Church, where his father had played the organ and where the sermons were more an attempt at modern philosophizing than doctrinal instruction. Even this little remnant from the Roman experience soon got lost in the fascinating sophistication of the Bennett's London flat and the life of a highly disorderly Cambridge freshman.

Before leaving the European scene I would like to recall one other encounter which, early though it was, may have left its mark. At the end of 1930, while Tom was awaiting the results of his scholarship exam, Tom Bennett, already exercising his role of guardian, arranged for Tom to go to Strasbourg, to broaden his culture and perfect his German. Bennett did not realize how close to death Owen Merton was, and it probably did Tom good to be away from that agonizing situation for a bit. With diplomatic ambitions, it was important for Tom to develop his facility with languages. A relative of Bennett's arranged for Tom to stay at a sort of university hostel run by a Protestant pastor, Professor Hering. Among the residents was another man who was a bit ahead of Tom in the search for the freedom of faith. Louis Bouyer, who would become a leading liturgist and one of the architects of the reforms of the Second Vatican Council, was impressed by Merton, although they did not find too much in common at that time. To him Tom seemed rather shy. Bouyer would enter the Catholic Church three years later. Much later he would resume his acquaintance with Tom through correspondence. It is always encouraging to find another searcher on the journey.

Strasbourg would touch off other resonances in Merton's soul. It was Tauler's city. Its streets were known to Eckhart. These were two of the voices that Tom later identified as "singing" him into the Church.

Merton was in the deepest sense of the word a literator. Writing, reading, books were part of the fabric of his life. Oftentimes books had more impact on him than personal encounters, or at least they enabled experiences to surface and articulate themselves more clearly and powerfully. At the end of the *Secular Journal* he would sum up his road to conversion by listing the books he had read along the way. These were other voices that sang him into the Church.

William Blake would be one of these voices. He would return repeatedly to sing to Tom, putting him in touch with some of the deeper aspirations of his spirit. Tom's father first introduced the boy to Blake's *Songs of Innocence* when he was ten. Later a master at Oakham would further the acquaintance. In many ways Blake mystified the young student. The poet was a revolutionary and yet he detested those who seemed to be the greatest and most typical revolutionaries of his time. The day would come when Thomas Merton would mystify people in the same way. Blake remained the one religious vestige in Tom's life during the irreligious period he went through after his father's death. Blake's continuing and deepening impact, especially as his metaphors unfolded, was such that in the end Tom decided to devote his graduate studies to this poet and wrote a master's thesis on "Nature and Art in William Blake."

Another repeated influence, still more Catholic than William

Blake, would be Dante Alighieri. Again it was Tom's father who made the first introduction. When Tom went up to Cambridge for the scholarship exams, even before taking the exams he purchased a copy of Dante's *Divine Comedy*. The course he took with Professor Bullough reading Dante seems to have been the only course he enjoyed at Cambridge. Later Dante would give Tom the typology for his autobiography and his personal quest for true freedom.

Tom found many friends at Columbia and some of the friendships proved to be deep and long lasting—indeed, lasting a lifetime. Ed Rice is the only one who stands out as a Catholic, but any influence he may have had on Tom's conversion is not apparent. Rice tells us how surprised he was when one day someone ran into him on campus and told him Merton was looking for him. Merton wanted Rice to be his sponsor at baptism. Rice had had no idea Tom was preparing to enter the Catholic Church.

His three close Jewish friends, who stood by him at the Baptism, each brought a significant influence to bear on Tom's journey toward the baptismal font.

Bob Lax was undoubtedly the closest and most influential of Merton's friends. In the early 1980s Paul Wilkes made a documentary film on Tom's life. Wilkes traveled more than 50,000 miles and interviewed twenty-four people to capture the context and reveal the depths of an extraordinarily rich and fascinating life. The resulting television production was beautiful and touching. The interviews were subsequently published: *Merton By Those Who Knew Him Best*. The sense of Bob Lax that emerges from the documentary and his published interview, as well as from *A Catch of Anti-Letters*—the letters that passed between him and Tom from 1962 to 1967—is an attractive one. Lax, a gentle and deep man, was a searcher. He searched deep into his own tradition: the Torah, the cabala, Hasidism. And he reached out from it to other traditions: Catholic theologians and mystics, Hindus and Buddhists. Everything interested him. And he shared all his interests with Tom. This friend gave Tom background for his Catholicism. Lax himself would follow Tom into the Catholic Church.

It was Bob Lax who recommended to Tom the reading of Aldous Huxley's *Ends and Means*. Tom was already familiar with the author; he had enjoyed Huxley's novels. The book had a profound impact on him. He wrote a review for *The Columbia Review* and a letter to

Huxley. *Ends and Means* had created a stir among Huxley's admirers. Some predicted an imminent conversion to the Catholic Church; others saw him about to embrace Buddhism. He did praise the Catholic tradition, with its rich spiritual teaching, high sexual morals, and general discipline. He was, however, pointing more to the Catholicism of the Middle Ages, for he saw the Church as "certainly not progressing . . . becoming worse, not better."

Huxley's somewhat less qualified endorsement of Buddhism set Tom to reading Father Wieger's translations of Buddhist texts. It is difficult to say how much the young man got out of them at this point; probably not very much. His opening to the East at this time occurred more through Bob Lax's roommate at Columbia, another Jewish friend, Sy Freedgood. By some curious turns of events, Sy's Long Island family found themselves hosting an Indian swami, Bramachari. Soon the swami was the stowaway resident of the two students' room and the fascination of all their friends, including Tom Merton. Tom draws a delightful picture of this swami, clad in his traditional *kavi* and sitting cross-legged atop a trunk, in serene meditation in the midst of the chaos of end-of-term packing. This kind of presence and freedom intrigued Tom. It would be the sort of role he would later play in the midst of the agitated political movements of America of the 1960s, sitting quietly in his cloister. Even in his own personal life, which became so full of events, he would sit quietly at the center of his soul, remaining a serene and peace-bestowing presence.

At that earlier time Tom probably did not distinguish too much between Hinduism and Buddhism, and so, left perplexed by the Buddhist texts he was reading, he asked the Indian master to recommend some reading to help him along in his search for deeper spiritual understanding. He was taken aback with the direction he was given. Like all good masters, Bramachari encouraged the young man to stay within his own tradition and deepen his spirit there. He urged Tom to read the *Confessions* of Saint Augustine and the *Imitation of Christ*. Tom did. Both volumes became lifetime companions. The *Confessions* were in mind as Tom wrote the first draft of his autobiography, a fact that one of his censors did not appreciate. He would continue to read the *Imitation* regularly until he entered the monastery. Once there, it would be read to him each day at the end of the midday meal.

The third of the Jewish trio, Bob Gerdy (who was also to follow Tom into the Catholic Church) spoke to his friends in the spring of 1938 about a course he was taking that was being taught by an exchange professor from Manhattanville. The professor's name was Dan Walsh, and the course was on scholastic philosophy. Bob was enthusiastic. The fall found all four friends signed up for Philosophy 177, Walsh's course on the philosophy of Saint Thomas Aquinas — the only course Tom took that year that was outside of the English department. It was the beginning of an important friendship for Thomas Merton. Walsh would be the first to endorse Tom's vocation to the priesthood and point him toward Gethsemani. By one of those wonderful turns of Providence, Tom would be at Dan Walsh's side helping him to prepare for the priesthood some thirty years later.

Merton's own wonderful experience of the Middle Ages as it still lived in parts of France and elsewhere on the continent, Huxley's endorsement of those better times in Catholic history, and Bob Gerdy's enthusiasm for Walsh's course all combined to lead Tom to reach out impulsively and buy a copy of Etienne Gilson's *The Spirit of Medieval Philosophy*. The bonds of anti-Catholic prejudice were slacking, but that day, the day he purchased the book, they got a real wrench. The book was stamped with the mark of the Church, one of the aspects of the Church that Tom found most offensive and one that was in the future to cause him no little pain and grief; the book had been submitted to ecclesiastical censorship. A powerful revulsion contended with a desire to seek the freedom of truth. Tom was perplexed: how could this eminent man of reason submit to such censorship? The insight he finally gained was one that he himself would deeply live in the years to come: it was the willingness of one who is truly a seeker of the freedom that comes from acceptance of the Truth to accept the apparently restrictive structures of an institution that in fact would support him in his quest for the freedom in truth.

Gilson challenged Tom in many ways and made clear to him his God-given responsibility. God created the human being "with a power of choice analogous to that of the angels," wrote Gilson, because God wanted that person responsible for attaining his or her end, free to choose either the way that leads to happiness or the way that leads to misery. Tom was responsible. And great minds,

minds as diverse as Aldous Huxley and Etienne Gilson, were pointing to the same way to happiness. Huxley spoke to his heart, with his
deepening social sense as well as his emerging spiritual longings. Gilson spoke to his head, for Tom was becoming a powerful philosophical thinker (John Tracey Ellis would say that Thomas Merton was one
of the five great original thinkers of the twentieth century), and to
his artistic sense, so well-rooted in the Catholic tradition.

The freedom he had found after the experience at Cambridge to
choose his beloved books over carousing was, indeed, important for
Merton. It opened the way for these books to speak to him and put
him on the way to true freedom. The summer of 1938 was spent in
much reading, following the leads of the previous semester. Huxley
had led him to the somewhat suspect Catholic writer, but one of the
deepest writers of the later Middle Ages, Meister Eckhart, and to the
anonymous *Cloud of Unknowing*. And Gilson pointed to the wholly
unsuspect Aquinas and to Maritain's *Art and Scholasticism*. Things
were coming together for Merton.

There was one more author who played a part in Tom's finally
coming to the freedom of the faith, not perhaps as important as any
of these others, but an occasion of grace. As a boy in the streets of
Montauban his fellow students would point to the black-robed
clerics they saw in the streets and whisper, "Jesuits!" The epitome of
all that was sinister about the Roman Church, all anti-Catholic prejudices could be honed to a fine point when directed toward these
sons of Saint Ignatius. In this regard, as in so many others, things
changed with the move to England. Tom had a long bout of illness
while he was at Oakham. A solicitous headmaster, who appreciated
the particular genius of his young charge, kept him well supplied
with books. One day the master put in Tom's hands a challenging
volume of English verse by a little-known author, Gerard Manley
Hopkins. Tom was astounded to discover that Hopkins was not only
a Catholic but a Jesuit. Years later Tom would tell the novices at
Gethsemani that he felt a sense of community with all poets. It was
this sense of community, this call of one poet to another, that broke
through prejudice and gave Tom the freedom to be open to Hopkins. Tom would return to him. In the summer of 1938 he read James
Joyce's *Portrait of the Artist as a Young Man*. There was much he could
identify with in Joyce's masterpiece. Surprisingly though, freed
from his prejudice against the Jesuits, Tom found that he rather

liked and drew inspiration from the Jesuits in Joyce's book, the ones Joyce himself so mocked. That fall Tom returned to Hopkins, taking up G. F. Lahey's *Life of Gerard Manley Hopkins*. The volume is not so much a flowing biography as a linking together of Hopkins's own writings, especially his letters, and letting them tell the story. One rainy October afternoon Tom was reading a letter Hopkins had penned to John Henry Newman seventy-two years earlier, almost to the day, in which Hopkins, after recounting the decisive steps taken by three of his friends to enter the Catholic Church, announces that for him, too, any further delay is impossible; he asks Newman to receive him "at once." Tom was at that moment freed from all his own indecisiveness. He was out the door and down the street to Corpus Christi Rectory to tell Father Ford *viva voce* that his own decision was made.

Death had been a frequent visitor to Tom's life, and it played its role in helping him to realize the limits of human freedom, at least the kind of freedom he envisioned for himself as a young man. When his mother died, no thought of prayer entered his head. In reality, her death was experienced as a sort of liberation, giving him more of the kind of freedom he was then seeking. It was a different story with his father, who had taught him to pray. His father's death was a holy death, somehow in the shadow of icons, of the great and merciful Judge. In death he led Tom to suspect another kind of freedom. In the fall of 1936 Tom had a sort of nervous breakdown. It involved a struggle with death, the fear of physical dissolution, even with a certain attraction to suicide. Pop's death, soon after, brought Tom to his knees, as did his grandmother's, ten months later. Tom had come to know the need of something beyond, something that can free one even from death. Otherwise, all other freedom would be illusory and, even in the longest of lives, short lived. With faith, Tom found that there was a liberation that reached even beyond the grave or the crematorium.

Merton's journey into faith involved a gradually attained freedom from a prejudice against the Catholic Church. As he moved along he did look at the Protestant churches. When at home in Douglaston, he tried a number of them, hoping to have a better experience than he had had at Montauban and Oakham. But, as he records in his *Secular Journal*, he found in the preaching a lack of the metaphysics that he later came to learn, thanks to Huxley and Gilson, existed in the medieval Church and gave the Church's teaching a solid foundation. The choice, however, was not all that simple for him. In his imaginary return to England in his novel, Merton visits both Protestant and Catholic churches. The Protestant church is old and beautiful; it appeals to his aesthetic sense. And yet he finds it empty. The Catholic church is full, even crowded, but it is all in poor taste. Tom seemed to respond to his difficulties by building up in his mind a certain intellectual prejudice against Protestantism. It was not like the strong and deep prejudice that was early bred into him against Catholicism and from which he had a long struggle toward freedom. But it comes through, embarrassingly so for most Catholics today and especially for a more mature Merton, in *The Seven Storey Mountain*. In time, he prayed for, sought, and found a truly ecumenical heart, one finally freed from all prejudice.

Embracing the Catholic faith did not immediately free Tom from his enslavement to his old habits and passions. One has only to read of the rather dissolute summer he spent with his friends in 1939 to realize this. It was undoubtedly an improvement over the previous year, when Lax couldn't get Tom to even visit a nearby Franciscan campus. Yet the Catholic Church did give him a means and a challenge to grow. And he did, rapidly. Again, one has only to compare the summer of 1939 with that of the following year to see the growth into freedom through self-discipline and spiritual practice. In the second summer Tom would often go apart to pray and think, read and meditate. He would retire early so that he could be up in the morning to hike into town for mass and Communion. The previous year the drunken crew often hadn't gone to bed until morning and had slept much of the day.

Most important of all was the fact that Tom had learned that true freedom lies not in following the dictates of your own passions and emotions, of your own thoughts and ideas, but in aligning your mind and your heart with reality, with truth, with God. God is truth and "the truth shall set you free."

When we acknowledge God's rights over us, then we are free. The assent of faith in no way truncates our true freedom but rather enhances it. The faith gives us a sure place on which to stand to look out openly and freely at all else, with no need for defensiveness. We need depend no longer on what others think, say, or do. There is a sureness in ourselves. We have a sure knowledge on which to base

our lives, a knowledge that is based on the most solid of all founda-
tions, on him who can neither deceive nor be deceived. We are freed
from ultimate doubt, from the fear of being wrong in regard to what
ultimately matters.

The assent of faith does not mean we give up our right to think
and express our own thoughts. The only thing that has the right to
demand the assent of the human intellect is the truth. All the truths
of the faith are necessarily true, even if the intellect cannot comprehend them, because they are attested to by God. Therefore the will
can rightly demand assent, even in the midst of questions. As Cardinal Newman said, in the face of the assent of faith, ten thousand
questions do not make a single doubt. Everything below faith is
questionable. The human mind has the right and duty to question,
including the right to question the teaching of the magisterium of
the Catholic Church in matters that are not of the deposit of the
faith. That authority was objectively wrong in the well-known case
of Galileo, even though it was acting according to the ordinary
magisterium of the time. If the intellect does not see the validity of
the truth set forth by the ordinary magisterium it has to
acknowledge that fact in order to be true and honest. It also needs
to acknowledge that although the magisterium is not infallible in
such instances, neither is the human intellect that is failing to
understand it. The perceived weakness in the cogency of the arguments of the ordinary magisterium may be in the arguments or it
may be in the understanding of the hearer. In order to be truthful,
the intellect must admit this. The magisterium should not be threat-
ened by such truth. In its pastoral role it should seek to set forth its
teaching more adequately to help understanding. The magisterium—*magister*—is teacher. To teach effectively one must go to
where the student is and lead him or her forth. The word *education*
comes from the Latin *educare*, to lead forth. It challenges the hearer
at least to look at his or her presuppositions.

I think the new Code of Canon Law is wrong when it commands
the obedience of the intellect. It is the will that obeys; the intellect
reasons. The American Bishops' presentation in their pastoral on
peace is more accurate and appropriate. The bishops in no way
negate their teaching authority. First, they set forth with sureness
the principals that all must accept in faith. Then they set forth the
conclusions they draw in the application of these principles and

their line of reasoning. Having done this, they call upon all Catholics to carefully examine the conclusions and the reasons leading up to them and in the light of the Gospels responsibly to make their own decisions.

It has been curious for me to see people who ask Church authorities to crack down on dissenters and bring them into line suddenly, when they themselves do not like the teaching that is being set forth by our bishops, not only dissent but even deny the magisterium's affirmation of its right to teach in these matters. We have here a twofold denial that could have far reaching effects.

The Founder of the Church did promise to be with his Church until the end of time. We have a sure basis for our faith. Yet he also described his Church as a field with weeds as well as wheat, as a net with good and bad fish. There will always be a mixture. Even the ordinary teaching role — that one not infallibly protected by the Lord from error — suffers from the misuse of power.

Merton admired a certain spirit he found in Blake: "His rebellion for all its strange heterodoxies was fundamentally the rebellion of the saints. It was the rebellion of the lover of the living God, the rebellion of one whose desire of God was so intense and irresistible that it condemned with all its might all the hypocrisy and petty sensuality and skepticism and materialism which cold and trivial minds set up as impassable barriers between God and the souls of men." In some way this inspired his own response. A man of complete fidelity and orthodoxy, Tom realized that the true lover is never a "yes" man. A subservient conformity is not the way of love any more than it is the way of truth. Tom agonized and spoke out where he saw the teachers failing. He spoke the word of truth in love. He called for a deeper examination of the principles of faith, a clear presentation of the reasonableness of the conclusions.

Tom was happy in his faith. From the time he received the gift of faith he never had any difficulty reconciling it with that other gift with which he was exceptionally well endowed, the gift of intellect, of reasoning. In *The New Man* he wrote: "If God made us intellectual and free, it was in order that we might develop our freedom, extend our powers and capacities of willing and loving to an unbelievable breadth, and raise our minds to an unheard of vision of truth. . . . It is paradoxically by the grace of God that we finally achieve our full spiritual freedom."

In *Conjectures of a Guilty Bystander* Tom said his conversion to Catholicism started with the realization of the presence of God *in the here and now,* in the world and in himself. He saw that his main task as a Christian was to live in full and vital awareness of this ground of being. He saw himself as a progressive with a deep respect and love for the tradition, a progressive who wanted to preserve a continuity with the past. He loved the Middle Ages, he loved the Greek and Latin Fathers. He wanted to be open to the values of the modern world while retaining a traditional Catholic position. In this he later felt very much in harmony with Pope John XXIII. Yet he wasn't backward looking: "The Christian is the one who has 'decided for' the Parousia, for the final coming of the Kingdom." His whole life was oriented by this decision. He prayed, "Thy Kingdom come!" Tom's conversion to Catholicism marked the end of a long struggle, a breakthrough to a new freedom, an end that was in truth a beginning, an opening to a process, to a whole life of conversion. Almost thirty years later he would write, "I think I will have to become a Christian." His next step in 1938 was to begin to look for the way in which he would be truly free to live out the process of conversion. It would lead him to a life marked by conversion, one that would call upon him to make a solemn vow of conversion.

5. The Freedom of Monasticism

According to Thomas Merton, the Christian's first mission is to live as a person who has been freed by faith from the world's myths, idolatries, and confusions in whatever way God gives him or her to live that freedom. It matters not whether it is in the world or in the cloister.

The word *world* has various meanings in Merton's writings and in this book. It can have its ordinary meaning: this globe and every person and everything sharing its space—nature, creation. Or the word can have the meaning given to it by Saint John in his Gospel: that part of creation that has come under the domination of Satin. That is the meaning it has the first time it is used in the preceding paragraph. And finally, it can be used in contradistinction to the monastic enclosure, a space set apart by monastics where they seek to create an environment conducive to contemplation, akin to the City of God, the City of Love. That is the way *world* is used the second time in the preceding paragraph. Both these usages come directly from *Conjectures of a Guilty Bystander.* Obviously, the monk is not free from the world as nature, as creation, nor is he free from human society, just because he has moved into a cloister.

In his novel, *My Argument with the Gestapo,* Tom has B. ask Merton, "What have you been doing?" Merton's response could well sum up what Tom was doing from the day of his baptism (November 16, 1938) until the moment of decision on December 7, 1941. "Trying to find something, I don't quite know what." He experienced himself as "an exile all over the earth." He didn't yet realize how true that was. Once he found what he was looking for, he would sing every evening, of himself and his brothers, *exules filii Evae*—"exiled sons of Eve."

What Tom was seeking was how to live fully the freedom of the faith. His experiences in the course of the months and years immediately following his baptism showed him it was not an easy thing to do, especially when one is immersed in the world. Tom uses the Dante image of purgatory in two ways during this period. In one, he sees his baptism as his emergence from hell and this period as the purgatory leading to the paradise of the cloister. In another sense, he is still struggling in the outer limits of hell and will emerge to the purgatory of monastic life, which will bring him eventually to paradise. The former is perhaps the more accurate, for he is struggling during this period to free himself from the capital vices that still have their hold on him. Classically, the cloister, although oftentimes experienced as a purgatory, for the monk certainly still has a great need of purification, has been called the *paradisus claustralis*.

The first step toward that true freedom which is a gift of God, is an acknowledgment of our need of his grace. This Tom did in approaching the baptismal font. Then we must live up to that grace, to the new nature that has been given us in baptism, that of the free children of God. We become by baptism godly, in the strictest sense of the word, and we need, in order to be true to ourselves, to live godly lives. In order to spiritualize our activity, to bring it under the Spirit of God, we have to develop our awareness of spiritual reality. This spiritual awareness, which depends first of all on faith, is impossible if we do not have a genuine knowledge of ourselves. Without this we cannot see to make the choices we need to make. If freedom cannot see to choose, it is not fully free. To use one of Merton's images, the lamp of our personal liberty is fed with the oil of the doctrine of the Church, the teachings of faith, which give us spiritual awareness. But we can receive that oil and it can be enkindled by the flame of the Holy Spirit only if we know ourselves, humble ourselves before God, and let him purify us, clearing away the pride that dominates our minds and hearts, so that there is space in our minds for the inpouring of the oil of true doctrine, and our hearts are free to respond to that doctrine in love.

In the struggles that marked these transitional years for Tom, he learned much about himself, and in his reading he learned much about the doctrine of the Church. He came to learn, both in theory and in practice, that the sacraments, especially Mass and Communion, are the places of encounter where the Spirit of God turns doctrine into life. The more he entered into the spirit of the liturgy, the better he understood the personalism of the Catholic faith. A mere outward, formalistic participation in the rituals of the Church would not foster growth; in fact, it would do just the opposite. It would stifle freedom and stunt spiritual growth. It would evade that

moral and spiritual commitment that the liturgy demands. Freedom and slavery are incompatible. Slavish conformity to rites and
precepts without commitment to the consequences obstructs the
interior action of grace and prevents us from entering into a vital
relationship with the Spirit of God. It prevents us from finding and
being our true selves in the actualization of our capacity for a relationship with God in love and commitment.

Merton first came to learn something about this in the books he
read. He worked hard at internalizing what he read. He spent time
regularly in meditation. He used the traditional forms of the rosary
and the Stations of the Cross. He guided himself through the *Exercises* of Saint Ignatius. He came to know the power of the mass above
all by participation. During the summer of 1939 at Olean, New York,
living in what he later described as an early hippie commune, intent
upon producing a novel, he contented himself with Sunday mass. In
the following summer he withdrew to some extent from the general
activities of the commune—for a couple of weeks he even went to
live in a dorm with young Franciscan novices at Saint Bonaventure's
College—and got to bed early so that he could be up and off to mass
in town or at the college each morning.

Entering more and more deeply into the meaning of the mass,
Tom began to conceive a desire to be a priest. Yet there were other
considerations: his past and his present. Would a past such as his be
a lifetime impediment to such a ministry of holiness? And wasn't he
still too much of a man of the world, drawn to the things of the world
and in need of them? Could he give them up? And if he gave them
up, could he live in the world and stay away from them? Many questions, plus the fear to answer them.

Finally, he approached Dan Walsh. He had, in response to Bob
Gerdy's enthusiasm, signed up for Dan's course in the fall of 1938.
He liked the course, he loved the professor. Dan not only taught
Catholic philosophy, he was a true philosopher. He lived what he
taught. The two became more than professor and student; they
became friends, meeting often. On one occasion Dan took Tom to
a talk by Jacques Maritain, the father of the scholastic renewal. Tom
only had a moment with Maritain that evening, but many years later
the venerable scholar would make the long pilgrimage to Gethsemani to sit before the fire in the little hermitage on Mount Olivet,
much to Tom's delight.

With some fear but with confidence in Dan, Tom met with his mentor in a corner of the lounge in the old Biltmore Hotel and told him of his interest in the priesthood. Dan surprised the young man. He had been thinking along the same lines: Tom had the makings of a priest. Dan went further and began to speak of the religious orders, and in particular of the Trappists. Tom expressed his fear of austerity. He thought he needed meat, and he was probably right. Tom suffered a good deal from the fasting and abstinence he would undertake as a young monk and later have to abandon. There is a rather defensive letter from Dom James Fox to Naomi Burton Stone assuring her that Tom was getting "a wonderful hot dinner at noon-time with plenty of meat" each day in the infirmary refectory. Dan responded to Tom's fears and to his poetic sense and directed him toward the Franciscans. There life was relaxed enough. In fact, Tom, in that ambivalence between idealism and realism that marked much of his life, would soon enough have his difficulties with the Franciscans' "laxity."

For the moment Tom followed Dan's advice, even though it was countered by the pastor at Corpus Christi Church where he had been baptized and by the priest in his own parish church. They both wanted the gifted young man for the diocesan priesthood. With a letter from Dan, Tom approached the Franciscans on Thirty-First Street and eventually applied for admission to their province. His past caught up with him, however, or at least the way he presented it (as a vocation father, listening to the way Tom recounted the case, I suspect it was more his presentation than the facts) and he was advised to withdraw his application.

The parish priests may not have been off the mark in urging Tom to consider the priesthood plain and simple instead of the Francis-cans. Actually, in pursuing a life with the friars, Tom was seeking two things: the priesthood—one can be a Franciscan without being a priest; there are Franciscan brothers—and the monastic life. Tom was clearer about the first in 1940—and that is probably what Father Ford and Father Kenealy saw; he was not so clear yet on the monasti-cism. Like many called to the Cistercian life, the first hearing of it, such as Tom received from Dan Walsh, incites a certain fascination—why else would Tom have headed for Gethsemani for a retreat and then visited Our Lady of the Valley, another Cistercian monastery in Rhode Island—and at the same time a certain fear.

Does one really want to go that far? I know that was my initial reaction and I found it in many inquirers whom I served as vocation father.

Tom first came to the awareness of his priestly vocation. With a good bit more struggle he opened to the more radical call to a monastic way of life. But when he did finally return to Gethsemani in December 1941, he was as certain of the one as the other. Since the Second Vatican Council there has been much discussion on the topic of monastic priesthood. Most of it has had to do more with theory than practice. Some have argued that when a man accepts a monastic vocation he must give up any notion of a priestly vocation. If the abbot one day calls him to serve the community as a priest, fine, but otherwise the monk should give no thought to it. If a man feels sure he has a priestly calling, then he should not become a monk or be accepted into a monastery, at least a contemplative monastery. Others do not go so far, but merely insist that the candidate see his priestly vocation as secondary and dependent on the abbot's call, much as a diocesan candidate depends on the bishop's call. I think that we must remember that vocation is God's business. He can, and often enough does, call men to be both priest and monk. The young man who perceives such a double call, in order to be true to who he is—for it is the divine call deep in our being that essentially constitutes who we are—will want to respond to the double call. A vocation father who, because he has adopted one or the other theory about monastic priesthood, will not hear the double call the candidate is receiving, does violence to the work of God in a fellow Christian whom he is supposed to be serving. Tom clearly had a call to both priesthood and monastic life. In those days a double call was not problematic. We went to the other extreme. In order to become a monk the candidate had to have a priestly vocation. Otherwise he was placed among the lay brothers, even if he did not feel a call to that beautiful life of humble service but rather felt a call to the full choral life of the monk.

When the Franciscan vocation father apparently closed off all hope of the priesthood, Tom found the freedom to look at the other part of his vocation, which proved to be a call to be a monk. As my grandmother frequently said to me, "When one door closes, another opens." When our attention becomes riveted on a particular goal, an attachment to attaining that goal can rob us of the freedom to consider not only other goals but even enriching complementary facets of the goal we are pursuing.

Curiously, the monastic seems to have been constantly present with Tom on his journey through life. His life began in the shadow of a monastery. The medieval abbey of Saint Michael de Cuxa stood in ruins above the small town of Prades, where Tom was born. In the summer of 1939, when Tom spent only a short time at Olean and returned to New York to work on his thesis, he spent many an hour haunting the cloisters of Cuxa, for they had followed him across the Atlantic and now stood, reconstructed, above New York City in Fort Tryon Park in a museum called the Cloisters. Cuxa was there, Tom would write in his autobiography, "when I most needed to see what a cloister looked like and what kind of a place a man might live in according to his rational nature and not like a stray dog." (He was rather hard on his earlier promiscuous habits.)

When Tom settled back in France with his father in 1925, the monastic element was still present. Owen had decided he would build his own home on the outskirts of Saint Antonin. To this purpose he bought the remains of a small monastic chapel and incorporated them into his home. Thus Tom passed in and out of an old monastic doorway and looked out upon the world through a monastic window frame for the little time he lived in that house in the Aveyron valley.

In the miserable summer of travel with Pop and the rest of the family in 1926, the only recorded moments of joy for Tom and his father were found in Dijon. Neither probably knew that the Abbey of Citeaux lay just outside the town's walls, a short bus ride away, and that the wine cellars of Saint Bernard's Clairvaux lay right in the town. Indeed, if they had visited the municipal library, they could have held in their hands the very Bible Saint Bernard read from and they could have visited his mother's tomb in the crypt of Saint Benigne. It is an interesting association, if nothing more.

The reading of Sir Arthur Conan Doyle in the course of another, even more miserable summer, may have had more impact on the young man. It was the summer of 1929, when he was lodged in the bleakness of Aberdeen, left behind with all the uncertainty of a father going to a London hospital. He consoled himself that summer by reading many novels. In Doyle's novels he may have met the Cistercians for the first time, in a sympathetic context.

His first visit to a Cistercian monastery came less than three years later, in early 1933. It was a time of most special grace. Tom had experienced his dead father's presence, which had opened the way to repentance and heartfelt prayer. The morning after this experience he had climbed the Aventine (one of the seven hills of Rome) to visit the Church of Santa Sabina. It was the first time in his life he had gone to a church precisely to pray, not to sightsee, not to attend a service but just to pray. His prayer was short—the only one he knew, taught to him by Grandmother Merton on her one visit to Long Island: an Our Father. But what better prayer? It may have been one of the best prayers of his life. After the prayer he looked around a bit and peeked into the sunny cloisters of the Dominicans adjacent to the church. Tom continued visiting churches and eventually got to Tre Fontane, the church that marks the traditional spot of the Apostle Paul's martyrdom, a good way outside the walls of Rome— Tom went out in a tour bus. Bernard of Clairvaux had sent his monks to Italy to start a Cistercian monastery in the 1130s. They never reached the site he had in mind. The pope installed them in this early Greek monastery. Bernard visited there and in the course of his visit had one of his great visions. A chapel now stands on the spot where the saintly abbot is said to have seen the heavens open and angels ascending and descending, as had the ancient patriarch Jacob. In 1145 the Cistercian abbot of Tre Fontane was elected pope, and ever since then the pope has been the abbot of the monastery. The day Tom visited it he was too shy to ring the bell of the guest house and speak to a monk. Just visiting the church and hearing about the monks' lives made a strong impression on him. On his return journey to the city he informed the young lady sitting next to him that he was going to become a Trappist monk. The telling may have been largely for effect, but the fascination was there. The seed of the vocation had been sown, just as the seed of the faith had been sown a few days earlier. It would have to lie dormant under a lot of manure, for some years, however, before it would sprout and be seen.

In the fall, after his time at Aberdeen, Tom began his studies at Oakham, which stood, as did many of the schools in England, on an old monastic site. In fact, the infirmary in which Tom first read Hopkins was one of the ancient monastic buildings that had survived. Back at Ripley Court, where he had prepared for Oakham,

Tom had what he jokingly spoke of as "his first intimate contact with monastic life." Christopher Pearse, the headmaster's brother-in-law, was an amateur excavator and was working on the nearby Augustinian Priory of Newark. He put Tom to work measuring the drains. More pleasant were the bicycle rides Tom took on his own to the ruins of Saint Alban's Abbey.

The summer of 1932 brought Pop back to Europe, but this time it was for a quiet and boring time at Bournemouth. Tom did manage to fall in love again. After seeing Pop and his own ladylove off at Southampton he went wandering in the New Forest. He found himself, finally, lying on the lawn in front of the ancient Cistercian Abbey of Beaulieu, bewailing his lonely fate. Then he got up and wandered about the monastic ruins, enjoying the soothing, the peaceful atmosphere, little suspecting he would one day find true peace within a Cistercian cloister. He went on to the Isle of Wight to stay with a school friend. There, too, on the island, stood the ruins of another medieval Cistercian abbey.

If Aldous Huxley did much to open Tom to a more sober life and even a Catholic life, he also did his share to move Tom along toward his monastic vocation. *Ends and Means* spoke of the Cistercians a number of times, always with respect. Huxley admired the monks' civilizing influence, their industriousness, and, above all, their simplicity— something that would attract Tom and be the subject of one of his earliest literary endeavors when he became a Cistercian. Huxley showed himself insightful in regard to the reason for Cistercian simplicity: "bare: aids to devotion (in other words fetters holding back the soul from enlightenment) are conspicuously absent." As Saint Bernard had pointed out, popular piety needed the support of pictures and statues, colors and images, but the monk needed only the cleared space to directly encounter the living God. He also saw that the purpose of community was to foster and support the search for enlightenment or spiritual attainment. "Communities have been formed for the purpose of making it possible for their members to live more nearly in accord with the currently accepted religious ideals than could be done 'in the world.'" Speaking further of this quest for enlightenment or, as we might say in our more ordinary terminology, for true contemplative experience, Huxley made statements that must have been challenging to the lusty young collegiate:

The individual cannot transcend himself unless he first learns to be conscious of himself and of his relations with other selves and with the world. A measure of sexual continence is the pre-condition of awareness, and other forms of mental energy, conative and emotional as well as cognitive. . . . Chastity is one of the major virtues inasmuch as, without chastity, societies lack energy and individuals are condemned to perpetual unawareness, attachment and animality."

That is quite a statement for a man who proclaimed himself a "rational idealist." Yet Huxley did not make too much of chastity. He saw this virtue, along with courage, prudence, temperance, and the like, as minor virtues because they could also serve wrongdoing, "unless they are directed by the major virtues of love and intelligence." In time Merton would agree with all of this, substituting faith for intelligence. The ways of God are wonderful; he can lead a man such as Huxley so far and then use him as an instrument to call forth a man such as Merton. "My ways are not your ways . . . says the Lord." When an energetic young man such as Tom, who is definitely on the way, hears a man such as Huxley say, "The group within the society which suffers the greatest continence (I suspect at that point, Tom would agree with Huxley in seeing continence as a suffering), displays the greatest energy and dominates society," a society that practices continence begins to have meaning for him. Tom was to discover a new kind of freedom, the empowering freedom of self-mastery.

The evening Tom asked Dan Walsh about the priesthood, Dan responded by telling Tom about a retreat he had had with the Cistercians at Gethsemani. Dan was enthusiastic about his experience, but Tom was not quite ready to consider a life of such austerity. This was, in fact, not the first time Tom had heard about Gethsemani. His grandmother's companion, Elsie Hauck, came from Kentucky. Tom had become friendly with Elsie's family and her mother had told Tom about a visit to the abbey, where she had bought her rosary beads. Some popular myths as well as reality probably colored Tom's feelings. When he did finally go for a visit and see for himself, it would be a different story.

Having embraced the faith and made a new start, Tom was trying more than ever to move toward the truth. He wanted to be free from the lies we tell ourselves and that we tell others and that we try to live. Even though he had received Dan's encouragement in regard to a priestly vocation and was moving apparently steadily toward the Franciscan novitiate, he feared that the whole thing might be a lie. That is why he rushed back to New York to tell his Franciscan vocation director everything. He did not yet understand the freeing and freedom of the monastic way of life. It does free the sinner. Monastic profession has been called a second baptism. This is why, traditionally, a man receives a new name when he becomes a monk. Thomas Merton would die. All his past would be gone. Father Louis would be born. But in its effects it wouldn't be an instantaneous act. Nor would the effects be produced within nine months or the two years in the womb of the novitiate. It would be a lifetime process till he was born to eternal life. Entering a monastery, we do die to the old self, to the world, yet we are not yet fully alive. There will be a Resurrection. Tom began to realize this in the later years, and took to again signing himself as Tom—but that was still a long way off.

Feeling the door to religious life was closed to him, Tom tried to carve out for himself a life as near to it as possible, a life close to, if not within, a religious community, a life of simple routine and practice, a life for the most part removed from the world. He moved in with the Franciscan community at Saint Bonaventure's College, followed most of their religious exercises, quietly went about his rather simple work of teaching freshmen, and read, prayed, and meditated. And he listened to God.

Tom listened a good bit through writing. He pulled things together for himself in his writing. In the summer of 1941, he attempted to do this in a largely autobiographical novel, which happily did survive when all his others were destroyed. As Merton says to one of his interlocutors in the course of the novel: "I will keep putting things down until they become clear." The volume has many monastic references; the contemplative life is praised in detail. Merton, the character, expresses Tom's feelings at the end of that summer: "I have no plans. My plans change from day to day. I may leave. I may stay. I am finishing the first volume of my series of journals."

Catherine de Hueck came to Saint Bonaventure's campus that summer. She offered Merton another alternative—one that, in fact, his friend Bob Lax would take up: to be a part of Friendship House. Tom visited the house in Harlem. His idealism and realism were coming closer together. God help us if we ever lose our ideals—where will life go? We will settle down in the "real" and go nowhere.

On the other hand, if we strive to make our dwelling exclusively in the realms of the ideal, we will never settle anywhere. The challenge is to hold fast to the ideal, lovingly embrace the real, and happily live in the tension of the daily challenge to bring the real closer to the ideal. Tom would write to Catherine with great beauty, "the place I want to be is somewhere where the angels are not only pres-ent but even sometimes visible: that is slums, or Trappist monaster-ies, or where there are children, or where there is one guy starving himself in a desert for sorrow and shame at the sins and injustice of the world." Prior to his visit to Gethsemani, Tom had read about the Cistercians in *The Catholic Encyclopedia*. He had also read about two orders of hermits, the Carthusians and the Camadolese. The eremitical call had begun to stir in him. It, too, was part of his voca-tion. It would cause Tom much stress before the powers that be would finally see how it could be reconciled with his Cistercian calling to Gethsemani. In 1941 the eremitical dimension of his vocation was not yet clear to Tom, so it was not part of the immediate problem.

Another aspect of his vocation was problematic. Tom was also called to be a writer. That was at issue. Would life in Harlem allow the time and space he needed to write? More, would the Cistercian life totally rule it out? The answer to that last question seemed obvi-ous. It is, in fact, obvious. There would be no sense embracing a monastic life while still clinging to *anything*. Tom would have to give up his writing if he was going to find the freedom of the monastic life. But what he would learn—and it would take a long time to learn it fully, because it would in fact take him a long time to give up his writing and turn it completely over to the Lord—was the fact that giving up something does not necessarily mean you do not still have it.

A delightful story indicates that Tom did have some intimation of this. Shortly after he was admitted to the postulancy he decided to test the waters. He knocked on the father master's door. When he walked in there were two people in the room: the master of novices, Father Robert, who would one day be the abbot of Holy Spirit Abbey in Conyers, Georgia, and a novice, Frater Walter, who would later be novice master of Gethsemani and then abbot of the Abbey of Our Lady of the Genesee in Piffard, New York. Tom placed a small collection of his poems on the father master's desk, saying, "I thought you might like to read some of my poetry." As he went out the door, Robert turned to Walter: "Read his poems, indeed. Who does he think he is?" There was many a hearty laugh over that in later years.

Tom still had hopes, but for the moment he was ready to let every-thing go. In October he had written to Catherine, "Writing and talking and teaching come *after* works of love and sanctity and charity, not before. And the first thing of all is our own sanctification, which was the lesson I got out of my retreat with the Trappists, and keep finding out over and over again every day." The writing was still there, but subordinated. He was ready to come to Harlem and take his chances. He would work and love—and write when he could. But his heart was more strongly elsewhere. Sanctification was first and he knew where the best path to sanctity lay for him. On the eve of his departure from Saint Bonaventure's he would write again: "I don't desire *anything* in the world, not writing, not teaching, nor any kind of consolation or outward activity. I simply long with my whole existence to be completely consecrated to God in every gesture, in every breath, and every movement of my body and mind, to the exclusion of absolutely everything, except Him: and the way I desire this, by His grace, is the way it is among the Trappists." He had opened his hands and let go of everything. They were now wide open to receive everything. Again and again he would be tempted to hang onto something and he would have to remember or be reminded to let go. It is only when we are totally free that we can receive the totality of God who, in his immense love, wants to give us all—himself and everything else in him.

It may seem paradoxical that a man who is intently in search of freedom should enter upon one of the most strictly regulated forms of living to be found in the Church. But as Tom pointed out in one of the papers collected in *Contemplation in a World of Action*, a life of freedom is necessarily a life of self-discipline and self-denial. This may sound contradictory to those who take only a superficial view of freedom. But when we realize the true depths of the Christian idea of freedom, we realize that it is essentially bound up with such asceticism.

Monastic life is a life marked by charismatic freedom. It is for those who are free enough to walk away from society, from some of the values society holds most precious, from many of the comforts of life, from what others think and do and say. It is a life in which the person is free of some of the routine cares, responsibilities, claims, and demands of life that are less fruitful or even somewhat deadening, in order to be more awake, alert, alive, and sensitive to what really is, and to his own experience of that.

It is easy to see the freedom the enclosed life gives the monk from many of the distracting and confusing things that plague the every-day life of the city dweller. Because of the simplicity of life-style and the fraternal cooperation found in the monastic community, the monk is liberated from a whole network of needs, servitudes, and demands that secular life imposes on people. When Tom was speak-ing at the Center for the Study of Democratic Institutions at Santa Barbara a few months before his death, he spoke of this: "What you become a monk for is first of all, and I will say this without any quali-fication, it is an unconditional breaking through the limitations which are imposed by normal society. You become a completely marginal person in order to break through the kind of inevitable superficiality of social life." From this vantage point it is easy for the monk to take a critical attitude toward the world and its structures and point out where its claims are fraudulent.

One of Tom's novices, who became a real friend, has in our times become well known, if not notorious in the eyes of some. Ernesto Cardenal had to leave the novitiate at Gethsemani because of his failing health. But the monastic ideal remained alive in him. He returned to his native Nicaragua to establish a community that adopted a radical form of monastic living. It was when this commu-nity was savagely destroyed by the forces of the dictator that this man of peace took his place among those fighting to establish a new democracy in the oppressed country. Many have wondered what Tom would have thought of Cardenal's new role. In writing an intro-duction for one of Cardenal's books, Tom wrote, "A monastery is an ideal school of freedom, in which the monk learns to obey in the incidentals of life in order to be free in what is essential, that is, free to love." That a man who was long enrolled in a school of freedom should have ended up enrolling with freedom fighters when every other route to freedom seemed to be denied his people should not seem too surprising. What is certain is that Cardenal was living out of that freedom to love, a freedom from self strong enough to enable him to be willing to lay down his way of life and even life itself for love of his persecuted sisters and brothers. Would it have been yet a greater freedom to be able to let these things be taken from him without his taking up arms?

Tom points out here another obvious freedom the monastic life endows us with: freedom from having constantly to make decisions about the incidentals of life. I remember one day sitting in the office of a busy bishop. Our conversation was repeatedly interrupted by phone calls. As the bishop set down the phone for about the tenth time, he put his hands to his head and moaned, "Decisions, decisions, decisions!"

But, one might ask, Don't you get tired of being pushed around all the time by bells? There is more than one way to listen to bells. As Tom points out in *Thoughts in Solitude*, bells speak to us of our freedom, which responsibilities and cares can make us forget. The bells say, Business does not ultimately matter. Rest in God and rejoice, for this world is only the figure and promise of the world to come, and only those who are detached from these transient things can possess the substance of an eternal promise. Of course, one does not always like to hear the bells. When Father Augustine got back to Gethsemani from the foundation in Georgia for the first time in years—it was the occasion of the centenary of the mother abbey—Dom James gave him and Father Louis permission to speak until they heard the bell. As Tom led Gus into the vault he used as an office he carefully closed the door, saying, "We'll never hear the bell in here."

The bells are probably the clearest symbol of obedience and an actual call to it. They have traditionally been said to be the *vox Dei*—the "voice of God." Again, there may seem to be a paradox here. The highest form of freedom is found in obedience, obedience to God. Nor is obedience to others in authority or even to the brethren an abdication of freedom, but rather its prudent use. Our obedience is always practiced under certain well-defined conditions, above all, the true demands of love. The lowest form of freedom is the ability to choose good *or* evil. This Tom exercised with great abandon and with great cost in his adolescent years. Perfect spiritual freedom lies not in this but in the inability to make any evil choices. True freedom consists in being able to love perfectly and accept what is really good and hate perfectly and reject what is evil. This is the kind of freedom that God has, or rather is. It is in this context that Tom goes so far as to say, "God is Freedom." In his commentary on Saint Bernard's treatise on grace and free will, Tom notes that this kind of freedom comes only from perfect obedience to God. It is something that begins on the outside—obeying the Church, superiors, brethren—but it cannot stop there. That is not enough. We must come to that deep listening where we can constantly hear the Spirit in our depths and obey his every movement. One enters, then, into a strict cloistered life or a solitary life in order to protect the inner atmosphere of silence, listening, and freedom, in order that the Spirit may do his work in us and guide us in all that we do.

What monastic life does is to help us achieve a certain freedom of spirit, the true freedom of the spirit of which Saint Paul and Saint John speak in the Sacred Scriptures. In order to have such a freedom, in order to hear the Spirit, we must be ready to stand in the truth. The monastic life seeks to lead us into that kind of truth through an authentic life of self-denial, denial of the false self, so that the true self can emerge. The freedom we are looking for is not a kind of spontaneous following of our natural tendencies and feelings and emotions. Christian freedom is the freedom found on the Cross. It is the freedom that comes when we fully give ourselves to Christ on the Cross and thus can rise with him and share his freedom—the freedom to act spontaneously in the Holy Spirit. True discipline crucifies our superficial and selfish self and opens to us the freedom of a life that is not dominated by egoism, vanity, willfulness, selfishness, passion, aggressiveness, jealousy, greed, and the like. This means a solitude of some sort, being apart from the crowd, not cherishing the comfort of the various social idols, not depending on the approval of others.

There is necessarily for the one who follows such a life of apartness a certain amount of loneliness. When Tom was speaking to the community at Gethsemani on the Georgian Letters of Pasternak, he insisted that the monastic life is a lonely life. But we should want this. It forces us back on our own "naked spiritual reserves." It is here that we find out who we truly are and what we have to give to others. This also puts us in touch with what is one of the real consolations of the monastic life: we can see that God does, in some obscure way, give us what we need. It is a point at which our despair meets God and blossoms into hope.

It is also the place where true humility is born. And it is humility that sets us free to serve God and to know him most fully, for it leaves us open for the inpouring of his sure knowledge, unfiltered by any of our prejudicial blinders. All our illusions show up and we can abandon them and give ourselves over to a life that is wholly to God's glory and ours in him. We are indeed free. Free to listen to the Word of God in our hearts, to hear how much we are truly loved. Free to see ourselves reflected back in the eyes of the Divine Love. Free to come to know how magnificent we truly are.

Monastic ascesis, then, is a way, a practice, a technique, a practical vehicle to carry us to enlightenment. This is provided, of course, that it is lived in a healthy manner. We are, unfortunately, prone to turn our practice into a morality, a list of dos and don'ts. With such thinking, if we succeed in carrying out all the dos and avoiding all the don'ts, we begin to pat ourselves on the back and become established in an illusion of holiness. If we fail in our attempts, we are apt to become discouraged and thrown down, and, what is worse, harden ourselves against our brothers who seem to be succeeding. In fact, there is no question here of success or failure. It is a question of using the practices as best we can to make what progress we can. We use the practices to the extent that they truly serve our ends, are truly leading us toward enlightenment. A consequence of this, which I fear is not readily seen in many monasteries, is that we need not expect to follow all these practices all our lives. More and more the Holy Spirit will take over in our lives. No matter how prevalent—or valid—is the statement that we are novices all our lives, that we are always beginners, it is stultifying to treat a monk ever as a novice. A young monk should be able to look foward to something more, to a time of greater freedom in the Spirit, to a greater freedom to enjoy the Divine Presence unimpeded by observances and practices. We need to come to trust the Holy Spirit. We do what we should but we should not hang onto our doings when they impede the freedom of the Spirit within us.

After the Second Vatican Council Father Louis wrote a significant article on "Renewal and Discipline in the Monastic Life." In it he pointed out that we should not practice monastic discipline just because it is part of the tradition or because of some commitment or for some quid pro quo or for moral perfection or to acquire virtue. No! We should use the disciplines of the life insofar as they aid us to deepen and expand our freedom and capacity for the experience of God, for awareness and understanding, a deeper entering into the mysteries, for that transcendence that leads to the death of the old self in the fullest possible way and to the greatest freedom to enter into the life of the risen Christ animated by the Holy Spirit. Monastic discipline, monastic observances are always a means. We must never make them an end in themselves, for to do this would be to construct idols, which would prevent our ever coming to know and experience the true God.

All of this is essentially true for every Christian. It is only the way in which it is done, in which it is lived out, that is particular to the particular states in life. The monk does it the way he does it because he senses this is the way in which God is calling him. It is the way that works best for him. And it enables him, in God's providential plan, to be a sign for the world. We renounce other forms of freedom in order to have monastic freedom, the freedom of the contemplative life. It means we must accept restrictions, restraints, self-denial, and sacrifice so that inner freedom can grow and blossom within us in the freedom of the Spirit. In our life Christ is to be all-sufficient. It is a life of awareness that one thing is necessary, that Jesus Christ is necessary, that to live for him and in him is all. "To live in him takes care of everything."

Monks have a prophetic role. We are called by God to live the way we live to be a sign to the world. As Merton points out in *Contemplation in a World of Action*, "We monks should be able to reassure modern man that God is the source and the guarantee of our freedom and not simply a force standing over us to limit our freedom," as unfortunately all too many see God. The monk should be one who not only seeks full realization but "has come to experience the ground of his own being in such a way that he knows the secret of liberation and can somehow or other communicate it to others." If many contemplative communities are closed to sharing their life or the fruits of their contemplation with their sisters and brothers in the world, is it perhaps because they doubt they have something to share? They have not been trained and encouraged to seek realization and are not experiencing the ground of their being, where they will so experience their oneness with all that they will sense an impelling need—the need of true love in the oneness we are in Christ-God—to share all that they are and have with all. The monk, Thomas Merton, Father Louis, o.c.s.o., can and does offer to communicate, not only to his sisters and brothers in the world, but to his fellow nuns and monks, the secret of liberation, the way to true freedom, if we would but have the courage and freedom to hear him.

These words from "The Inner Experience" can most appropriately be applied to their author: "In liberating himself, he becomes able to show others the way to the same liberty because his life bears witness to a supreme liberty and enables them to know it, obscurely, and to burn with its desire."

And to his fellow monks and nuns, he addresses these powerful words:

Anyone who undertakes to be a monk knows by the very fact of his vocation, that he is summoned by God to a difficult, life-long work in which there will always be anguish and great risk. If he evades this work, under any pretext whatever (even under the pretext of conforming to an exterior ritual or ascetic observance which does not really suit his inner needs), he must know that he cannot have any peace with himself or with God because he is trying to silence the deepest imperative of his own heart.

Thomas Merton's vocational struggle was an open one, a struggle for freedom, to be free enough to do what he really wanted to do and do it as his true self. At first he could not hear the call to be a Cistercian. Then when it was first expressly set before him he backed off from it, because other considerations still had too great a hold on him. He tried to settle for something that made less demands, but his own truth would not let him. In the end he let go of everything, even for the moment his writing, and he was free. And what a remarkable freedom we see in him in that moment of decision. In a matter of hours he gave away all, disposed of all, left his career and jumped aboard a train, with no assurances, only a humble heart that came truly seeking God. The gate could not but open, for this is the one thing that Saint Benedict would have the novice master ask: Does he truly seek God? Tom, in many obscure and dark and confused ways, and then in ways that became more and more lightsome, did truly seek God—and he would go right on seeking him, the God who is Freedom. Saint Bernard, in his *Parables*, indicates four stages in the return to true freedom. First there is repentance. This began for Tom in Rome, though it was not yet well grounded. Then there is the flight. Tom, a bit rashly we might think, hurtled South on the night train in the opening hours of a world war. But ahead would be his own battles, long and hard fought, filled with their own terrors. In the end there would be the victory, with all its strength and wisdom. Thomas Merton, a true son of Saint Bernard, like his father dared to seek freedom even in the apparent prison of the cloister. He became the freest of the free and the inspiration of a countless multitude, calling them forth to the true freedom of the children of God, in that Son of God, our Lord Jesus Christ.

6. Free to Be to the World

In 1098, when Robert, abbot of Molesme, resigned his crosier and led twenty-one of his monks out into the swamps of Citeaux, he had it in mind to create an opportunity to practice the way of the Rule of Saint Benedict as fully as possible, not for the sake of the Rule itself, and certainly not so that the monks could pride themselves on being observant, but for that to which the practice of the Rule is to lead: "So that when all these steps have been climbed, the monk will soon reach that love of God which, being perfect, drives out all fear."

Repeatedly through the centuries, Robert's sons forgot this. At times they were lax in their observance. At other times they prided themselves on their observance, forgetting their purpose. In the saddest of times they fought over its observance. When Thomas Merton arrived at Gethsemani in 1941, the observance was good. I do not know though how clear it was in the mind of the monks what the purpose was of their observance. The new postulant was one day powerfully to remind them and all of us, in what was to be a most significant time of renewal, that observance is indeed secondary, is a means to an end, and even the observance of the Holy Rule can and must be set aside or changed when it no longer serves its purpose.

In accordance with the Rule, when Tom arrived he was kept for a few days in the guest house, where he was put to polishing floors and the like. Father Joachim, the guest master, was a little surprised when the new postulant asked him if he could have a copy of the sermons of Saint Bernard, and in Latin. He was even more surprised when he brought the volume to Tom's room and found him writing poetry. These first days in the monastic quiet were among some of Tom's most creative, and he produced what I think are some of his best poems.

It was not Father Robert, his novice master, but the abbot himself, Dom Frederic Dunne, who encouraged Tom to continue to use his artistic talents. Nor was it Father Robert who most discouraged him from using them. That was Tom himself. Again and again he argued with himself, creating a great imaginary split between Thomas Merton the writer and Frater Louis the monk. In the moments when the monk was winning out, he would resolve never to write another poem — for to write poetry was frivolous — nor would he keep a journal — that was self-serving and prideful. What was at hand was torn up and tossed upon the pyre of self-immolation. As a result, we do not have any surviving journals from Tom's earliest days at Gethsemani. His oldest notebooks, heavy, hardbound ledgers, date from the time immediately after the end of his novitiate.

When a man first enters the monastic community, he is called a postulant. In the days when Tom arrived, the constitutions of the Order provided that a man who was entering to be a choir monk, as was Tom, would spend a month as a postulant. During this time he remained in his secular clothes so that it was obvious to everyone that he was new and learning the basics. This also allowed time for the necessary testimonials to arrive from the pastors and bishops of the places where the new man had lived prior to his entry. The 1917 Code of Canon Law, which was still in force in 1941, required getting these testimonials from all the bishops in whose dioceses the postulant had lived since he was fourteen. In Tom's case this proved quite an undertaking. His postulancy was prolonged until February 21. On that day Dom Frederic gave the white habit of a novice to Tom — along with his new name: Frater Maria Ludovicus. As he did, he told him and his companion for the occasion: "Each of you will influence this community for better or worse, for good or bad, but you have got to have an influence on the community." Who sitting in the chapterhouse that morning could have guessed how much Frater Ludovicus would affect that community and every other community of the Order. But the beaming new novice would have much more to go through than two years of novitiate and three years of temporary vows before he would be the monk who would make that kind of difference.

Frater Louis's earliest notebooks are interesting. They come from his first years as a professed religious, 1945–1946. They give us a fairly complete chronicle of his reading, many of the pages being dated. He was usually reading more than one book at a time. Often the book he was reading was in Latin and so would be the notes he took from it. Robert Daggy, curator of the Merton Collection, noted that little has been done with these books for that reason. During his first days of relatively independent study after his profession—for his studies during the novitiate were carefully regulated by the father master—leaving little time for anything else—Tom turned to a study of freedom. At first his sources were scholastic texts from the master of the Franciscan school, Duns Scotus, whom he had grown to love in his years at Saint Bonaventure's, but more and more as time went on he turned to the Cistercian Fathers, especially Bernard of Clairvaux, but also others. He pursued many avenues of theological and mystical thought. As he went along he turned to some of the other mystics who would remain longtime friends: John of the Cross, Denis the Carthusian, Ruysbroech, Tauler, and many others. He read rapidly, covering an amazing amount in the little time he had for reading. His notes are clear and concise, catching the essence of the texts he was reading. During this period, too, he studied the theme of freedom in the Scriptures, especially the Gospel of Saint John and the Epistles of Saint Paul. These notes served him later when he became master of the students. The first course he gave was on the Epistles of Saint Paul.

During this early period, Tom's study was more scholastic than existential. On entering into the freedom of the cloister, he embraced an ideal, and that ideal was to bind him for many years. He had turned his back on the world, and not just that world which was under the bondage of Satan, but insofar as he could, on all that was outside the cloister and even much of his own humanity. Reaction can be as enslaving as attraction.

I remember an enlightening experience I had back in the days when we were first struggling with renewal in our monasteries. I had received permission—things were a good bit more open at Spencer than they were at Gethsemani—to attend a sensitivity training workshop. In fact, this was my second time at this particular workshop. In the opening hours of the workshop, the participants were left on their own, just to mill around and get uncomfortable, so that they would be more open to receiving help. As this was my second experience, I was more at home with what was going on and therefore a bit more sure of myself. Another young priest, who was quite lost, latched onto me and we became close companions on the journey. After a couple of days the group rather savagely pointed out

Father's dependence and challenged him. We were soon wrestling on the floor. He turned completely against me. After a day in this reactive state, the facilitator helped him to realize that he was still allowing himself to be dominated by me in his reaction. It was only then that he was able to step back and see that he was free to like or dislike me, cultivate a friendship or the opposite. I am happy to say he opted for friendship, a friendship in which there was no longer dependence or domination, but a freedom to love.

Frater Louis's first years in the cloister were marked by his reaction to the world and reaction to himself as a poet and as an existentialist writer. This, despite the fact that during this period he wrote, as I have said, some of his better poetry and his most significant autobiography. The breakthrough came first in regard to writing. He writes of it in *The Sign of Jonas*. It happened only after his first real experience of writer's block, which he suffered in part because he was working for the first and last time on an extensive speculative book, using technical theological language. With the publication of *The Ascent to Truth* he knew that this was not his way. For the future he would write "in terms of spiritual experience ... traveling in byways of poetry and intuition," focusing "not upon dogmas as such, but only on their repercussions in the life of a soul in which they begin to find concrete realization ... using my own words to talk about my own soul." At least in his writing, Tom had now found the freedom to be himself.

Bob Lax, in the interview he gave to Paul Wilkes in connection with the television documentary on Merton's life, says:

When he [Tom] first got to the monastery he might have thought that he could live just a contemplative life cut off from the rest of the world. That may have been an illusion that ... anyone could expect would soon wear off. ... When he got back to a more universal point of view ... that was the Merton we already knew before he got there and it was just parts of him coming back.

Tom did try to deny parts of himself and most of the world in his earliest monastic days. It took some years for him to reclaim it all. He had embraced an ideal. And as he himself wrote later in *School of the Spirit*, a book he reserved from publication (though large parts of it actually appear in *The Climate of Monastic Prayer*): "conformity to any ideal, even the highest, means that a man must somewhere stop growing or rest content to be something less than a man. It is only when we have conformed and are assimilated to the infinite God that we can grow in wisdom and love without end. For the Word is Infinite Light and the Holy Spirit is in a sense Infinite Freedom."

Even in the very year in which he would have his great breakthrough, he would publish, in *Thoughts in Solitude*, this restrictive outlook: "A monk must never look for wisdom outside his vocation. If he does, he will never find wisdom, because for him wisdom is in his vocation. . . . It is by living his life that the monk finds God, and not by adding something to his life." Could such a monk have entered into the fight for racial equality or into the peace movement? Could such a monk have gone to the Orient to consult with masters of other traditions?

Tom needed a breakthrough to get "back to a more universal point of view." And it did come. And it was, in a way, another tradition that opened the way for him: the rich Christian tradition of the Byzantine East.

The importance of the influence of Byzantine spirituality and especially that of the Fathers of Eastern Christendom on the development of Thomas Merton's well-integrated spirituality can scarcely be exaggerated. From its first serious awakening, Tom's Christian life was marked by the influence of the Christian East. When he was in Rome in the spring of 1933, still very much a hedonist, it was the great Byzantine mosaics that called him forth and changed the tourist into a pilgrim. In *The Seven Storey Mountain* he tells us:

I was fascinated by these Byzantine mosaics. I began to haunt the churches where they were to be found. . . . And now for the first time in my life I began to find out something of Who this Person was that men called Christ. . . . And now I think for the first time in my whole life I really began to pray—praying not with my lips and with my intellect and my imagination, but praying out of the very roots of my life and of my being, and praying to the God I had never known.

How much the glimpse he had of mosaics in the sketches on his father's bed prepared an opening for this experience cannot be said, but his father was very much a part of it all.

At the end of his journey, in the last book that he prepared for publication, *The Climate of Monastic Prayer*, Merton opens with the Fathers of the Desert and goes on to share the kernel of the teaching of the *Philokalia*. As we progress through the text, which offers a clear and concise history of contemplative spirituality and the teachings of the masters, we come upon such names as Isaac of Niniveh, Saint Ammonas, Evagrius Ponticus, Saint Basil, Saint Gregory of Nyssa, the Pseudo-Dionysius, Saint Nilos, and others from the Byzantine tradition.

It might be said that the influence of the great Fathers of the Eastern Church first came to Father Louis mediated through the Cistercian Fathers, whom he read extensively in his early years in the monastery. As his studies moved forward he came, in part with the help of Etienne Gilson's *The Mystical Theology of St. Bernard*, to recognize and identify these Fathers' sources. But I think it can also be said that it was the Fathers of the Desert, whose delightful, pithy, and profound sayings so attracted him, that opened Tom to pursue the evolution of this strong, rich current of spirituality. Keith Egan, in his interesting and informative series of taped talks, *Solitude and Community: The Paradox of Life and Prayer*, said of Merton, "He began to read the literature that came out of the desert, the Christian desert of the fourth century. And one of the most important books he wrote is his shortest and that is *The Wisdom of the Desert*. . . . The study that lies behind the writing of this little book was transforming and changed Merton's life forever."

In 1960, when he published his short collection of *Sayings*, Tom wrote a rich introduction of twenty-two pages. He traced the spiritual path laid out by the fathers in their sayings. It begins with a clean break, compunction, a lament over the madness of our attachments to unreal values. Through solitude and labor, poverty and fasting, charity and prayer the old superficial self is purged away and the true secret self is permitted to emerge into true freedom. The monk moves thus toward purity of heart—

a clean unobserved vision of the true state of affairs, an intuitive grasp of one's own inner reality as anchored or rather lost in God through Christ. This leads to QUIES, the sanity and praise of a being that no longer has to look at itself because it is freed and carried away by the perfection of being that is in it. And carried where? Wherever Love itself, the Divine Spirit, sees fit to go. Rest, then, was a kind of simple no-whereness and no-mindedness that was freed from all preoccupation with a false or limited "self."

The terminology Tom uses here is not that of the Desert Fathers. By the time he was writing the introduction, the fathers had opened Tom to other, broader influences. But first they opened him to their own immediate heirs. Tom went on to expand and deepen his vision through the theology of the Christian East with the Cappodocians, especially Saint Gregory of Nyssa, and with Evagrius Ponticus, who really belongs to the desert tradition, and, above all, with Maximus the Confessor.

In his study of the teaching of Saint John of the Cross, *The Ascent to Truth*, Merton devotes many pages in the first and third chapters to those "great theologians of darkness: Saint Gregory of Nyssa and Pseudo-Dionysius." The former he hails as "the most important and the most neglected of the early Christian mystical theologians, the Father of Christian apophatic mysticism." Tom mainly uses Gregory's scriptural commentaries, those on Ecclesiastes, Psalms, and the Song of Songs. He traces out Gregory's journey from light to darkness with the Mosaic imagery of the burning bush and the pillar of cloud, and then seeks to elucidate it with the teaching of Saint John of the Cross. He speaks of *theoria physike*, distinguishing the positive and negative aspects of it. But at that time this important element of Eastern Christian spiritual teaching had not had the impact on him that later was to be highly significant.

Some years later Tom had the opportunity to study these fathers more fully and reflect more profoundly on them as he prepared and gave a course to his fellow monk-priests on Christian mysticism. We have only the notes of these lectures, but the notes are quite full and, although they lack his usual literary style, they do have his candid clarity and forceful impact. It is here that he highlights the central place of Saint Gregory more in detail, indicating Gregory's influence on the Cistercian Fathers—on Saint Bernard through Origen, on William of Saint Thierry through the Pseudo-Dionysius and John Scotus Erigene, and on all Cistercian fathers through Cassian and through Evagrius—on the Syrians through Saint Macarius, and on the Greeks in general through Maximus the Confessor. Here he studies extensively and deeply the meaning of the *spiritual senses*, disagreeing with the interpretations or understanding of previous Western teachers such as Poulain and Gaillard. Tom adopts a more integrated view, seeing these senses closely allied with the bodily senses that have been freed and purified by mortification, virginity, and passive purification, and elevated and spiritualized by grace and the operation of the Holy Spirit till they approach a full restoration of that state of paradise where God was enjoyed by the senses "deifying the body" (Saint Gregory Palamas).

More important is the breakthrough insight he attains into *theoria physike* under the tutelage of Evagrius Ponticus, whom he strongly defends, and Maximus the Confessor. He now sees that the spiritual life has three levels:

Bios praktikos—praxis— the purification of the body, of the senses, of the passions—*apatheia—*the *puritas cordis* of John Cassian, something more than detachment, a positive openness to reality, to the Divine. *Theoria physike—*a spiritualized knowledge of the created, a sort of natural contemplation, which does reach on to the divine *oikonomia*, God's plan for things, and the *logoi* of things, the divine place within things. At its highest it reaches to the contemplation of the spiritual. *Theologia—*the contemplation of the Trinity without form or image.

I believe that it was his understanding of *theoria physike* that enabled the zealous, ascetic, world-despising young monk, who constantly fought with his own human gifts for poetry and literature, to reintegrate his natural appreciation and love for the wonder of creation and all that God made and to go on to become the very full and integrated person he became. He himself said, "We can in fact say that the lack of *theoria physike* is one of the things that accounts for the stunting of spiritual growth among our monks today."

He went on to say: "It is by *theoria* that man helps Christ redeem the *logoi* of things and restore them to Himself. . . . This *theoria* is inseparable from love and from a truly spiritual conduct of life. Man must not only see the inner meaning of things but he must regulate his entire life and his use of time and of created beings according to the mysterious norms hidden in things by the Creator, or rather uttered by the Creator himself in the bosom of His Creation." I would like to quote more extensively from Father Louis's notes in this place because I think this matter is central to an understanding of his spiritual development and outlook.

Man by *theoria* is able to unite the hidden wisdom of God in things with the hidden light of wisdom in himself. The meeting and marriage of these two bring about a *resplendent clarity* within man himself, and this clarity is the presence of Divine Wisdom fully recognized and active in him. Thus man becomes a mirror of the divine glory and is resplendent with divine truth not only in his *mind* but in his *life*. He is filled with the light of wisdom which shines forth in him, and thus God is glorified in him. At the same time he exercises a spiritualizing influence in the world by the work of his hands which is in accord with the *creative wisdom of God* in things and in him. No longer are we reduced to a purely negative attitude toward the world around us, toward history, toward the judgments of God. The world is no longer seen as purely material, hence as an obstacle to be grudgingly put up with. It is spirit there and then. But grace has to work with and through us to enable us to carry out this real transformation. Things are not fully spiritual in themselves, they have to be spiritualized by our knowledge and love in the use of them. Hence it is impossible for one who is not purified to "transfigure" material things. On the contrary, the *logoi* will remain hidden and he himself will be captivated by the sensible attraction of these things.

In this last sentence I think we see the difference between these Greek Fathers, and Merton with them, and the currently popular creation theology. The Fathers and Merton emphasize that it is impossible to enter into a true *theoria physike*, a true appreciation of the creation and the presence of God in creation, without first embracing the *bios praktikos*, that purification that produces *apatheia*, a purity of heart that enables us to appreciate the overwhelming beauty transfiguring the creation without being ensnared by it. Otherwise, we are in danger of resting in the creation and becoming attached to it and ourselves rather than finding all in God and God in all, being attached to him alone.

Also, the Fathers and Merton never stop at the *theoria physike*, the wonders of creation, even transfigured by God, but are ever conscious of this as a stage on the way to *theologia*, to finding our true place within the life of the Trinity, we who have been made one with the Son in baptism, we who have been "deified." In this context and in this context alone does *theoria physike* or creation theology attain its full meaning and human life come to have its full meaning. I quote Father Louis again:

The "will of God" is no longer a blind force plunging through our lives like a cosmic steamroller and demanding to be accepted willy nilly. On the contrary we are able to *understand* the hidden purpose of the creative wisdom and the divine mercy of God, and can cooperate with Him as a son with a loving Father. Not only that, but God himself hands over to man, when he is thus purified and enlightened, and united with the divine will, a certain creative initiative of his own, in political life, in art, in spiritual life, in worship: man is then endowed with a *causality* of his own.

As I have said, I believe that Father Louis's "discovery" and full perception of *theoria physike* had a profound formative and liberating influence on him. There is much evidence to this.

Out of the course that he was teaching came one of his more significant and weighty volumes, *The New Man*. When Dan Walsh received a prepublication copy from Tom, he remarked to Father Flavian, "*The New Man*—the new Merton!" In this study Merton depends heavily on Western Fathers and theologians: Saint Augustine and Saint Bernard, Aquinas and Ruysbroeck. But the names of Eastern Fathers keep cropping up: Clement of Alexandria, Gregory of Nyssa, Cyril of Jerusalem, and others. The Byzantine influence is perhaps more profoundly marked by the frequency with which he employs Greek words in the text. We find *pneuma, pneumatikos, metanoia, antitypos,* and *parousia,* all used more than once. More significant is the extensive use of *parrhesia,* which Tom aptly defines as "free spiritual communication of being to Being."

Russia had a special place in Tom's heart. Through the writings of Father Sophrony, he came to know and love a Russian monk who lived on Mount Athos in this century, Father Siloan, the procurator of Aghios Ponteleimonos. Father Siloan never lost his love of solitude even in the midst of serving a monastery of hundreds of monks. In his preface to Sergius Bolshakoff's *Russian Mystics,* Tom gives evidence of his extensive knowledge of Russian monastic history. Saint Nilos, in his controversy with institutional monasticism represented by Saint Joseph Volokolamsk, was of special interest to Father Louis. He could sense an ally in the person of Saint Nilos. But for Tom, Saint Seraphim of Sarov was "without doubt the greatest mystic of the Russian Church." In him there was a balance between the ascetic traditions and austerity (*poddvig*), between repentance and tears and a humanism filled with joy, open to life, gentle, and profoundly compassionate. Tom found in him evangelical and patristic purity, pure and traditional theology, ingenuous amazement at the divine light shining through the darkness. Saint Seraphim's was a mysticism of light (albeit based on the apophaticism of Pseudo-Dionysius and Maximus) that approached the Invisible as visible in a creation transfigured by Divine Light.

Father Louis's interest in Russian writers, though, ranged far beyond the monastic and even the religious properly so called. In the late 1950s he made an abortive attempt at learning Russian so that he could read contemporary Russian writers in their original language. *Conjectures of a Guilty Bystander* is sprinkled with names such as Belinsky, Lenin, and Berdyayev, along with the pages devoted to Evdokimov. His next published journal, *Woods, Shore, Desert,* includes a quote from Yelchaninov in the prelude.

Without a doubt Merton's favorite among the modern Russian writers was Boris Pasternak. Tom wrote three articles on this poet and novelist whom he saw as "immensely more important than Sholokov." He found Pasternak's witness to be "essentially Christian." The Christianity Pasternak presented was "reduced to the barest and most elemental essentials: intense awareness of all cosmic and human reality as 'life in Christ', and the consequent plunge into love as the only dynamic and creative force which really honors this 'Life' by creating itself anew in Life's — Christ's — image."

Tom senses a oneness with Pasternak and expresses it powerfully and beautifully in the first letter he addresses to the Russian, some months prior to the explosion over the Nobel Prize awarded to Pasternak in October 1958:

I feel much more akin with you, in your writing, than I do with most of the great modern writers in the West. That is to say that I feel that I can share your experience more deeply and with greater intimacy and sureness. . . . With other writers I can share ideas, but you seem to communicate something deeper. It is as if we meet on a deeper level of life on which individuals are not separate beings. In a language familiar to me as a Catholic monk, it is as if we were known to one another in God.

I believe this is so because by this time Tom has integrated the outlook and experience of *theoria physike* and Pasternak comes out of that same living tradition; they experience creation in the same basic way and express this in their poetry and prose. Tom points to this in his first article on Pasternak: Pasternak, whether he knows it or not, is plunged fully into midstream of the lost tradition of "natural contemplation" [Father Louis's English expression for *theoria physike*] which flowed among the Greek Fathers after it had been set in motion by Origen. Of course, the tradition has not been altogether lost and Pasternak has come upon it in the Orthodox

Church. The fact is clear in any case: he reads the Scriptures with the avidity and the spiritual imagination of Origen and he looks on the world with the illuminated eyes of the Cappodocian Fathers [Saints Basil, Gregory of Nazianzanus, and Gregory of Nyssa].

Merton grasped this sophianic view of the cosmos—a creation impregnated by Sancta Sophia, Holy Wisdom, the Word and Love of God—in other Russian writers such as Soloviev and Berdyayev, but he identified most strongly with Pasternak's spirit, so akin to his own. This is why he shared with him in his second letter a secret he had shared with only three others. Because of its special bearing on this important breakthrough in Tom's life, I quote the passage in full:

It is a simple enough story but obviously I do not tell it to people—you are the fourth who knows it, and there seems to be no point in a false discreetness that might restrain me from telling you since it is clear that we have so very much in common. One night [Friday 28, 1958] I dreamt that I was sitting with a very young Jewish girl of fourteen or fifteen, and that she suddenly manifested a very deep affection for me and embraced me so that I was moved to the depths of my soul. I learned that her name was "Proverb," which I thought very simple and beautiful. And also I thought: "She is of the race of Saint Anne." I spoke to her of her name, and she did not seem to be proud of it, because it seemed that the other young girls mocked her for it. But I told her that it was a very beautiful name, and there the dream ended. A few days later when I happened to be in a nearby city [Match 18, Louisville], which is very rare for us, I was walking alone in the crowded street and suddenly saw that everybody was Proverb and that in all of them shone her extraordinary beauty and purity and shyness, even though they did not know who they were and were perhaps ashamed of their names— because they were mocked on account of them. And they did not know their real identity as the Child so dear to God who, from before the beginning, was playing in His sight all days, playing in the world.

Father Louis adds with humor, "Thus you are initiated into the scandalous secret of a monk who is in love with a girl, and a Jew at that! One cannot expect much from monks these days. The heroic asceticism of the past is no more."

In *Conjectures of a Guilty Bystander* Merton had reported the Louisville experience but not with such intimacy:

In Louisville, at the corner of Fourth and Walnut, in the center of the shopping district, I was suddenly overwhelmed with the realization that I loved all those people, that they were mine and I theirs, that we could not be alien to one another even though we were total strangers. It was like awaking from a dream of separateness, of spurious self-isolation in a special world, the world of renunciation and supposed holiness.

Tom had had a somewhat similar or sort of initial experience of this almost ten years earlier, in August 1948, when he accompanied Dom Gabriel Sortais to Louisville: "I met the world and found it no longer so wicked after all. Perhaps the things I had resented about the world when I left it were defects of my own that I had projected upon it. Now, on the contrary, I found that everything stirred me with a deep and mute sense of compassion." With his ever-deepening insight into *theoria physike*, and with the impact of the rich imagery of a dream, the 1958 experience worked a profound and lasting change in Thomas Merton.

The last journal that Tom himself prepared for publication, *Woods, Shore, Desert*, is a magnificent witness to the full flowering of *theoria physike* in his life and outlook. It conveys his cosmic and earthy contemplation in the way it can best be conveyed: through poetics and artistry. This severe critic of technology (and in many of his criticisms I think he was right on the mark) does not hesitate with the true freedom of a son of God to use a bit of technology— the camera—to produce some real art that powerfully highlights and shares his contemplative insight.

As Rowan Williams said in his comparative study of Evdokimov and Merton, "Merton's spirituality ... would not be what it is without his devoted and careful study of Greek patristic thought and the Desert Fathers." And, I would add, all that flowed out of them. And Merton not only studied the Desert Fathers, he assimilated and integrated them in a way that produced a profound and profoundly beautiful lived synthesis. Tom now resonated with Teilhard de Chardin and praised him for "taking matter into account as basic."

This is where Tom also joined the Shakers—in spirit. In *Conjectures of a Guilty Bystander* he recounts a winter visit to Shakertown, camera in hand. He is open to what is: "I have no way of explaining how the bare, blank side of an old frame house with some broken windows can be so indescribably beautiful." Then in the first sentence of the next entry in his journal he does explain it: "All being is from God." With this he goes on to set forth as rich and powerful and positive an expression of creation theology as I have ever read, noting that it "starts not from a *question about being* but from a *direct intuition of the act of being*," such as he had on the corner of Fourth and Walnut, the experience of "one who has experienced the baffling, humbling and liberating clarity of this immediate sense of what it means to *be.*"

Before the experience of March 18, 1958, Tom would write of "the indignity of being a member of the human race"; after, he would write, "It is a glorious destiny to be a member of the human race." Before, he would write, "The contemplative and the Marxist have no common ground"; his last talk would be devoted to monasticism and Marxism. Again, he would praise de Chardin for proclaiming the Good News in a way that was accepted by both scientists and Marxists.

Tom would join Teilhard in his prayer "to be widely human in my sympathies and more nobly terrestrial with my ambitions than any of the world's servants." He had entered into his depths and found one Person, drawing all together into a common humanity, all part of one creation, all coming forth from the one heart, the heart of Christ-God. As he would write in "The Inner Experience": "The life of contemplation in action and purity of heart [the goal of the monastic life as set forth by Saint John Cassian] is then a life of great simplicity and inner liberty. One is not seeking anything special or demanding any particular satisfaction. One is content with what is. . . . He soon learns *not to want to see* anything special in himself." This is freedom.

Recently a book of essays on Thomas Merton was published with the title *Getting It All Together.* The title expresses the essence of the spirituality that Merton lived and offers to us through his many books and articles.

Perhaps not everyone would be ready to recognize Father Louis as a realized man or, as Catholics might say, a canonizable saint. He doesn't fit some of our more conventional pictures of the "holy monk." To find him, just a few days before his death, spending his evening in the bars of Colombo and staying at the most deluxe hotel in a city plagued by much dehumanizing poverty is a cause of scandal for some. Others are scandalized to find this Catholic monk taking off his shoes and going barefoot and reverent in a Buddhist sanctuary and, even more scandalous, experiencing God there in a profound way.

Yet those freer from preconceptions, more open to the reality of the man, did not hesitate to proclaim what they experienced. Dr. Koko Soedjatmoko, the Indonesian Ambassador to the United States, who spent a day with Merton about three months before his death, made this remarkable statement: "If there is one impression that has stayed with me all along it is a memory of one of the very few people I have known in this world with an inner freedom which is almost total. It was, I felt, an inner freedom which was not negative, in terms of something else, but it was like water that constantly flows out of a well."

A person much closer to Merton, a disciple who became his father, Abbot Flavian Burns, said, "Thomas Merton was for me a spiritual master, and I would say he is the most extraordinary spiritual master I've met, a living master. . . . I think he was a saint."

Michael Mott in his authorized biography of Merton reports that to almost all he met in Asia, even in brief encounters, Merton was a "living example of the freedom and transformation of consciousness which meditation can give."

Merton speaks powerfully to us. That he does so is attested to by many facts. The sale of Merton's books, almost all still readily available in paperback twenty, thirty, and forty years after their publication, goes on unabated. It would be hard to count the number of centers around the country that now bear the name of Merton, and the many conferences that are regularly being held in his memory or to study his heritage. Colleges across the nation offer courses about Merton and his literary and social contribution. The list of doctoral and master's theses about him keeps growing. Merton speaks powerfully to us precisely because he did "get it all together"—he was an integrated person, a Christian humanist, a Cistercian in the best sense of the name.

Ours is a humanistic age. One is tempted to say that it is excessively humanistic, but that would not be quite accurate. Although it is true that an exaggerated value is placed on some dimensions of human life, the unfortunate truth is that humanity for what it truly is, is not appreciated adequately. Our age has discovered, or rather rediscovered, the value of some of the dimensions of human life that the Church and society as a whole have not respected or valued in recent centuries. In cultivating and enjoying these values, other truly basic human values have sometimes been left behind, with sad and even *de*humanizing consequences. Even where this has not been the case, where we have become more humane, more in touch with the aspirations of the human mind and heart, there has been a growing sense of a need for something more. To attain that something more, is it necessary to turn our backs on what we have found? Can the experience of the appealing aspects of human life be a part of our existence even while we reach for and enjoy the transcendent, for that something beyond, which we need? Is a renunciation of the good things of this world the only route? Do we all have to become monks? Do monks themselves have to turn their backs on good human experiences in order to be true to their quest, to their vocation?

Father Louis's answer was no. Indeed, as he moved more away from the world and even from his community at Gethsemani, moving into his hermitage, at the same time he moved more toward the world in concern and compassion, and he opened himself to some of the deepest friendships he was to know.

Father Louis's concerns did not stop with the global, but extended to the cosmic. The cosmic is much fuller than the global. It is the context within which we can truly embrace the global and make it our own, integrating it with all its human, political, social, economic, and religious concerns. The deepest aspirations of the human spirit are more than global. They are infinite. We desire not only to know all, to be in touch with all that is going on, we want to care, to embrace all in love. Merton had an amazing, insightful knowledge of "what was going on," amazing for any person but especially for an enclosed monk—perhaps this highlights the role of the monk and the truth that one needs to get apart to see, to get a true perspective.

It was the great mosaic icons that first awakened Tom's faith in Rome. The icon of the Cosmic Christ, the all-embracing icon of the Byzantine church, an embrace of society, world, and all creation, is a reality that powerfully expresses in classic hieratic form the ultimate stance of Thomas Merton—if we soften the classically severe features of the Pantocrator with the Oriental smile of the Buddha!

7. A Life Free from Care

On July 1, 1964, about a year before Thomas Merton moved fully into the hermitage on Mount Olivet, he wrote to Father Brendan Connolly, the librarian at Boston College. Tom had donated one of the manuscripts of *The Seven Storey Mountain* to the Boston College Library in response to the request of his young poet friend Francis Sweeney. It was a donation that paid off. Tom developed by correspondence a friendship with successive librarians at Boston College, and they became an inexhaustible source for the books he wanted in order to pursue such varied studies as ancient Irish monastic rules or the writings of William Faulkner. In this particular letter Tom told Connolly that "after years in religious life one is more inclined to live and accept the spirit of one's Order than to talk about it." He went on to say: "The one thing I find it most difficult to write about at the moment is the Cistercian Order and its spirit."

In his early days Father Louis was put to writing about the order and its spirit. There were various translations and biographies, brochures for prospective candidates, material in connection with Gethsemani's centenary celebration, and the liner notes for a record of the monks singing as well as the accompanying commentary. Many thought they were at last hearing the voice of the great monastic author when they listened to the record, but he only wrote the text; another monk read it. Later he was embarrassed by the triumphalism in much of this early material. Yet it did contain some of the most insightful writing that had yet been printed about a much misunderstood vocation in the Church.

By the time Father Louis was moving into another expression of the Cistercian charism, one provided for by the Holy Rule, he was little inclined to write about it. "I find it hard after all to just sit down and bat out on a typewriter what seems to me the monastic ideal," he wrote to Connolly, "not because I have not thought about it but because I have thought about it so much that I sometimes wonder if anything I say about it has any meaning." When we stay with something—or someone—long enough, in a living way, we come to an experience of depth that makes human expression virtually meaningless. This is, of course, all part of entering into the contemplative dimension of our own being.

One thing, though, that Tom had become very aware of is that there are "two aspects to our life": the one, more personal and solitary; the other, communal. "We have emphasized the fact that these are two aspects of the same thing . . . they are both right." He went on to say that we have to discover for ourselves and for our communities how to reach the right combination of the two elements so that "each one of us will be able to live fully the expression of the vocation to which he or she has been called." Tom proclaimed as the *Magna Carta* of monastic life this text from the Gospels: "There are many mansions in my Father's house."

Father Louis was a good community man. He had learned from one of the Cistercian Fathers, William of Saint Thierry, as well as from penetrating the meaning of true charity, that those who care about others not only want to love them but to be loved by them, for our friends can become more loving by loving us. "The vocation to charity is a call not only to love but to *be* loved."

Father Louis had a very special relationship with his community. It is something an outsider rarely gets a chance to see. I remember well a parallel experience. Dom Jean Leclercq, one of the men who most fully understood and supported Tom, is well known for his travels. He has been one of the most tireless apostles of monastic renewal since even before the Second Vatican Council. He has willingly traveled to the most distant outposts to encourage any small community he has heard is trying to live the basic monastic charism in a new way. He also has done more than his share to encourage the large, entrenched, traditional monasteries to meet the challenges of a rapidly evolving world. I had known Dom Jean for quite a few years, welcoming him to Spencer and sharing many meetings with him, before I had occasion to visit him in his own abbey, the large, traditional Benedictine community of Clervaux in Luxembourg. It was a revelation to see how beautifully this monk of world renown blended into his brotherhood. I found he was deeply loved by all his brothers, especially the lay brothers, even though he was absent much of the time. They told me he regularly wrote home long letters, sharing all his experiences with them. He seemed to never forget anyone's birthday or feast day, always sending an appropriate greeting. He always made an effort to be home with his brothers for the major feasts. On the day of my visit, everywhere we walked around the abbey glad smiles greeted Father and his guests. He obviously loved his brothers and was loved by them in a warm, fully human way.

The same was true of Tom. One of the brothers recounts the first sight he caught of Father Louis. The first bell for the evening office of vespers had rung and the monks were flowing toward the church, walking, as is the custom in Cistercian monasteries, along the two sides of the wide cloister. Coming in the opposite direction, right down the center, full of smiles and making signs to just about everyone (the cloisters are a place of stricter silence) was this obviously happy monk, enjoying the fact that he was out of step, going in the opposite direction of everybody else. Everyone seemed to brighten up a bit as Father Louis passed them.

The bond a Cistercian monk has with his community is a special one. On the day he is consecrated a monk, he makes a solemn vow of stability, promising to remain with his particular community for the rest of his life. The only ordinary exception to this is if a group of monks from the monastery undertakes to establish a new monastery. Even then the monk retains the right, as long as he lives, to return to his original monastery. It is a kind of belonging that could be reduced to a juridical formula. But for the monk who enters into the deeper meanings of being called by God to be a committed part of a particular community, the bonding becomes something much deeper than the sum of the human relations and the years of living through all sorts of things together. There is a particular oneness in Christ that is meant to be exemplary of the oneness that we are all called to be part of in the one Christ.

Gethsemani was and is a human community, with the usual disagreements, antagonisms, and jealousies. Yet Father Louis was, in spite of this, universally loved and respected—with varying degrees of appreciation. Tom served on many monastic councils and committees in the community. This was undoubtedly one of the great asceticisms in the years prior to his escape to the hermitage. At such meetings he was not listened to as an oracle, but met healthy opposition to many of his plans and ideas. Not all agreed with the judgments he made about candidates during his years as novice master. If he seemed at times naively unaware of his reputation outside the monastery and the excitement he could cause, it is understandable, because he was so constantly cut down to size by the brethren who surrounded him day in and day out. Community life does much to ensure the sense of realism that is true humility.

A good bit has been written about Father Louis's relationship with his second abbot, Dom James Fox, much of it distorted. It was undoubtedly a most complex relationship. One thing, certainly, cannot be denied, and that is that Dom James had not only a deep love for Father Louis but also a profound respect for him as a spiritual master. Weekly, for more than fourteen years, the abbot knelt at Father's feet as a penitent before his father confessor, placing the guidance of his life in the Spirit in Father's hands. Thinking of some of the notes Tom wrote to the abbot in his more agitated moments, one would very much like to have been a fly on the wall listening in on these encounters. It must have been a ministry that challenged Tom a great deal, making demands on his own humility and compassion. Tom had a way of bringing a light touch to such weighty moments, calling upon an immense repertoire of stories, especially about the older brethren.

Father Louis always had a special affection for the older monks—a common monastic trait. He had a way of drawing out the more shy and less attractive ones,—young and old. Old Brother John was born on the same day as Tom, but fifty years earlier. Each year Tom would visit the infirmary to celebrate the day with the venerable ancient. Father Timothy tells of how much it meant to old Father Idesbald, something of a community oddball, to have received a card from Brother Louis when he was off somewhere in Asia.

Dom James was concerned that Father Louis be not too much out of the community. Perhaps he discerned how much Father really needed community. Tom always liked belonging. As a kid he and his friends formed a club in Douglaston. At Oakham he formed a literary society. He was always much in the midst of friends at Cambridge and Columbia and spent summers with his friends in a tightknit commune in Olean. At Gethsemani he was deeply involved in the lives of many of the monks as master of the students, then novice master, as the confessor of many, and as confidant and friend. Yet the brothers' involvement in his life was always partial.

When Father's first books were read in the refectory at Gethsemani, many in the community did not know that Frater Louis was Thomas Merton. *The Seven Storey Mountain* and *The Sign of Jonas* were not put out in the community library. *The Sign of Jonas* was passed around in a brown wrapper among those in the know. Father Flavian likes to recount a story in regard to this. Flavian was, at the time, a serious young junior. Among his immediate contemporaries was the jovial Frater Herman Joseph, later to be Abbot Thomas of Gethsemani's fifth daughter house, New Clairvaux Abbey, in Vina, California. One day Flavian found Frater Herman Joseph in the garden, rocking with mirth, reading the brown-covered book. He remarked upon this "scandalous" conduct to their scholastic master, Father Louis, only to learn that it was Tom himself who had passed his contraband book on to the delighted junior.

Father Louis, because he was in some ways so guileless and created so much goodwill and good feeling around him, was not aware of the reactions that some of the special permissions he received caused among the brethren. This was one of the reasons Dom James gives for restricting Tom's desire to travel. Travels would have caused only more reaction on the part of the older monks. Tom didn't readily see this. He rather saw that some of his gifted young students were being given opportunities to travel and to further their education outside the monastery, and the farthest he was allowed to go was to Louisville to the doctor. In the late 1950s the order had built a large house for students in Rome. Most of the American monks who went there went for graduate studies in some special field: theology, scripture, philosophy, patristics, or the like, and took every opportunity to see the other houses of the order and explore the great cultural treasures of Europe. Tom, with difficulty, was able to get a quick trip to New York to see the renowned Zen master Dr. Suzuki. Anyone else who wanted to see Thomas Merton had to make the long trip to the Kentucky knobs.

The confidence that pervaded the relationship between Father Louis and his abbot was strong enough to give Tom the freedom to speak out and speak out with a certain vehemence at times, knowing that this would not be misunderstood as disrespect or a questioning of the true authority that belonged to the abbot as abbot. Tom did challenge the cultivation of an attitude that seemed to expect the brethren to let the abbot do all the thinking in the mon-

astery, an attitude that expected the monks to accept all the teachings of the abbot without questioning: the good monk did his job
and said his prayers—that was enough. There was no encouragement for a monk to develop as an independent thinker. That was to
change, thanks in good part to Father Louis, and thanks to direc-
tives of the Church requiring that monks who were to formally
teach other monks in the monastery were to have ecclesiastical
degrees. During Dom James's early years most of the Cistercian
superiors in America, both of the older abbeys and of the new foun-
dations, were men who had been trained and formed in diocesan
seminaries or other religious orders before they entered the order.
Tom was not interested, however, in just forming some independent
and responsible thinkers to lead the communities. He wanted every
monk to be able to think for himself and be able to give a reason for
the faith that was within, for the life he was living. At least, he
wanted everyone to have the opportunity to develop his mind in the
things that pertained to his vocation to the extent to which he
wanted and felt called.

Few monks will be heard as Thomas Merton has been. Few will be
heard at all, because as soon as they begin to think aloud in the community in any way that does not reflect the thinking of the abbot,
they are quickly labeled by others as being in some way out of line.
The social pressure in most of our communities to conform is very
great. Few monks or nuns have the stamina not to succumb to the
pressure that can be exerted not only morally but even physically,
with so much work being imposed on the "thinker" that he or she
has little time to think or express his or her thought. Tom was fortunate in that his first abbot appreciated thinkers and writers and
encouraged them. He had so launched Father Louis as a writer that
it was inevitable that Tom would be able to continue to pursue his
literary work under Dom Frederic's successor. Yet the common life
chopped up Tom's day into little pieces, and the demands of the
brethren and the work he was assigned left him really none of that
gracious space so necessary for serious literary output. The situation would have been impossible for most. When Tom did try to do
a more profound, scholarly sort of book he suffered a virtual breakdown, a long period of writer's block, and concluded that that type
of writing was not possible for him. Many of his later books are
drawn from brief daily jottings in a journal or are collections of

essays or letters. All of this is undoubtedly part of the reason he sought greater apartness and solitude—to find the freedom to think and write. By the time he did get his hermitage on the hill, he had become too famous and was immersed in too many causes and involved with too many people to be able to find much truly free time.

The day Father Louis formally took his leave of the community to live full time in the hermitage, August 20, 1965, he remarked that he had spent his whole monastic life up to that time in formation. First he was a novice and then a student. Even before ordination he was teaching courses and soon after he was appointed master of the students, and then novice master. Tom had clear ideas on formation, drawing from the living Cistercian tradition. He had a special affinity for Adam of Perseigne, a twelfth-century novice master who later became abbot of his community. Drawing from Adam's writings, Tom wrote an essay on formation. The title is telling: "The Feast of Freedom: Monastic Formation According to Adam of Perseigne." In it Tom gives his most formal statement as to what formation is about:

To form . . . is then to draw out the inner spiritual form implanted in his [the disciple's] soul by grace: to educate—that is to say, to "bring out"—Christ in him. It is not a matter of imposing . . . a rigid and artificial form from without, but to encourage the growth of life and the radiation of light within the soul, until this life and light gain possession of his whole being, inform all his actions with grace and liberty, and bear witness to Christ living in him. It takes account of the whole man, called to find his place in the whole Christ.

The individual was supremely important and had to be encouraged to live to the full his or her own unique expression of the beauty of Christ-God within. Yet for Father Louis, this could never be apart from others. Our oneness in Christ, which is incarnate in the communities to which we belong, is the essence of who we are. Tom returned to this in the talk he gave a few hours before his death. There he said that Christianity looks "primarily to a transformation of consciousness—a transformation and a liberation of the truth imprisoned in man by ignorance and error. . . . The traditional religions begin with the consciousness of the individual, seeking to transform and liberate the truth in each person, with the idea that it will then communicate itself to others." For Father Louis, the monk, above all, should be able to help others in this, for the monk should have "come to experience the ground of his own being in such a way that he knows the secret of liberation and can somehow or other communicate this to others."

This role in formation coalesces with the traditional role of the spiritual father. In 1952 Father Louis became spiritual father of the scholastics and began to speak of "my children." This seems a bit incongruous for these young professed, as Tom brings out in the same passage, were going through very much the same experiences the thirty-five-year-old Merton had gone through just five years before. But at that point in his development Tom was still very much a product of the pre-Vatican II Church and not yet the prophet of the renewing Church. It was a paternalistic Church, within which spiritual direction tended to be maternalistic. But even at that period Tom had some worthwhile things to say about spiritual direction. His thoughts were published in an article in the journal *Sponsa Regis* and then republished in the book *Spiritual Direction and Meditation.*

When Dom James, after almost twenty years of abbatial rule, was about to retire to a hermitage, Father Louis made it clear that he was not open to being elected abbot and assuming the role of spiritual father of that large monastic community. But this was an older and wiser Merton, who had moved toward the eremitical life himself. In 1952 he was very happy to be appointed spiritual father of the scholastics or young professed monks. And three years later he volunteered for the job of father master of the novices. Thus he had held within the community the two offices under the abbot that most called forth the services of a spiritual father.

This call to ministry in the community was a great grace for Tom. He speaks of it candidly in *The Sign of Jonas*: "Their [his "children"] calmness will finally silence all that remains of my own turbulence. . . . They refresh me with their simplicity. . . . I make resolutions to speak less wildly, to say fewer of the things that surprise myself and them." He found his ministry a stimulus to live more faithfully: "I am obliged to live the Rule in order to talk about it." He accepted his failures: "I have not always seen clearly and I have not carried their burdens too well and I have stumbled around a lot and on many days we have gone around in circles and fallen into ditches because the blind was leading the blind." He was confronted by his limitations: "On all sides I am confronted with questions I cannot answer, because the time for answering them had not yet come. Between the silence of God and the silence of my own soul stands the silence of the souls entrusted to me. Immersed in these three silences, I realize that the questions I ask myself about them are perhaps no more than a surmise." In all this Tom found fulfillment, at least for a time, of his greatest desire, the desire for solitude: "All this experience replaced my theories of solitude. I do not need a hermitage, because I have found one where I least expected it. It was when I knew my brothers less well that my thoughts were more involved in them. Now that I know them better, I can see something of the depths of solitude which are in every human person, but which most men do not know how to lay open either to themselves, or to others or to God." And again: "I know what I have discovered: that the kind of work I once feared because I thought it would interfere with 'solitude' is in fact the only path to solitude." But he adds: "One must be in some sense a hermit before the care of souls can serve to lead one further into the desert."

Father Louis was aware of the advantages and the disadvantages of living in a large community—and Gethsemani was, by contemporary monastic standards, a very large community. A large community provides a lot of space. Many can be doing other things and the basic common life will go on. A large community has greater resources of all kinds: more spiritual fathers and friends, and opportunities to use one's talents and gifts. But personally, the large community, especially one where communication among the brethren is limited, has many drawbacks. One can easily get lost in the crowd. One monk at the monastery at Spencer wagers how long a monk might lie dead in his cell before anyone would discover him. It is difficult for the average monk to sense himself making any difference in the community. Apart from the heads of the departments, most have little personal involvement in the work. They belong to the WPA: we putter around—filling in here and there, doing what they are told to do. At the time of Gethsemani's boom, the cellarer or work boss had, at times, to invent work to keep the mob of novices busy. The monk is confronted with the fact that the work and the observances and everything else in the life would go on without him. The community gatherings, whether for liturgy or meals (where there is reading while the monks eat in silence) or the abbot's chapter talks, are all very formal, encouraging virtually no creative participation on the part of the monks. Tom said he couldn't go into the chapter meetings without falling asleep, "and it wasn't a good sleep either."

All of this is, of course, looking at the question from the natural point of view, which certainly remains valid for one living out of faith. Yet the faith does bring in another dimension. No matter how much, on the natural level, our life in community seems to be making no difference, if we are a living part of the community—and that means a loving part, for life is love—we are making a difference in the fullness and the quality of life of the community. The community would be diminished if we were not there. Being there does not necessarily mean our physical presence—though ordinarily it does—but our loving presence. We are by personal commitment a part of this particular community and hold it before God as our community, deeply committed to its well-being. Thus a Cistercian hermit continues to be a significant part of his community, whether he has only withdrawn to the hill across from the abbey as had Father Louis or lives halfway around the world, as does Spencer's hermit in Norway.

Merton was profoundly convinced that it is God who calls us to community and to a particular community. And it is a call to love. In researching for the writing he was to do for Gethsemani's centenary celebration he came upon more than one skeleton in the family closet—"dreadful stuff." But, he pointed out, the community did get through all that stuff. It was a remarkable sign of God's great love for the community. And he felt called to love the community of Gethsemani as much as he could. And he did. Christ's aim, our aim is to overcome sin and death by love. This love grows and is manifested in the loving labor of creating community, the place of the ongoing struggle, by those chosen, the weak ones of this world. A Christian community cannot function without personal love. True Christian community is built by God, on God, through faith. We find ourselves with people whom we might not have chosen as the special sharers of our love. Our struggles in community usually come from preferring things, including our own ideas, over people, the people whom God has given us to love—to love as he loves them, laying down our lives for them. Christian community for Father Louis, his community, was not identified solely with the community of Gethsemani. It was in a very particular way that community, but only as a part of the larger community of the faithful and, indeed, of the whole human family. He was profoundly aware of himself as belonging to other communities: the international community of writers — this led to special relationships with writers in South America, Russia, and other places — and the community of the civil rights movement and the community of the peace movement.

A contemplative community is more difficult to achieve than most other communities. Writers can share their writings and their struggles as writers. Monks who teach find solidarity in facing together the challenges of running the school. But the challenges of the contemplative life are largely solitary ones, the deep challenges of faith and identity. Moreover, contemplatives come together and form a community precisely to help provide and ensure contemplative space for one another. So sharing is restricted. Observances are structured so as to leave one another alone to be with God. The bonding is very much in faith and for the most part at the level of faith. This faith is certainly confirmed as we experience the blessings that God pours out on the community in spite of all our human weakness. Perhaps the greatest confirmation of this faith is the death of an old monk. We have long known his weaknesses and his fallibility, but in the end we see peace and serenity and complete joy. This high ideal of faith has its own built-in danger for community. We are all too prone to judge one another in the light of this ideal and thus be very hard on one another. A deep, realistic sense of our own spiritual poverty and misery is the greatest safeguard here.

Father Louis experienced an ambivalence in going forth to the greater freedom of the hermitage. He wanted the freedom that that apartness would bring. Yet he also wanted to experience the love and support of the brethren. "It all comes down to our actual relationship with our brother. I don't believe in the Abbey of Gethsemani, Inc. But I do believe in my brothers. I stand or fall with them. I need them and they need me." He liked to be heard in regard to significant community decisions. He had for years been on the abbot's council in an era when it was perhaps even more important than now, when the whole community gets more of a hearing. He suffered a good bit at times because he sensed an alienation from

the community—real or imagined. He was pained by his disagreements with the abbot and others. Apartness is the distinctive note
of the monastic vocation, and it is often in this kind of apartness
within the community—which befalls us rather than being sought
—that God completes the work that apartness or solitude is meant
to achieve in us.

In spite of these mixed feelings, Tom went forth to his eremitical
life with courage and joy because he was profoundly convinced this
was the way God was calling. He was also convinced that the community needed a hermit. He felt the hermit was a witness to the community that the individual member can move ahead in the depths
of the life at his own pace and in his own way and does not have to
move along with the slowest ship in the convoy. So, too, for the monk
who is called to share out of the fullness he has been receiving in the
community. The community needs the constant witness of such out-
reach to remind each monk that he is called to live his life to the full
for the whole Church and for all of God's people. Each monk's
unique call to image Christ must be respected. The monastery and
the community exist for the individual; its strength and its fullness
lie in the strength and fullness of the individuals who make it up. In
turn, the individual grows by being a member of the whole and
sacrificing himself in many ways for its well-being.

Tom also saw the hermit as a witness that the monk is called to a
life free from care. In the midst of a cenobium, with the many community observances and activities, we are too prone to take on all
sorts of cares and concerns. "Monastic life should be free from care
and we fill it with care," he told the community the day he formally
laid down the burdens of his charge as novice master—which he
said was the best job in the monastery—and climbed Mount Olivet
to take up permanent residence. He had already written to Catherine de Hueck:

It certainly is a wonderful thing to wake up suddenly in the solitude of the
woods and look up at the sky and see the utter nonsense of *everything*,
including all the solemn stuff given out by professional asses about the spiritual life: and simply to burst out laughing and laugh and laugh, with the
sky and the trees, because God is not in words and not in systems, and not
in liturgical movements, and not in "contemplation" with a big C, or in
asceticism or in anything like that, not even in apostolate. Certainly not in

books. I can go on writing them, for all that, but one might as well make paper airplanes out of the whole lot.

It sounds a bit romantic. But we certainly do need to stop at times, sit back, and take a long distance look—and we will probably start laughing at all our nonsense. The monk is called to take this distance habitually in order to give witness to the rest of the Church and human family that it is something important to do. And he needs the hermit to remind him that this is what he is supposed to be doing.

Tom grew up in an era when powerful totalitarian states were emerging: Nazi Germany, fascist Italy, communist Russia. Mass media and consumerism were also relentless in instilling in people a conformist mentality. Such an age had a special need to be reminded—and reminded by the forceful witness of a life—that we have an inalienable right to that solitude which is absolutely necessary if we are to attain interior freedom. To be a person implies responsibility and freedom, and both of these imply a certain interior solitude, necessary to have a sense of personal integrity, a sense of our own reality and of our ability to give ourselves to others and to society as a whole. Through the ages there have been great voices speaking to us out of solitude, a whole succession of Christian saints, Asian sages, Zen masters, and humanists, such as Thoreau. Tom felt it was important for the monastic order to produce and support such living witnesses. He realized his thoughts on this were not generally espoused in our order, yet he was profoundly convinced that they were authentically monastic. Thanks to him, and Dom James's very active support in this, the eremitical vocation is again recognized in the Cistercian order, but its voice is largely muffled and not allowed to reach much beyond the monk's own community. There is too strong a desire or need within the "Stricter Observance" to keep everything under control, including the life of the hermits within the order.

When Tom wrote to Catherine de Hueck of his eremitical aspirations, he said his hope was simply to get out there and live the life without a lot of rules, and so on. His steps toward the freedom of the hermitage had been slow. Early on, when new duties began to crowd in upon him and his relative solitude in the rare-book vault was lost—the young professed began coming to see him there when he became their father master—he was allowed to escape to an old construction shed that had been dragged out to the woods just beyond the enclosure wall. Saint Anne's, as it was christened, became very dear to him.

In early 1960 the idea evolved of constructing something up on the hill behind the abbey that could be reached by a separate road directly from the highway, a place where Tom could meet with the various groups that were continually coming to see him. He saw this as one of the important roles or aspects of monastic hospitality, influencing the influencers. "I am more concerned with dialogues with selected groups of people—intellectuals, etc., and *not* with large numbers or with a movement. This may sound like an aristocratic approach but I think it is a traditional monastic one. I think the monk is concerned with *personal* contacts with people who exercise influence over groups, rather than directly with groups." An example of this personal sort of dialogue would be the six-day meeting Tom hosted in the fall of 1965 for the leaders of the Fellowship of Reconciliation. The group included such people as Jim Forest, director of the International Fellowship (Jim has published a pictorial biography of Tom), the Berrigan brothers, Abraham Joseph Muste, and J. Oliver Nelson. At the conclusion of the meeting, Tom asked them to sing "We Shall Overcome"; he had never heard it sung. By this time Father Louis had concluded that "literature, contemplative solitude, Latin America, Asia, Zen, Islam, etc., all these things come together in my life. It would be madness for me to attempt to create a monastic life for myself by excluding all these. I would be less a monk. Others have their way of doing it but I have mine."

The center on the hill was to be a gesture toward the ecumenical awakening in the Church, because many of the groups Merton was meeting with were ecumenical. Tom felt that "especially in the field of ecumenism this dimension of friendship, spontaneity and spiritual liberty is of the greatest importance and too much emphasis on organization can be stupefying." Not that ecumenical dialogue was to be reduced to a simplistic discussion among people with good intentions but little else to offer. At Calcutta Father Louis insisted that interreligious dialogue should be "reserved for those who have entered with full seriousness into their own traditions and are in authentic contact with the past of their own religious community—

besides being open to the traditions and to the heritage of experience belonging to other communities." From the depths of our own tradition we are to listen to the depths of the traditions and heritage of others. For Tom the dialogue had to go far beyond the Christian churches. Saint Paul said we have to be all things to all men. Tom interpreted that to mean that to some extent he had to be a Moslem with the Moslems and a Jew with the Jews. In this he was one with Pope John XXIII. He didn't claim this was necessary for everyone, but he did think it was part of the apostolate of the contemplative. Just praying was not enough. The contemplative needs to seek a deeper understanding and identification with all. A person is "catholic" in the best sense of the word when he or she has a unified vision and experience of the one truth shining out in all its various manifestations, some clearer than others, some more definite and more certain than others. "He does not set these partial views up in opposition to each other but unifies them in a dialectic or insight of complementarity. With this view of life he is able to bring perspective, liberty and spontaneity into the lives of others." The fully integrated person is a peacemaker in the full beatitude sense. Tom felt enriched by these contacts. "In my contacts with these new friends, I feel consolation in my own faith in Christ and his indwelling presence. I hope and believe he may be present in the hearts of all of us."

At first elaborate plans were drawn for the "conference center," but Tom, with the help of others, gradually simplified them until they reached the modest proportions of a three-room cinder block cabin — not too elaborate for a hermitage. It was built in the late fall and Tom formally took possession of it on Saint Lucy's day, December 13, 1960, the nineteenth anniversary of his entering the community. At first he was allowed to spend only a few hours there each day. He had also a private room in the abbey where he enjoyed some solitude — and slept much better at night. The time he spent in the hermitage on Mount Olivet gradually increased. In time he received permission to spend his nights there. However, even after he was relieved of his duties as master of novices he had to come down to the abbey each day to say mass and eat dinner in the infirmary. Dom James was quite concerned about Tom's health and equally sensitive about criticism concerning his care for Father Louis. On one occasion he wrote a rather long, defensive letter, not lacking in humor, to Naomi Burton Stone about Tom's situation after Ed Rice had paid a visit to Tom in the hermitage in early 1966:

He [Ed Rice] happened to wander up to Fr. Louis's hermitage after supper—or about supper time—and of course there was no sunshine. It was a rather gloomy day—and Fr. Louis pulled out a can of sardines and a few sandwiches and they munched. But he didn't realize that Fr. Louis had a wonderful hot dinner at noontime with plenty of meat and vegetables. And all monks eat only one meal a day [actually they ate three times a day] without meat. Then the good Father Louis takes back to his hermitage at noontime for his supper a big bag of sandwiches so that there are no dishes to wash—don't you see? Fr. Louis just loves all of this. If it were any different he couldn't stand it. Of course, he doesn't have running water or New York City plumbing [he had an outhouse where he had some interesting encounters with a snake] and he does not have a steam heating system—but he has a tremendous big fireplace, and he tells me that the logs are still always burning in the morning with plenty of embers. He has an electric stove which he tells me: "I never turn on—I don't need it." And even with zero outside, he tells me: "Why I had the window open all night—just put on more blankets. I couldn't sleep otherwise." Do you think that Ed Rice is going to write about this gloomy aspect in an article in *Jubilee*? Lord, I will shoot him if he does.

Eventually a chapel and indoor bathroom were added to the hermitage and Tom was allowed to say mass and take all his meals there. Still, there was a good bit of traffic up and down the hill. Tom continued his Sunday talks in community right up until his final departure.

Tom draws for us an enchanting picture of himself in his first days in the hermitage. In "Rain and the Rhinoceros," which appears in *Raids on the Unspeakable*, he tells of his sitting before the large window in his little hut, reading by a Coleman lantern—he did not yet have electricity there. The rain is pouring down, filling the room with its musical drumming on roof and trees. Tom is reading Philoxenos, a sixth-century Syrian father, seeking to understand better the solitude that has so drawn him and that now he is finding more and more. It is Philoxenos's ninth *Memra* addressed to dwellers in solitude, the one on poverty. Tom hears again that "there is no explanation and no justification for the solitary life, since it is without a law"—it is a truly free life.

As Merton wrote to Catherine de Hueck, he had hoped to live in the hermitage without many rules. He did, however, quickly draw up for himself a daily horarium and submit it to Dom James for approval. Whether he submitted successive editions of his schedule to the abbot, I do not know, but right up to the last summer of his life he kept revising his program in little ways. He always had a horarium. He found it freed him from many little daily decisions. With a time set for each thing he wanted to get done, he was able to proceed without wasting much thought or energy on repeated planning or decision making. A rule of life of this sort is a real help, provided, of course, one lives it with due flexibility, appreciating it as a supporting trellis, not allowing it to become a confining cage.

Father Louis's daily rule followed very much that of the abbey across the valley with one significant exception. Tom scheduled himself to anticipate matins, or the night office, and pray it in the evening before supper. This left the dark, quiet hours of early morning—he rose at 2:15—free for deep, silent prayer and meditation. His daily schedule included the rosary and psalter—he prayed the psalter through, fifteen or twenty psalms a day. New Testament, meditation, and examen received an hour before he retired at 7:00 P.M. He allowed himself some time for light reading after lunch, when many of the monks took a nap. In his prayer forms Tom remained traditional, preferring to pray the office and the mass in Latin.

The important thing in all this is not to make too much of what one is doing. More important is the simple being. Tom's prayer was essentially one of being. Speaking of Philoxenos, he stressed that the number one thing in all of this is the call to union with God—and this call is to everyone: *Venite ad me*. In comparison with this, the particular call, the particular path we are called to follow in coming to union is secondary. Yet it is important, because we must be true to ourselves in order to remain free to respond totally to God's call to union.

During his first full days in the hermitage, Father Louis read some of the Stoic philosophers, who had had an indirect influence on the Cistercian school of spirituality. In Epictetus, a contemporary of Saint John the Evangelist and, like him, exiled to Greece, Tom found wisdom. The philosopher urged his followers to carefully distinguish between what was truly theirs and what was not. The only thing that is truly ours is our freedom. We should not surrender it at any cost. If we surrender our freedom for what is not our own, we betray ourselves. If we choose anything over our freedom, that thing comes to dominate us and we lose our freedom. We begin to depend on having it for our happiness. That is a bad state to be in. When we fall into such a state, we begin to despise ourselves for being dependent. The real answer is to will that all things come to be as they are brought to be by the "great disposer." Will what he wills and we will always have what we want. For the Christian with the revelation this wisdom is brought to a greater fullness. This willing what the great disposer wills becomes the surrender of personal love. Surrendering our freedom to God is the way to be absolutely free. Tom saw Epictetus as very positive, a man who had a great sense of gratitude to God, albeit a sort of impersonal, universal, natural deity. We do not then find freedom by setting ourselves against the world, holing up in some inner sanctuary, but rather through entering fully into and enjoying the "great festival of life" with others, seeing God in and through all.

As Father Louis stepped further apart from the community and in that respect further from society, to find greater freedom, he found a greater freedom to be with others. In this freedom he was seeking a fuller healing and greater integrity. In the first days of 1964 he wrote in his journal: "I need to find my way out of a constructed solitude which is actually the chief obstacle to the realization of true solitude in openness and inner subjectivity. False solitude is built on an artificially induced awareness of unrealized possibilities of relationship with others. One prefers to keep these possibilities unrealized. (Hence, false solitude is a short-circuit to love.)" How false and fragile and truncating is a solitude that defines itself by not being in relationship with other members of the one we are in Christ! So much energy is used in maintaining such a posture that there is little free space left to be open to true love, certainly not the free and unlimited space that is needed for the all-consuming and all-fulfilling Divine Love. Tom wrote in his journal in his first days on Mount Olivet: "It does not matter how I may or may not be classified, in the light of this simple fact of God's love and the form it has taken in the mystery of my life ... the only response is to go out from one's self with all that one is (which is nothing), and pour out that nothingness in gratitude that he is who he is." It is only when our solitude is undefined, when it simply is in our being, and therefore totally open and vulnerable to all that is—which is God—

that it is true solitude. We stand alone in our solitude because there is no "other"; we are in God and, in a sense, we are God, and all that is one with us in God. When we are our solitude, there is infinite space in us, in our lives, for God, for others, for all in God.

In this growing openness, freedom, and vulnerability, beautiful, new, richly human relationships came to be in Tom's life. The picture of the world-famous monk-hermit sitting on the floor in Tommie O'Callaghan's living room, reading the comics with her small son and helping his sister, Nancy, with her history homework (he had actually been to all those places she was studying) is for some charming and winning, and for others, who have a set image of the good monk, the good hermit, disconcerting. Brother David Steindl-Rast, who enjoyed a wonderful friendship with Tom in these later years and spent time with him just before Tom left for Asia, had brought out how much Tom disliked labels. If you label me, then you also automatically expect me to live up to the way you define that label. If you call me a monk, you expect me to act the way you think a monk should act. If you call me a hermit, you expect me to act the way you think a hermit should act. This is precisely the antithesis of the freedom of monastic and eremitical life. A monk, and even more a monk who has chosen the eremitical way, is by definition one who does not live by definition. He seeks to free himself from all the expectations of society so that he can be free to be fully to God and move always with the spontaneity of the Holy Spirit, the Spirit of God.

In his freedom Tom entered into a relationship during his first year in the hermitage that has raised questions for many. I agree with Father Flavian that too much has been made of Tom's friendship with a student nurse whom we will call Marge. (Michael Mott calls her S., but I find using an initial a little too impersonal.) Some feel that Tom took advantage of Marge, but I sense they both were fully aware of what was going on. Marge was generous in speaking with the authorized biographer and allowing him to make use of the letters Tom wrote to her and the journals he wrote for her. This collaboration on Marge's part, along with Tom's great care in documenting his experience and then seeing that that documentation was carefully preserved by his friend, who would be one of the trustees of his literary legacy, strengthens me in my understanding of what was going on.

I do not think there was ever any question or danger of this romance going beyond the reality of a passing romance that did not exclude a true friendship. Tom felt free and secure enough to open himself to this beautiful experience precisely because he was so solidly grounded in his commitment as a monk. And Marge, on her part, was secure in her relationship with her boyfriend. The romance Tom and Marge allowed to develop between them, with all its joy and its pain, would be a growing experience for them both, enabling them to move on in their chosen paths, better persons and better lovers for having had this experience together. I do not mean to imply that there was anything phony about the feelings of love that Tom and Marge had for each other. They were very genuine human feelings and emotions. They allowed themselves to have them to the full, and they were perhaps at times frightened and challenged by them. But they were lived out in the context of other, deeper commitments, which never wavered. Tom, who had never had a romantic relationship with a woman that was wholesome and satisfying, found the freedom now to allow himself just such a relationship, and he found a woman who was able to live it with him. Tom had written of romantic love in *The Seven Storey Mountain* in a passage that was deleted. He had said that "a man in a monastery is helped by having had some experience of natural and human love." He felt he had had little of that, at least of the right kind.

On the eve of his fiftieth birthday, in January 1965, Tom wrote in his journal: "I suppose I regret most my lack of love, my selfishness and glibness (covering a deep shyness and need of love) with girls who, after all, did love me, I think for a time. My great fault was my inability really, to believe it, and my efforts to get complete assurance and perfect fulfillment. So one thing on my mind is sex, as something I did not use maturely and well, something I gave up without having come to terms with it. That is hardly worth thinking about now—twenty-five years since my last adultery." If in early 1965 Tom felt his lack of integration in this area of his life was "hardly worth thinking about," a year or so later, with newfound freedom, he did decide to do something about it.

There was never anything sexual, in the sense of genital expression, in Tom and Marge's relationship. That would have been going beyond what they really wanted and it would have done violence to the more permanent commitment they each honored in themselves and in each other. It is true that Tom is exceptionally reticent in writing about his sexuality after his conversion from the licentiousness of his youth. It may be that his conversion was so complete in this area that, as we hear in some of the hagiography, he was preserved from any further difficulties. I would be surprised, however, if that was the case. In the passage just quoted, he does allude to a fall in the dark days after his rejection by the Franciscans. In his talks to the novices about chastity he calls for a straightforward, no-nonsense decisiveness in the matter of sexual temptations. I have little doubt but that that was the way he handled the matter in his own life.

My understanding of Tom and Marge's relationship may seem to some a bit unrealistic. I think it can be comprehensible only to those who have experienced the freedom that comes from a deep rootedness in God. In that freedom Tom wanted to do all that was necessary to become even more completely free, mature, and integrated. He was willing to experience the pain as well as the joy of such a romance in order to find a fuller healing of the wounds that remained from the violating relationships he had had with women, where he used them and acted in ways that were unworthy of his or their true humanity.

Some would feel that in doing what he did Tom was unfaithful to his commitments. That judgment would come in part at least out of their image of what a monk is and therefore what Tom should have been, how he should have acted. As I have already said, trying to live up to anyone's image of a monk, even or especially one's own, is the surest way not to be a true monk. Tom could well have seen all that he was doing as being very much in line with his aim of being a true monk, a man wholly integrated and free. After the fact he did have some misgivings and regrets. He did do some things that seem a bit devious. They were in relation to the demands of an institutionalized monasticism that did not leave him with the freedom to act as he thought he should. There is a question here, though, in regard to what was demanded of him in loyalty to his community. I am sure loyalty does not demand of a monk that he live up to all the expectations or definitions of his brethren. But where does one draw the line? The question of fidelity to his vow of obedience and its demands upon him can also arise here. I do not want to make any further judgments in the matter. I do feel confident that what Tom did in this relationship involved no infidelity to his basic monastic commitment, but rather showed a great courage and freedom in pursuit of his goal. Father Flavian has said, in another context, that Tom was truer to himself in his writing than in what he did. That may be the case. Perhaps we should apply to Tom himself what he wrote years before in *New Seeds of Contemplation:* "God sometimes permits men to retain certain defects and imperfections, blind-spots and eccentricities, even after they have reached a high degree of sanctity and because of these things their sanctity remains hidden from them and from other men."

For a monk who was such a good spiritual father and who spoke and wrote so well on the role of the spiritual father in the life of the monk, we might challenge Tom on his lack of openness with some guide regarding this relationship. But, as he noted in his last talk at Bangkok, there come times when everyone must stand on his or her own two feet. He would have been hard pressed to find anyone in the Gethsemani community at that time who would have been able to understand his freedom. Though he may have found one, but his confessor obviously is not going to volunteer any information.

One of the questions Tom had to face in entering upon this romance was how would it be brought to a close. He sensed he could rely on the institution to take care of that. I find it sad that at that time there was not a single telephone available to the monks where they could be assured of confidential communication. That has since changed and all the phones in the new system at Gethsemani allow for privacy. Even sadder, I think, was the prevailing spirit that would lead the brother at the switchboard, after he had accidentally listened in on a phone conversation between Tom and Marge, to report the matter to the abbot. Fraternal correction, helping a brother or sister, in true love, to see and correct their personal faults, is an important and compassionate part of Christ's teaching. But his teaching is clear. When we find another at fault, we are first to go to him or her privately. If the person does not hear us, then we are to seek two or three others to help us in this task of love. Only if this proves ineffectual are we to approach the Church in the person of the superiors. Such evangelical practice did not prevail in Cistercian communities. In fact, the chapter of faults, the strict rules of silence, and the practice of the superiors inculcated the opposite. One was to bring things immediately to the superior and the community. Happily, the chapter of faults is gone. But unfortunately, many superiors by their receptivity and their way of acting still encourage the brethren to bring misdeeds immediately to them rather than encouraging the brothers to reach out to each other in true fraternal love and assistance.

Tom, on one occasion near the end of his life, told the brethren how he lamented the lack of communication he had experienced among them. He understood this flowed out of the way they had been trained in the monastic life. Yet he hoped they could learn from the young men entering, who were so much more open to each other. Tom felt the way they had been operating in community was based on a false theology. We are broken persons and live in broken communities in a state of brokenness. We are alienated from ourselves and from each other. We do not readily fit together. We are like a bunch of porcupines trying to huddle together for warmth who are always driven apart out of fear of the wounds we can inflict upon each other with our quills. The ideal we were brought up with tended to consecrate our brokenness. We were to become united to God without any interference from one another. We went to great lengths to avoid such interference. Each sought to come to possess the ground of being, the contemplative experience of God, as if it could be his own. But the ground of being, our being in God, is totally common ground. It is gift, given to us all together, given in and through each other as members of one sole Body. We try to keep some little private area within us for us alone with God. This we see as recollection. What are we recollecting? If we want to be recollected, that is, centered and gathered in God, then let us drop all walls and be completely open, and we will find God in all and be centered in God, gathering, collecting all in God all the time. Certainly, Tom did not want to argue against some privacy, the value of some time apart, the precious time of deep, contemplative prayer. He was concerned about a false attitude. God is not exclusive, he is all-inclusive. God can be found within and in the quiet of the cell. But he cannot *not* be found in others and in all and still be found within and in the quiet of the cell. We cannot be selective as to where we are going to find God. God is where he is. We must be open to him where he is or we will not find him where we selectively decide to seek him. We all need to reach out and find God in each other, love and care for him in each other, listen to him in the reality of each one's response to the call of God that he or she is.

Marge's love for Tom did much for him. She truly and freely loved him as he was. With her he was not in the pigeonhole of monk or author or famous person. A nurse gets a special opportunity to get in touch with a person. When Tom was lying in bed being nursed in all the intimate ways, his humanity was very much in evidence. His "world greatness" and "monkness" (at least the trappings of it that are what most people use to box us in) were laid aside. He was simply a man who needed to be washed, relieved, have his back rubbed. In this nakedness—both literal and figurative—Tom's open, simple lovableness was fully exposed. He was a man easy to love and who very much wanted to be loved, loved for who he really was and not for what people made him out to be. His basic humanity, his maleness, his manhood were affirmed by this woman's love. When the foreseen encircling protection of the institution brought the romance to a painful but in many ways beautiful end, both Tom and the woman he loved and by whom he was loved were able to go forward with their lives, freer and greatly enriched by the beautiful experience they had shared.

And we are enriched by it too. It tells a world that is steeped in sex that it is possible to have a romantic relationship and not have to express it genitally. It tells men and women committed to celibacy that they can indeed fall in love and be true to that love and not have to abandon their commitment. Tom was conscious that his life was in some ways lived out for others. That is part of the reason why he documented it so fully, even this special relationship. As we hear his lessons though, we must be sure to hear them fully in context. Such a relationship was able to retain its beauty and be true to the commitments of the two involved only because there was a deep grounding in God, which meant a profound reverence for each other's integrity.

The reader may or may not agree with my understanding or interpretation of Tom's relationship with Marge. Admittedly, it is colored by a certain subjectivism on my part. But that is the advantage of a monk looking at a monk. As men living a similar life we are closer together. I could well see myself, in my commitment to continuous growth as a human being as well as a monk and man of God, opening to such an experience of human love.

Tom, being as fully human as he was, could not open himself to such a relationship in the way he did and not experience powerful and conflicting emotions. He did some foolish things during the period of his strongest infatuation. He made some outrageous demands on his friends that deeply embarrassed them and strained the friendship. He made painful demands on Marge—that is part of every love relationship. This may well have been one of the times to which Tom refers in a later circular letter when he says he once seriously thought for five or ten minutes of leaving the monastic state.

Canonically speaking, it would have been perfectly legitimate for Father Louis, as for any other monk-priest, to get a dispensation from his vows and commitment to celibacy and, with the blessing of the Church, enter into the married state. *Canonically speaking*—but the matter had to be weighed in the light of broader moral considerations, including his responsibilities to his community and to the millions who looked to him as a spiritual master. He had to take into account their needs and expectations, false as well as true. Most fundamentally, though, Tom had to look at himself. He was monk to the core. That is why he—and Marge—obviously set their relationship in a context that not only precluded its being of any long duration, but even forestalled its becoming a love affair in the sense in which that is usually understood. Passion and emotion were indeed theirs—witness Tom's poems for Marge, now published, as well as some of his foolish actions—but they were deliberately circumscribed. Tom could have broken out of the confines he deliberately left intact, as could have Marge, but they both recognized a deep commitment to keeping those confines essentially in place. In the end they were both true to their commitments and true to each other in the way they freely chose to be. Such is true human love, a love worthy of a man and a woman who are conscious of their human freedom and dignity.

Tom's "life free from care" had then its share of cares, little and great. He was still en route, he still had much growing to do. The context of greater freedom, which the eremitical life gave him, enabled him to move ahead perhaps more quickly and more daringly. Certainly, he moved ahead persistently in a quest for final integration and the full freedom of a son of God. It was not easy. It involved not a little struggle and pain. In a note dated 1966 Tom wrote:

To remain in solitude is to remain in freedom and love of direct obedience to God and not withdrawing to the safety and security of a "tissue of works." I came into solitude to hear the word of God, to wait in expectation of a Christian fulfillment, to understand myself in relation to a community that doubts and questions itself and of which I am very much a part. I came to solitude not to attain to the heights of contemplation but to rediscover painfully for myself and for my brothers the true eschatological dimension of our calling. For our need for genuine interior freedom is now urgent, yet this is something I am helpless to enter except through the cross and I must try to see and accept the cross of conflict—to renounce myself by renouncing "my" answers and while restraining the urge to answer, to reply—in order that I may silently respond, or obey. In this kind of obedience there is never a full understanding of what one has to do—this does not become clear till the work has been done.

I would not want the beauty and simplicity of Tom's life in the hermitage on Mount Olivet to be obscured by all these weighty considerations. Tom did have his struggles there: struggles with Dom James, struggles with his relationship with Marge and with many other friends, struggles with the peace movement and the civil rights movement, above all, struggles with himself. There were perhaps too many things happening, too many comings and goings. But the basic life of the hermit went on in great peace and joy. Tom rose in the night, hearing the matins bell from the abbey across the valley. He stirred up the embers in the grate, if it was cold enough for that, or he settled on the porch, if it was warm enough for that, and enjoyed those deep, rich hours of quiet prayer that are the joy of the monk even when they are dry and seemingly barren. He went for long tramps in the woods, was invigorated by hours of reading, meeting the minds of fellow travelers from many nations and times. The daily mail brought messages of love, concern, and affirmation—God was using him and his work. And there were satisfying, creative hours at the typewriter as poetry and prose came forth. It wasn't a life without its cares—fixing meals was one of them: it could be frustrating and it could be fun—but it was a life increasingly free from care for this monk who ever became more and more a child of God.

8. Final Integration

In his years at Columbia, when he was losing almost the last of those who were to him family (his brother would survive a few more years, only to become a war casualty), Thomas Merton established deep friendships that would last as long as he lived.

Some friends, such as Mark Van Doren, would always be looked up to as mentors. That does not mean the respect and esteem was a one-way street. In the telegram that he sent to Gethsemani at the time of Tom's death, Van Doren said that Tom was the best person he had ever met. It was to Mark that Tom entrusted some of the literary legacy he wanted to preserve as he prepared to be buried in a monastery.

Others, even from those early days, looked to Merton as the mentor. In time their number would grow to be legion.

In other cases it was purely and simply fraternal affection, as with Bob Lax. They mutually enriched and enlivened each other, and their affection ran deep. Father Flavian told me of a Christmas card Tom received from Bob. It contained only three words: in the upper corner, "Tom," in the lower one, "Bob"; and in the middle, "Hi!" It was that kind of friendship. When Tom died Bob's telegram arrived at Gethsemani: "Sorrow." With its one word it spoke more powerfully than the many other long and eloquent ones that arrived with it.

There was one man who was mentor, disciple, and friend: the feisty, happy little Irishman Professor Daniel Walsh. Flavian one day asked Dan, "Who influenced whom?" With a twinkle in his eye, Dan replied, "I guest we both read the same books." There was truth to that. The reason Tom was open to Bob Gerdy's enthusiasm for Walsh was because he had just read Gilson's *Spirit of Medieval Philosophy*, a book that was important to Walsh. Tom was, more than most people realize, a profound philosopher. Like Walsh's, once he had found the faith, Merton's philosophy was totally shot through with the fuller, richer insight that this transcendent vantage point gives one. Tom immediately, instinctively felt a great affinity with Dan

Walsh and placed his confidence in him. It was to Dan that Tom first dared to speak of his emerging desire for the priesthood. With more insight into Tom than Tom himself had at the time, Dan not only confirmed the priestly vocation but pointed toward Gethsemani. It took Tom many more months and much more struggle to see what his mentor saw.

Their friendship lasted through the years of greater silence, when Tom was being formed as a monk and his correspondence was strictly limited. In those first years he was held fairly close to the prevailing rule at Gethsemani: each monk could send out two letters four times a year. Walsh made the trip to Gethsemani to see his friend ordained in May 1949 and after that became a more and more regular visitor, until, retiring from his teaching post at Manhattanville, he came to live at Gethsemani to teach the young monks. He was soon teaching at neighboring colleges and at the seminary. Then suddenly, in a move that was unprecedented in modern times, the Archbishop of Louisville asked Dan Walsh to accept ordination to the priesthood. Tom had the great joy of helping his friend prepare for ordination and then assisting at the actual rite at Saint Thomas Seminary.

Everything in Tom's spirituality corresponds to Dan Walsh's philosophy or metaphysics of the person. It begins with being, with God as the creator of everything. What is first in intention is last in execution. If we want to know the reason for all that is, it is to be found in what God intended. For Dan Walsh, what God intended when he first decided to create was a Person. This Person is the Bride of the Word—as all the imagery in the Gospel of wedding feasts and the like brings out. In this concept of being, then, all of us are the one person together; each one of us in our individuality is at heart this one Person. We are told to love one another as ourself—not as *if* the other person is ourself but because she or he is ourself, our deeper self. As Merton wrote in the Japanese edition of *The New Man*, all are "created, redeemed, and loved by God, and all are 'one in Christ' in the sense that all are known to God as One Man, the universal Man, Christ, the Son of God."

We tend in our thinking and talking about person to think of the person as unique. We latch onto that. I am a unique person. No one else has ever been like me and there never will be anyone else like me. This is indeed true, but it is not the most important thing about ourselves, this finitude, this limitation. The more positive thing about us is that we are one, that we partake of the one Person. By spiritual rebirth we are brought into a deep consciousness that "we are not merely our everyday selves but we are also one with One who is beyond all human and individual self-limitation." What we have in common is far more important that what we have on our own. We do have our own personal vocation. We must accept our own uniqueness—with all the loneliness that that entails—but we accept it as part of a whole. We see that we are complementary to one another, that we complete one another, that we are all complete in that Person—and that Person is one with the Christ: "The two shall be one flesh." As Evelyn Underhill so beautifully wrote from her experience, "I knew the ocean of Love—the 'boundless living substance'—through me, and all of us, immersing us, in Love—it's true, 'the plural is never found.' But in honesty, Evelyn found herself adding, "but I shall incessantly fall into separateness again."

Dan and Tom's concept of the Person corresponds very well to the Eastern concept of the Self. Obviously, the Easterners do not put it in the context of the Bride of the Word. When we see how well they are grounded in this truth, however, we see how the Holy Spirit works in other ways besides the revelation he has given to the Church. We can, then, meet our Eastern brothers and sisters at a very deep level. And we can learn from them. Their notion of the Self is, for the most part, actually more suitable to the mystical life than the commonly prevailing Western notion of person, unless we get in touch with the deep understanding had by the Fathers of the Church and our later mystics.

Father Louis's interest in and sympathy with Eastern thought and practice were influenced by and influential in his preoccupation with the Christian mystical tradition. Eastern though served him better in his efforts to express that inner unity of all that is that our mystics have tried so hard to express. Expressions of this unity have been problematic for our Western theologians, who have ever been fearful of falling into pantheism. There is some legitimate concern here. We do need to be careful how we speak.

If one asks, then, what will we be at the end, I would answer that we will be one with God, we will be, in a sense, God. God will be all in all. The only thing different from what was before will be that then we will be in him. The distinction by which we avoid pantheism is that we can say, We are God, but we were not always God. God has been and always is God. By creation and recreation, by the transformation of grace, we become God. This is what Christ prayed for on the eve of his sacrifice that made all this possible, as he gave us the Eucharist by which it is perfected: "May they all be one. Father, may they be *one in us, as you are in me and I am in you,* so that the world may believe it was you who sent me. I have given them the glory you gave me, that they may be *one as we are one.* With me in them and you in me, may they be so *completely one."* The oneness we have in God in Christ Jesus is beyond anything we can comprehend, even as we cannot comprehend how the Father and the Son are one in the Trinity. It is a oneness we can hardly exaggerate. Yet it frightens us.

We should let God draw us into himself and let him transform us into himself and not hold back and worry about pantheism. Let us be open to where he can bring us and realize there is no way in which we can exaggerate what he intends for us. "Eye has not seen, nor ear heard, nor has it entered into the human mind what God has prepared for those who love him." The mystical writers in our own tradition and our own experiences in prayer will be much easier to understand, accept, and cooperate with, if we can free ourselves from overly dogmatic or static concepts of self.

For Tom, the all of life was simply living out what had happened at Corpus Christi Church on November 16, 1938. He was surrounded by three Jews and as he felt the waters flow over his head, he knew he was going through a rite of liberation, just as their ancestors had when they passed on through the Red Sea. He was incorporated into a people who are the Bride of God, a Bride whom God wants to lead into the desert to tell of his love, a Bride to whom God will be faithful no matter how unfaithful she is, as he showed through his prophet Osee, the constant lover of a harlot. The bonding is indissoluble and most intimate. Yet this bride is a people. Baptism is complemented by the sacrament of Confirmation. "The sacrament of baptism, the sacrament of unity in Christ, must be completed by the sacrament of chrismation, the sacrament of diversity in the Spirit." The gift of the Spirit grants us this complete liberty and freedom to be ourselves without infringing on others. It is a special gift of the Spirit to be free without violating the rights of others, to fulfill ourselves without violating love for others.

Exposure to Eastern thought can be helpful in enabling us to break down the blocks we have in our thinking. Tom can help us here. Tom was well aware he was a Westerner and that he wrote for a largely Western audience. He was deeply steeped in the Western Christian tradition. He was, indeed, a very traditional person. Yet he exposed himself as fully as he could in his circumstances to Eastern thought and practice. He was encouraged in this by masters such as Dr. Suzuki and excellent teachers such as Dr. Wu. And he did well. Some of the masters whom he met in Asia said that they had never met a Westerner who understood them so well. From the depths of his own tradition, which he lived and not just learned, he met them in the lived experience of their own tradition. His intellectual knowledge may fall short of that of the formal students of Eastern thought, but his understanding is deep and rich. That is what he seeks to share with us in his writings, always shedding more light on our own tradition and the way in which we can live it more fully.

The search for God and the search for our own true identity and the search for a relationship with others, with all persons, is really only one search. All that we seek lies within the one reality. All is based on the personal call of God, who is the author of all that is. It is good for us always to seek to purify our notion of God. The notion of God as the creator is basic. For those who have received the gift of Christian faith he is indeed the Father of our Lord Jesus Christ. But for everyone living in this world there can be a consciousness that he is the source of all that is and responsible for it. He is the cause of our being. The reason any of us exist is because God has called us into being. And the nature he has given us gives us a certain responsibility freely to respond, to be conscious of God all the time, even as at all times he calls us forth into being.

Dr. Suzuki was once giving a conference about meditation— coming to the center, the unity of all, through meditation. One of the participants asked, "What about society, what about others?" The eminent scholar paused and then replied, "But there are no others." If you have this experience of the Self and everyone as part of the Self, you can see what he is talking about. We are familiar with Sartre's saying, "Hell is other people." As long as we do not experience everyone as participating in this one Person, as long as we look upon them as other, there will be hell.

Many of the problems we have in day-to-day life come from not sensing how we truly are one in God's call and thus relating to those around us as other. Once we can see the unity, then with God's grace we can welcome all. Our differences have their reason in the divine plan.

The important thing about this part of Father Louis's teaching, and to me it is the key to understanding him and his mature spiritual teaching, is that it demands an openness to change. A transformation of consciousness must take place if we are to make progress in the spiritual life according to this thinking. We do not really have to have the philosophy, but it helps to understand it. It is not necessary because God himself is going to do the work. Where understanding is helpful is at the point where we tend to resist: when we get to the point where the Holy Spirit is going to break down the only self of which we have been conscious. We do not want to give up this false self. We cling to it because it is the only one we know. We think our salvation depends on it. But we must learn not to cling to anything. Not even, it would seem, to God himself. For if we are clinging to God, what we are actually clinging to is an inadequate concept of our God—not the real Lord who is already actually one with us. If we are not ready to give up our concepts of God, our desire to possess God as an object, we will not truly find God or our true self, which is actually one with God, or anyone else, equally one with him and in him.

To facilitate a consciousness of the true self and the experience of God, which is one with it, we need to free ourselves or rather to keep ourselves from resisting, the freedom that God gives to us. Tom told the community at Gethsemani that "the first step in the love of God is being human. My first obligation to God is to be me. If I love God without first being me I'm cheating him. I'm selling him a phony bill of goods."

Tom was a good philosopher, but his philosophy was always drawn up into and illumined by his theology, and the whole was not left in the abstract but became in him a living thing, a thing we sometimes call a spirituality. The same was true of psychology, another field that greatly interested him. He was very open. He followed the advice that Aquinas once gave to a student: "Don't be prejudiced by the sources of your information, but whenever something good is said, commit it fast to memory." He studied Aquinas and Scotus, the existentialists and the Eastern philosophers and drew what he could from each. He studied Freud and Jung and the transpersonal psychologists and drew what he could from them. He had a clear integrity and a power to integrate.

In December 1965, an Iranian psychologist, Dr. Reza Arasthe, asked Merton to write an introduction to a study on final integration. Tom declined, for his publisher, James Laughlin, had urged him to cut back on such writing. (Unicorn Press published a volume of Tom's introductions, *Introductions East and West*.) When Tom received Arasthe's published volume in January 1968, however, he spontaneously wrote a review article on it that was published in *Monastic Studies* a few weeks before his death. It was reprinted as the crowning piece of the first part of *Contemplation in a World of Action*.

Dr. Arasthe and Thomas Merton see final integration lying in a transcultural maturity that enables a person to apprehend his or her life fully and wholly from an inner ground. Such a person is, in a certain sense, "cosmic," a "Universal Man." He is Saint Paul's "all things to all men." This person has a deep inner freedom, the freedom of the Spirit; this person has an openness, emptiness, and purity, entirely docile to the Spirit. No longer limited by his or her culture, this person is truly "catholic," with a unified vision and experience of the One. Tom sees this precisely as the monastic ideal, this sort of freedom in the Spirit, this liberation from the limits of all that is merely partial and fragmentary in a particular culture. To indicate to Dr. Arasthe how consonant was their thinking on these matters Tom sent him a copy of "Rebirth and the New Man in Christianity" in which he says, "The 'new being' of the Christian, his 'new creation,' is the effect of an inner revelation which, in its ultimate and most radical significance, implies complete self-transcendence and transcendence of the norms and attitudes of any given culture, any merely human society."

In this same essay Tom recalls Saint Benedict's great theophany. When Saint Gregory the Great wanted to sum up the meaning of Benedict's life and teaching in the penultimate chapter of his *Dialogues*, he depicted the great abbot sitting at the window of his cell over the gate of Monte Cassino. As he prayed, the father suddenly saw the whole of creation come together under, as it were, a single ray of Truth. This was the symbolic image of the reality that is to be found at the top of Benedict's ladder of humility. Everything comes together. It is Bernard of Clairvaux's fourth degree of love, his highest degree of truth, when all is known and loved in and for God, in oneness in God.

This is clearly the goal of Cistercian life, to follow in the steps of Bernard and the other Cistercian Fathers, seeking to live the life and *Rule* of Benedict of Nursia in its fullness. And here, in this last article published in his lifetime, Father Louis indicts the monasteries for not, in fact, supporting and urging the monks on to this fullness of true freedom and integration.

To enter a monastery is to enter into the most restricted form of life there is. This restriction has a purpose. It is imposed in order to liberate us from attachment and from self-will. Does it? Father Louis answers yes and no. Institutional ascesis tends to go only so far. It frustrates and stifles growth beyond the median level when it refuses to allow anything beyond the communal pattern. Hence "for many authentic vocations the monastery has become merely a way station." For some women and men to stay in the cloister for life would be to renounce their full development. And yet, there is no guarantee that by leaving the monastery they will develop any better.

As Father Louis saw it, by their vow of *conversatio*, the sons and daughters of Saint Benedict have dedicated themselves to rebirth, growth, final maturity and integration. True monastic renewal lies in reshaping the structures so that they will not only permit such growth but foster and encourage it in everyone.

Such freedom begets a certain anxiety, especially in a superior, if the superior is the type who feels he must be on top of everything and the judge of all that goes on in the monastery. Such concern should not be allowed to become a neurotic anxiety, but serve as a good existential anxiety, a healthy pain coming from the perception that certain vital energies are blocked and there must be radical change in individual lives and in the community as a whole and its structures. Such anxiety is a summons to growth, to a fruitful, albeit painful, development. If the brethren do continue to grow and live out of their freedom they will develop a transcultural identity that is personal, original, creative, and unique, transcending the limits set by convention or prejudice.

I wrote an article some time ago entitled "Getting It All Together." It was about Tom's last week in India and Sri Lanka. For those who believe in the providential ordering of things by the Divine there can be no doubt that it was indeed providential that one of the greatest and most influential spiritual writers of the West spent the last weeks of his life in Asia. It is no exaggeration to say that the week he spent in South India, including Sri Lanka, was one of the most important in his life, building, of course, on all that had gone before. In some way it can be said to incarnate and express the essence of his heritage not only to the Christian community but the whole human family, as we seek to establish some global spiritual base on which to build word peace and humane economic order.

Father Louis wrote a paper for the Spiritual Summit Conference he attended in Calcutta just before his flight to South India. In it he said:

I speak as a Western monk who is pre-eminently concerned with his own monastic call, and dedication. I have left my monastery to come here not just as a research scholar or even as an author (which I also happen to be). I come as a pilgrim who is anxious to obtain not just information, not just "fact" about other monastic traditions, but to drink from ancient sources of monastic vision and experience. I seek not only to learn more (quantitatively) about religion and about monastic life, but to become a better and more enlightened monk (qualitatively) myself.

Tom did travel as a scholar. Indeed, there is a bit of humor in this, for he was constantly lamenting the sums he had to pay for excess baggage and making plans to unload some of the many books he acquired—as fast as he unloaded some, he would acquire more! Even in the midst of a heavy travel schedule, meetings of all sorts, and conferences that called for major papers, he managed to do a phenomenal amount of reading, serious study that prepared him for his encounters with spiritual masters of other traditions. He took his touring seriously and read up on the places he was visiting. He took copious notes and made interesting comments on his reading, never losing his rich sense of humor. He must have used every minute. His sweep was too broad to be intensive in any one area. But his keen mind and his deep spiritual sense, coming from years of contemplative experience, enabled him to penetrate, far deeper than most dedicated specialized scholars, into the spiritual traditions he was exploring.

He remained very much the writer. As I have just mentioned, he commented in writing on the many things he was studying and reading, seeing and hearing. He discussed ideas for future books.

He captured some of his experiences in poems. And as he moved along he wrote a journal for future publication.

Above all, he was a pilgrim. His secretary, Brother Patrick Hart, confirmed this in his introduction to *The Asian Journal*, writing, "Thomas Merton's pilgrimage to Asia was an effort on his part to deepen his own religious and monastic commitment." We might find this statement surprising on two scores. Anyone who has read Father Louis extensively would wonder about his need to deepen his monastic commitment. The man was monk, through and through. One could hardly be more dedicated to the monastic reality and to trying to live it. Yet it is of the essence of the monastic journey that the monk continually seek. The more he comes to know experientially what the fullness of monastic life rally means, the more he truly proclaims that he has not yet begun.

More surprising though, might be the fact that Tom was on pilgrimage as a monk who professed and followed Saint Benedict's *Rule for Monasteries*. Benedict did not speak kindly of monks who travel about, going from monastery to monastery. To counteract this "vice" he even required his monks to take a vow of stability, which Father Louis had done. Many have raised questions over the years and still do about Tom's stability. Tom's interpretation of the vow of stability, which we can find extensively spelled out in the notes from his talks to the novices about the vows, was the one commonly held today by the Cistercians and other followers of Saint Benedict. The vow of stability means fidelity to a community. It is not to be confused with enclosure, which is the expectation that the monk will find everything within the confines of the monastery, and therefore not go abroad. Although Benedict did provide for an enclosure and did say it is not expedient for a monk to go outside, he did nonetheless include in his *Rule* a number of chapters about monks going on journeys. The ideal would be for the monk to find all within his solitude, but the ideal is something we are always striving toward in this real world and never quite finding. Benedict, a man of great reality and balance, knew that, and so did the later and more mature Merton.

But perhaps we must say that Tom went beyond this. Not beyond his vow of stability: one has only to read some of his last letters to know his fidelity to that vow. He was firmly attached to his monastery and his monastic community and to obedience to his abbot.

Abbot Flavian strongly confirms this. But, also in the tradition of the Cistercian Fathers, especially Saint Bernard, he placed much importance on getting to know himself. He did indeed attain a very deep self-knowledge. In his later years he knew his needs and accepted them. His genius, his talents, his gifts needed to be called forth by living contact with great minds, great spiritual masters, by the richness of the world's spiritual traditions. In the *Asian Journal* he wrote, "I think we have now reached a stage (long overdue) of religious maturity at which it may be possible for someone to remain perfectly faithful to a Christian and Western monastic commitment and yet to learn in depth from, say, a Buddhist discipline and experience." We do not read anywhere in Tom's writings or journals of his using Buddhist or any other Eastern disciplines. We do read of great fidelity to the practices of the Christian and Cistercian tradition. But when he arrived at the point where he judged such disciplines must be usefully integrated into his spiritual journey, he courageously set out on a pilgrimage to explore this possibility. Throughout *The Asian Journal* we find him discussing spiritual practice with the great masters he encountered. He leaves some practices open for further exploration. Others he quickly decides are not going to be fruitful for him. Why complicate things, he asks. Simplicity, of which he wrote very early on in his own monastic journey, remained ever characteristic of him in his spiritual practice—something extraordinary when we consider what a complex and rich personality he possessed.

Father Louis did come to South India as a pilgrim, but as an exceptional pilgrim. This was not because of his fame. It was because of what he was seeking and the way he was seeking it. He came, as perhaps no person had before, as a pilgrim both to Christian origins in Saint Thomas and to the origins of other great spiritual traditions expressed in Shiva and the Buddha.

As Tom winged his way into Madras one of the first things he spotted was Saint Thomas Mount. Early the next morning he went there to celebrate the Eucharist on the site where tradition says this disciple of the Lord gave the supreme witness of his discipleship in martyrdom. Tom then went on to the cathedral in the Mylapore district of Madras to kneel in silent prayer at the tomb of the martyr-disciple. Artist that he was, he would express the depth of his experience in aesthetic terms. Of the chapel on the Mount he wrote: "One of the nicest things I have found in India or anywhere. A very lovely church, so quiet, so isolated, so simple, so fresh." Those were the qualities that appealed to Tom. For him they expressed primitive Christianity, pure Christianity, the Christianity he wanted to be in touch with and to live.

After kneeling at the tomb of the disciple, Tom traveled along the coast to the great Shivite temple at Kapaleeswara. Later he would cite this and Polonnaruwa, of which I shall speak shortly, as the high points of his pilgrimage. He had some difficulty in entering into Kapaleeswara in the way he wanted, because of the noisy crowds, and most especially because of the hawkers who wanted to sell him postcards and show him around the vast complex. He managed to escape from them and, in the small temple by the sea, he was allowed to enter into the creative mystery of Mother Ocean lapping against a great phallus, the central symbol of the Shivite temple. Out of the perfect circle, the completeness of God, comes forth this powerful burst of life that impregnates the whole of the creation, creation becoming ever more pregnant as it approaches again and again, in greatest intimacy, the tumescent intrusion of the divine into his creation.

Three days later Merton flew to Colombo, the busy port of Sri Lanka, and the next morning took the train up into the hills to Kandy. It was Saturday and the weekend was largely taken up with visits to the bishop, the seminarians, and the monks at Ampitiya, although he did find time to visit with a German bhikkhu. On Monday he drove with the vicar general of the diocese to visit Dambulla and Polonnaruwa. The next day he would begin the long journey to the place where, a week later, he would complete his earthly pilgrimage. He did not immediately write of the experience he had on Monday. Rather, two days later he would note, "Polonnaruwa was such an experience that I could not write hastily of it and cannot write now, or not at all adequately."

At Polonnaruwa, while the disinterested vicar hung back, Tom was able to enter into the sanctuary alone, which he preferred. The pilgrim took off his shoes and let the dampness of the living earth speak to him. At this point it is necessary to let Father Louis speak for himself:

I am able to approach the Buddhas barefoot and undisturbed, my feet in wet grass, wet sand. Then the silence of the extraordinary faces. The great smiles. Huge and yet subtle. Filled with every possibility, questioning nothing, knowing everything, rejecting nothing, the peace not of emotional resignation but of Madhyamika, of sunyata, that has seen through every question without trying to discredit anyone or anything—*without refutation*—without establishing some argument. For the doctrinaire, the mind that needs well-established positions, such peace, such silence, can be frightening. I was knocked over with a rush of relief and thankfulness at the *obvious* clarity of the figures, the clarity and fluidity of shape and line, the design of the monumental bodies composed into the rock shape and landscape, figure, rock and tree. And the sweep of bare rock sloping away on the other side of the hallow, where you can go back and see different aspects of the figures. Looking at these figures I was suddenly, almost forcibly, jerked clean out of the habitual, half-tied vision of things, and an inner clearness, clarity, as if exploding from the rocks themselves, became evident and obvious. The queer *evidence* of the reclining figure, the smile, the sad smile of Ananda standing with arms folded (much more "imperative" than Da Vinci's Mona Lisa because completely simple and straightforward). The thing about all this is that there is no puzzle, no problem, and really no "mystery." All problems are resolved and everything is clear, simply because what matters is clear. The rock, all matter, all life, is charged with dharmakaya ... everything is emptiness and everything is compassion. I don't know when in my life I have ever had such a sense of beauty and spiritual validity running together in one aesthetic illumination. Surely, with Mahabalipuram and Polonnaruwa my Asian pilgrimage has come clear and purified itself. I mean, I know and have seen what I was obscurely looking for. I don't know what else remains but I have now seen and have pierced through the surface and have got beyond the shadow and the disguise.

As on Mount Saint Thomas, so here—it is through the aesthetic experience that Tom enters into and seeks to express the mystical experience. The same qualities stand out: quiet, isolation, simplicity, and freshness. There is a wholeness. Tom said he could not express it adequately. He might have said, as had his Cistercian Fathers in speaking of such, Those who have experienced it know what I am talking about, and those who haven't, well, have the experience and then you will know.

Tom would not return to the experience in the few journal entries that follow. In a week he would be dead. What we find in the following entries and in some of those that go before, surprises us. On the next page Tom recounts trivial events from the local newspaper. On preceding ones he comments on the comics—including an old favorite, *Tarzan*. He is frequently caught up in sightseeing and touring. In Colombo he tries out the different bars and stays in the most luxurious hotel—this champion of social justice who is surrounded by the most abysmal poverty. His delightful poem coming from the train ride up to Kandy is teeming with life of all kinds, not omitting graceful girls and bathing women. As he comes down from Mount Saint Thomas he buys the *Selected Poems* of D. H. Lawrence, which he reads and quotes for us, and he discusses Blake with Raghavan. He reads again Hesse's *Steppenwolf.* He enjoys "really splendid" hotels, flying first class, overeating, and strong Bloody Marys. He finds time for the movies. What kind of mystic is this, what kind of completion?

The most complete kind.

Thomas Merton had made a long journey. He had pursued and tasted most of the desecrating pleasures of human life in his early days. He had been called forth by many causes. He had turned his back on the pleasures and the causes and sought that ascetic path we might expect him to be deeply immersed in in this hour of completion. But he had learned a deeper asceticism, that total response to God in all his manifestations, that left no room for posturing, for creating an image. For the clean, all things are clean. Father Louis was washed clean; he had attained true simplicity. He had it all together, at least for moments like Polonnaruwa, and for the most part, most of the time, in these last days. A simplicity of lack could never belong to this extraordinarily rich and complex person. He could only pursue the integration of the totally rich Divine Simplicity, a simplicity that brought all to harmony in the appreciation of its participated divineness.

On the same day that Tom wrote of his experience in the presence of the Buddha at Polonnaruwa he wrote to me from Singapore about the last book he would personally prepare for publication, *The Climate of Monastic Prayer*. This is a special book. He had begun it as an essay a number of years earlier. It was being written for his brothers and sisters in the Cistercian order and shared a more personal and intimate glimpse of contemplative prayer as he experienced it in the later years of his journey. When we decided in 1968, the year of his death, to begin Cistercian Publications, and we wanted one of his books to start off the Cistercian Studies Series, he proposed putting the essay into a larger context, producing a complete book on prayer. In the last two pages he wrote:

Prayer must penetrate and enliven every department of our life, including that which is most temporal and transient. Prayer does not despise even the seemingly lowliest aspects of man's temporal existence. It spiritualizes all of them and gives them a divine orientation. . . . The most important need in the Christian world today is this inner truth nourished by this Spirit of contemplation.

This is Thomas Merton's heritage, not only to the Christian world, but to the whole human family, a heritage of integration and spiritual freedom. A long-time Indian friend with whom he spent time in Calcutta, Amiya Chakravarty, wrote that "Tom never quite accepted the fixed medieval line between the sacred and the profane." Perhaps he did accept it for a time in his early days at Gethsemani, but it did violence to his nature. As we have seen, with the help of the Greek Fathers he moved back toward integration. He came to see grace and nature working in harmony. He came to appreciate that grace can and does manifest itself in all creation, in all cultures, in all religions. In the paper he read on the day of his death he said, "The combination of the natural techniques and the graces and the other things that have been manifested in Asia and the Christian liberty of the gospel should bring us all at last to that full and transcendent liberty."

His long quest and his open exposure to these elements did bring him to that freedom. Writing from New Delhi just a month before his death, Father Louis expressed a heartfelt desire: "I hope I can bring back to my monastery something of the Asian wisdom with which I am fortunate to be in contact." He was not able to do that except through his written words and his photographs. But through them, and far more, through his lived example, so crystallized in those last days in South India, he has left, not only to his monastery but to all of us, a heritage that invites us with attractive cogency to enter into a new freedom and fully enjoy the creative, loving presence of our God of Love in all things, to let them in and let them, through their reality, lead us into a new, transcendent freedom.

When I previously wrote about Tom's experience in those last days, one of our superiors wrote to me:

First of all, on the "gut level" I couldn't agree with Merton's manner of acting in Asia; eating in expensive restaurants, drinking cocktails in bars, etc. Sure it does represent a certain freedom. After all structures are means to be used for an end; and means can be dispensed with — and should be — when the means jeopardize the end. So to dispense with those means can be a sign of freedom. But also fidelity to the means can be a sign of freedom. The monastic life signifies a life of poverty, unworldliness and simplicity that can be lived even when we are outside the structures of the monastery. To be faithful to those interiorized structures is also an expression of freedom. I honestly feel that on that point at least, Merton wasn't consistent with himself. On the one hand, he wrote much about the poor and social justice; but on the other hand, when he had an opportunity, he traveled in the same circles as the people whom he was criticizing. At least to a certain degree and, seemingly, without much necessity. Interesting, his last conference mentioned that we should not be dependent on structures, to which I agree. At the same time, structures can express the very values we are trying to give witness to in our lives, so that they are not only a means but also an expression of our identity. At least so it seems to me.

I do not think Merton would argue with the good father. He amply respected others' positions. Tom had written in "Rebirth and the New Man in Christianity," that the Christian who has attained a radical experience of liberty "in the Spirit" is no longer "under the Law." That person is henceforth superior to the laws and norms of any religious society, because he or she is bound by the higher law of love, which is freedom itself, directed not to the fulfillment of his or her own will but rather to the transcendent and mysterious purposes of the Spirit, the good of all people.

There is no evil in anything created by God, nor can anything of his become an obstacle to our union with him. It is our attitude, our unfreedom, our self-centeredness that turns things into obstacles. In *New Seeds of Contemplation* Merton wrote, "A saint is capable of loving created things and enjoying the use of them and dealing with them in a perfectly simple manner, making no formal reference to God, drawing no attention to his own piety and acting without any superficial rigidity at all." Tom would have been the last person to say he was a saint. But his friend Bob Lax once told him as they walked down Sixth Avenue in New York, "What you should want to be is to be a saint." And Tom did decide to become a saint. Not a plaster of paris saint—not even in his most uptight state in his early days at Gethsemani did he seek that—but a true saint, the one who lives wholly in the freedom of God's love. He told the sisters in Alaska, "Somehow we have to learn to be guided by the Holy Spirit toward the freedom which can hardly be defended. And at the same time we are surrounded by conflict and criticism." He dared to try to live this way. And I would say, without canonizing him, he did a much better job than most of us in attaining to it.

But was he abandoning the Cross—that Cross which we are commanded to take up daily? By no means. His ascesis, his daily Cross, was "an ascesis of fidelity to life itself and to the human measure. . . . An ascesis not of rigor and restraint but of openness and response: not of solipsism but of self-forgetfulness, celebration and love. . . . An ascesis of generosity." He let go of the imaginary, the imaging and the role, of the abstract. He lived "to the present, the real, what is in front of my nose. Each time I do this I am more present, more real, more detached, more clear, better able to pray."

This morning at mass I heard again the story of the man who had lain for thirty-eight years among the sick, the blind, and the lame in the porticos around the pool of Siloe, awaiting the visitation of the Lord. The Lord finally came to him in the person of Jesus Christ. Jesus healed the man of the affliction that bound him and commanded him to take up his mat and walk. The superiors of the Jewish people, who were charged by the Lord to safeguard the observances, challenged the man with violating the Sabbath. He didn't need to take up his mat. He could have left it there till sundown—it had been there thirty-eight years! The Sabbath rest was and is extremely important. We so much need to enter into that weekly time of quiet, reflection, and prayer. The Jews have sought to safeguard it by surrounding it with multiple precepts based on the Divine Command. The Catholic Church has sought to sanctify the Sabbath observance by particular laws even in the new codification of Canon Law.

Yet Jesus did tell the man to take up his mat. Jesus did not come to abolish the law, but to fulfill it. He observed the Sabbath most fully on that day we continue to call the Holy Saturday, and then he transcended it on the next day in the power and glory of the Resurrection. Jesus did tell the man to take up his mat in violation of the law observance. Why? In that moment the people needed more the witness of the freedom that Jesus was bringing.

I know that right now our nuns and monks need far more the witness of Father Louis's transcendent freedom than they need the witness of observance. And so do, I think, some other Christians, although most have moved beyond the time when too much importance was attached to fish on Friday and mass on Sunday. Because observances have not been seen in their meaning, which is a dying to self through penance and mortification in order, through Christ's saving Passion, to live a new and transcendent life in the freedom of the Son of God, many nuns and monks still attach too much importance to them and do not live them as a means toward true freedom. We need to be jolted out of the complacency of good observance by the scandalous conduct of Father Louis. (On the eve of the election of a new abbot at Gethsemani in 1968 Tom told the community emphatically that he was "a professionally scandalous person.") We need to be challenged to a full living of our vow of ongoing conversion, a constant striving for that true freedom where we live according to the spontaneity of the Spirit of Jesus, who told the man to carry his mat on the Sabbath.

The superior's response in regard to Tom's conduct in Asia exemplifies the attitude that Tom was surrounded by in the order. Comparing the superior's words with the words from Father Louis's *Asian Journal*, which I quoted earlier in this chapter, one can feel the difference of spirit. More clear is the understanding of identity. The superior emphasizes the differences, the specific structures of monastic life as expressing our identity. Father Louis certainly did that in his earlier days, especially in the vocational brochures he was asked to write, but also in his more personal writing. But he moved beyond that to realize that our true identity is in Oneness. When the observance and practices, the means, are so linked with identity, they very quickly receive the emphasis, in spite of principles to the contrary. The result, as Tom pointed out in his piece on final integration, is that the expectations in regard to the observances become so great that it becomes virtually impossible for the monk or nun to move beyond them to that freedom where he or she can freely choose to use them or not use them. There is a truncation and deadening of the spirit. This is unfortunately the reality in many of our monasteries. Great emphasis is placed on the observance and little encouragement given to transcendence and integration. What differentiates the monk and nun from others is constantly stressed and not what makes them one with all in the Oneness that is God made flesh in his Bride.

Another difference is in the understanding of simplicity. There is a simplicity of deprivation and a simplicity of fullness. A thing can be simple because it is stripped down to its bare essentials. This has a beauty, if it is not taken too far and does not lead to deprivation of due being. In the spiritual life it is usually a stage that must be experienced in order to free ourselves from the acquired clutter of life so that we can begin to move toward the simplicity of fullness. The latter simplicity, that of fullness and integration, is found pre-eminently in God, who in absolute simplicity holds within himself all that is and ever will be.

When Father Louis was given the task of translating the report of the Cistercian general chapter on the spirit of simplicity, he did not content himself with translating the report and putting it out to stand by itself. Already he had a keen insight into the simplicity of fullness toward which the spirit of simplicity is meant to lead. His artistic sense breathed in deeply the incarnate simplicity of the ancient abbeys of the order. His eager, penetrating mind had already begun to search deeply into the Cistercian Fathers, especially Saint Bernard, and to find in them the fuller meaning of all of this. He surrounded the translation with an introduction setting forth what he had found in Saint Bernard (this text has been republished by Cistercian Publications in a volume entitled *Thomas Merton on St. Bernard*), texts from the writings of Saint Bernard, and pictures of the ancient Cistercian abbeys, especially the one constructed under the watchful eye of Bernard and set forth by him as an examplar for the new order.

Once he entered the Cistercian order he so immersed himself in the Cistercian Fathers that they became the very matrix of his life and thinking. In his early days, as he was assimilating this Cistercian spirituality, Father Louis wrote about the Cistercian Fathers explicitly. When he served the community as master of scholastics and as novice master he spoke about them constantly: his notes and his taped conferences are full of them. Later they cropped up spontaneously in his writings, the paradigm against which he evaluated what he was then absorbing. One of his favorites, Adam of Perseigne, showed up in the final talk Tom gave, a few hours before his sudden death.

When Tom first entered the monastery there were, as he said in the epilogue of *The Spirit of Simplicity*, few writings of the Cistercian Fathers available in English. He played an important role in remedying this situation by helping found Cistercian Publications, which has now published more than forty volumes of the Cistercian Fathers in English. The lack of translations did not hinder Frater Louis. He not only found no problem in reading the Latin texts in Migne edition, he believed that translations always lacked something of the original text. He constantly brought the Latin text into his classes and coaxed the students to translate them. How carefully he studied these texts is seen not only in his frequent use of quotations from them in his early writings and in the talks he gave his scholastics and novices but also in the underlinings and annotations found in the volumes of the Fathers that he used.

Bernard, Adam, Aelred, all the great Cistercian Fathers led Tom in the same direction. At the time of his death Tom was working on a monograph entitled "Saint Aelred of Vievaulx." The piece seems fairly complete and has been published serially in *Cistercian Studies*. In placing Aelred in context Tom gives a fine synopsis of Cistercian history and especially Cistercian literary history from the foundation of Citeaux in 1098 up until the death of Thomas Becket in 1170. I think one of the most valuable elements of this work is the insight that Father Louis has as a later Cistercian writer into these early Cistercian writers. His thoughts can be applied to Tom himself as a Cistercian writer:

The rich and elegant vitality of Cistercian prose—most of which is sheer poetry—betrays an overflow of literary productivity which did not even need to strive for its effects: it achieved them, as it were, spontaneously. It seemed to be second nature to St. Bernard, William of St. Thierry, Adam of Perseigne, Guerric of Igny, to write with consummate beauty prose full of sound and color and charm. There were two natural explanations for this. The first is that the prolific Cistercian writers of the Golden Age were men who had already been thoroughly steeped in the secular literary movements of the time before they entered the cloister. All of them had rich experience of the current of humanism that flowered through the twelfth-century renaissance. . . . There is a second explanation for the richness and exuberance of theological prose in twelfth-century monasteries of Citeaux. If contact with classical humanism had stimulated a certain intellectual vitality in these clerics, it also generated a conflict in their souls. The refined natural excitements produced by philosophical speculation, by art, poetry, music, by the companionship of restless, sensitive and intellectual friends merely unsettled their souls. Far from finding peace and satisfaction in all these things, they found war. The only answer to the problem was to make a clean break with everything that stimulated this spiritual uneasiness, to withdraw from the centers in which it was fomented, and get away somewhere, discover some point of vantage from which they could see the whole difficulty in its proper perspective. This vantage point, of course, was not only the cloister, since Ovid and Tully had already become firmly established there, but the desert—the *terra invia et inaquosa* in which the Cistercian labored and suffered and prayed.... The tension generated by the conflict between secular humanism and the Christian humanism, which seeks the fulfillment of human nature through ascetic renunciation and mystical union with God, was one of the proximate causes of the powerful mystical writing of the Cistercians. However, once these two natural factors have been considered, we must recognize other and far more decisive influences, belonging to a higher order.... It is the relish and savor that only experience can give, that communicates to the writings of the twelfth-century Cistercians all the vitality and vividness and impassioned sincerity which are peculiarly their own.... The White Monks speak with accents of a more personal and more lyrical conviction that everywhere betrays the influence of an intimate and mystical experience.... It is the personal, experiential character of Cistercian mysticism that gives the prose of the White monks its vivid freshness.... Since the theology of the Cistercians was so intimately personal and experiential, their exposition of it was bound to take a psychological direction. All that they wrote was directed by their keen awareness of the presence and action of God in their souls. This was their all absorbing interest.

Could anyone describe Tom and his writings better?

In his authoritative biography, *The Seven Mountains of Thomas Merton*, Michael Mott cites Carolyn Hammer, the wife of Tom's close friend and neighbor Victor Hammer, as saying, "They sometimes found Merton's wide range of enthusiasm disturbing." I think this might well relate something of Mott's own experience and account for one of the weaknesses of his excellent work. Toward the end one begins to get the sense that he is cataloging Tom's many activities without seeing how they fit together. The key to their unity lies in the great simplicity to which Tom had attained, a simplicity of fullness with its empowerment to be free and to love. It was a final integration, a transcultural maturity, a deep inner realization of the oneness of all in the One. This enabled Tom to find unity and peace in all that he did, to pass through a multitude of things, experience them not so much as multitude and diversity but as one, the One to whom he constantly responded, in one simple, universal love. Perhaps in giving so much space to the human fallibility of the monk, which Tom himself always readily and honestly acknowledged, Mott has not sufficiently brought out how successful Tom was in the essential quest of his life for that true freedom which is found in final integration. In the midst of his relationship with Marge, the relationship that most exposed his humanness, Tom wrote, "Life is not futile if you simply live it. It remains futile however as long as you keep watching yourself live it. And that is the old syndrome: keeping a constant eye on oneself and on one's life, to make sure that the absurd is not showing." Tom was in his later years not afraid to let the absurdities of life, of his own life, show through. And as he did, something else showed through.

Rabbi Lou H. Silberman wrote, "From the first moment I laid eyes on him [Father Louis] in the dark corridor of the guesthouse I knew I was in the presence of someone who lived with an inner center of calm—of peace—not in any static, self-satisfied way, but in a dynamic, open, sharing way." As I have already noted, the Indonesian ambassador to the United States, who spent an afternoon with Tom shortly before Tom began his final journey, reported a similar experience: "If there is one impression that has stayed with me all along it is a memory of one of the very few people I have known in this world with an inner freedom which is almost total." Mott reported that to almost everyone Merton met in Asia, even in brief encounters, he was "a living example of the freedom and transformation of consciousness which meditation can give."

In his introduction to the Japanese edition of *The New Man*, Merton wrote, "There is in the depths of man's heart a voice which says: 'You must be born again.' It is the obscure but insistent demand of his own nature to transcend itself in the freedom of a fully integrated, autonomous personal identity." Tom's quote brings us back to the familiar and deeply moving scene when one of the leaders of the Jewish people, crippled as we all tend to be by human-respect and peer pressure, came in the dead of night to secretly explore the hope a new young rabbi held out and that echoed a voice deep within himself. In the flickering light of a single lantern the two men sat face to face, cross-legged on the ground. One who was respected as a master in Israel inquired of one of the youngest of rabbis, "Can a man be born again?" The rabbi's response is a word of hope for us all. It can be frightening, too. "I tell you most solemnly, unless one is born through water and the Spirit he cannot enter the Kingdom of God.... You cannot tell where the Spirit comes from or where it is going. That is how it is with all who are born of the Spirit." When we attain true freedom, we live in the spontaneity of the Spirit. And we do not know whether we are coming or going. And others don't either. Such Spirit-born persons usually are not good, observant monks or run-of-the-mill Christians — though they may be — the Spirit can lead them that way, too. Usually they are a bit of a problem for superiors or fellow pilgrims who want to have everything under control. Yet there is within every one of us, if we dare to be free enough to listen, an instinct for newness, for renewal, for a liberation of our creative energies and power. We long to awaken in ourselves the force that will change our lives from within. If we dare to listen, we will soon enough realize that the change we seek is actually a recovery of that which is deepest, most original, and most personal in ourselves. To be born again is not to become somebody else, but to become ourselves, our true selves in the One who is Christ.

Our longing is to be true to ourselves, our deepest selves. To do this we must die, die to the false self with which we have so sadly and so strongly come to identify. The false self must die — with Christ on the Cross: that is the meaning of our participation in the Mass. Then the true inner self, the self animated by the renewing Spirit, can emerge with Christ from the tomb. This is the Paschal mystery that is at the heart of all that is Christian and truly human. It is not enough to remain the same self, the same individual ego, taking on a new set of activities and a lot of religious practices, no matter how good. As Father Louis wrote in *New Seeds of Contemplation*, "The obstacle is in our 'self,' that is to say, in the tenacious need to maintain our separate, external egotistic will." We must be reborn of the Spirit who is free, and who reaches to the very depths of everything. He wants to reach to the inmost depths of our heart and take our heart to himself by making himself one with our heart, creating for us a new identity, by being himself our identity. When we are completely freed from our old self by a true death to self in Christ, then we will be able to live totally in the spontaneity of the Spirit. And, no matter how we might seem to be to others, we will be fully integrated. It will be the final integration, that integration into complete oneness with God — and in him with all others — in Christ Jesus our Lord.

Epilogue: The Challenge
of Thomas Merton

"Talk about strident. I do not realize how strident I have been until I get into print. . . . I could after all have been more circumspect and moderate, and there are smoother ways of saying the same thing. I lash out with a baseball bat. Some professor of non-violence I am." These words from a letter Tom wrote to Ping Ferry in 1962 might apply to some of the passages of this book; I hope not many. Living with Tom, even just in his writings, one cannot help but get infected by his spirit, his enthusiasm, his total dedication.

Father Louis is a giant of a man. Indeed, his mind stretches to infinite horizons, and his heart goes beyond. As Jean Leclercq wrote in a review of one of the biographies, there is little hope of getting Thomas Merton between two covers. Even when our considerations are centered on a particular theme, such as we have here, there is still much too much, both in extent and in depth, to be captured. That is precisely why many of us like to keep returning to Thomas Merton — he always has more for us. If what I have written here has no other consequence than encouraging you to return again to his writing and to plumb them more deeply, I will be quite happy.

The day Father Louis died, Father Flavian sent two of the brothers out to Dom James's hermitage to bring him back to the abbey. As they were driving in, Dom James, with his characteristic piety, but more out of the need to fill in some of the aching spaces of silence, remarked, "Now Father Louis knows more theology than any of us." In response one of the brothers shot back, "He always did!"

Thomas Merton was a good theologian. Evagrius Ponticus, a fourth-century Desert Father, wrote, "The theologian is the man who prays." Prayer carries us far beyond the organized concepts of the mind into the limitless experience of God and allows the heart to make its contribution. Tom heeded well Saint Paul's admonition to test everything and retain what is good. He was open to everything and everyone and with great freedom allowed all to enrich his living and lived synthesis.

For a theology to be relevant in the most proper sense, it needs to speak to the actual questions that are confronting us as we seek to live in the Spirit according to our true nature. It must be a theology of the journey. There can be no divorce between theology and spirituality or ordinary, everyday Christian living. Tom spoke to the questions that were the very real questions for many in his times. Not for all, for sadly many of his fellow travelers were not sufficiently alive to perceive and live with the questions. Some preferred to live in the pseudosecurity of answers rather than in the life-giving and freeing space of the questions.

Are the questions Thomas Merton spoke to the questions we are asking today? Most certainly. While the crucifying struggle for civil rights rages on in other countries, the same battle is again coming to the fore in our own country. Years of relative quiet have allowed some serious erosion. Prejudice still holds strong, even in the hearts of some otherwise dedicated followers of Christ. Peace has never been more elusive on a globe pockmarked with ongoing wars and violence of all sorts and ravished daily by massive preparations for a war that would indeed end all wars.

Father Louis spoke to far more basic questions than these, questions that will always remain in the human heart even when, by God's infinite mercy and our greatest human effort, we do finally attain civil rights for all and peace on earth. The human heart will ever struggle to understand and achieve true freedom, self-determination, the empowerment that enable us to make a difference with our lives and do what we most want to do. Tom's great contribution to us all is to invite us to get in touch with the contemplative dimension of life—the deeper, transcendent reality that alone gives life enough meaning. More meaning than just getting ahead in the world or making it in a relationship. That can be challenge enough for a time but not for a lifetime.

Tom brought new sense and challenge to the question of monasticism, not only for those living it, but for those who see potentially contributing women and men "throwing their lives away" in the cloister and wonder about it. Why was Thomas Merton a monk? And why did a monk have such impact?

Who is the one having the greatest impact from within the American Catholic community? Is it the television star, Bishop Fulton Sheen? Like Tom, he was a man steeped in philosophy, which gave him the ability to set forth the truths of the faith with brilliant clarity. Or is it Father John Courtney Murray? He was a man far less well known, but the impact of his theology on the Fathers of the Second Vatican Council continues to challenge anyone who takes the call of that council seriously. Comparisons are odious. Each has his own particular and significant influence. Merton continues to speak powerfully to us today because he did "get it all together"—he was an integrated person, a Christian humanist, a Cistercian in the best sense of the name—a true monk.

The monk is a man apart, a man who can hear all that transpires—if he is listening: listening to the human heart, to God, to God in the human heart, and to the human heart in God. He can hear the questions of that heart. He can situate them. He can bring shafts of light to them, because he is listening to God, seeing God's plan for us, seeing us deeply, perceiving our truest aspirations. The Monastic Fathers have made it clear that we can know others only if we first know ourselves. Tom strove with all his being and with great courage to attain this self-knowledge. He embraced monastic discipline and asceticism so that he could be fully freed from the false self and totally embrace the true self in God. From out of the freedom and security of this Divine Embrace he was able to see all, love, and live compassionately.

One of the characteristic searches of our time has been for roots. Alex Haley's stirring search, shared by unprecedented millions on television, spoke to a rootless people. The attraction of many of the masters from Asia has been that they are well rooted. They speak out of an ancient, powerful, and living tradition. The attraction to them has now waned because their roots are not our roots. Tom's spirituality of integration is especially attractive to us in America today because it is well rooted and the tradition it is rooted in is our tradition. Cistercian spirituality as it blossomed forth in the twelfth century was one of the most complete and beautiful expressions of Christian tradition. In Father Louis it went on to integrate the richness of the later centuries.

Tradition, living tradition, is a constantly growing, self-enriching reality. The word is derived from the Latin *traditio*, which means a handing on. Each of us recipients is to receive the tradition fully into ourselves and allow it to come alive in us. Tom, in his earliest days at Gethsemani, sought to receive fully and to possess the Cistercian heritage. And he went on from there. In the spirit of the Cistercian Fathers of the twelfth century, who brought together the heritage of Antioch and Alexandria, of Christianity East and West, of incarnationalism and transcendence, Merton sought to integrate the spiritual riches of the ensuing centuries. In 1957 he wrote that he wished to "unite *in myself*, in my own spiritual life, the thought in the East and the West, of the Greek and Latin Fathers." When he reported this in *Conjectures of a Guilty Bystander* in 1965 he added "the Russian with the Spanish mystics."

Tom did not need the encouragement given by the Second Vatican Council to begin reaching yet further. His early life prepared him for it—his travels with a father, a New Zealander, who came from the other side of the world and down under, his readings, and his friends. Tom was a global man, a cosmic person. As long as he lived he reached and he reached, to other classes, to other races, to other creeds, to other nations, and to other cultures. This reaching would lead him to die in faraway Bangkok, on a journey with ever-widening horizons.

With the world becoming a global village, we are more and more conscious of the one human family. We want to be fully a part of it, embracing the values as well as the cares and concerns of each and all. Tom gives us a profound, cogent theological context for doing this.

The question is asked at times, How much influence did Father Louis actually have in his own monastery and in his own order? One of the monks, who loved Tom, replied that he did not think Father had had much influence on Gethsemani; he thought only Father Flavian followed Father Louis's teaching. I might question the accuracy of this monk's reading but the answer is telling, for it was Father Flavian whom the Gethsemani community chose to succeed Dom James as their abbot. I think Tom brought about a basic shift in the monastic culture of our American monasteries, beginning with Gethsemani. This was evident in the late 1950s and early 1960s, when young monks of different monasteries met together at the general house in Rome for study. Father Louis, comfortably reading French and a number of other European languages, was up to date with the thinking that was to blossom forth for the whole Church at the Second Vatican Council and that was already having an impact on some of our European monasteries. He had brought this to bear on his teaching as a father master at Gethsemani and the young monks had been formed by it. While the monks from the other American monasteries were still reading Father Faber and the like, or at best Dom Marmion, the Gethsemani monks were well into the Cistercian Fathers and the whole patristic heritage. Tom made the Fathers come alive for them. Those who came from Gethsemani to study at Rome were more interested in monastic and patristic studies than in the scholastic studies many of the other monks were still eagerly pursuing. Today in all our monasteries the emphasis is on monastic studies. With Father Louis's encouragement and assistance I got Cistercian Publications underway, so that now the Cistercian Fathers and Cistercian studies are readily available in English and are widely used. This has, in fact, flowed beyond the Cistercian communities with the founding of the Institute of Cistercian Studies at Western Michigan University and the well-attended annual Cistercian Studies Conference at the same university.

Using well his intellectual and other gifts, Merton grasped clearly what was at the heart of the monastic life and expressed it powerfully in a way that was intelligible to a wide audience. The organ of perceiving meaning is the heart, just as the eye is for sight and the ear for sound. It is the heart that perceives meaning, and the intellect, the will, and the emotions all together form the heart. Purpose in life is not enough; we need meaning: something that speaks to our mind and to our sensitivities and calls forth the response of our will. Tom, with his intellectual clarity and his poetic insight, was able to put across the values of the monastic call in such a way that we perceived them as meaningful. He called us to a deeper and fuller living. "Monastic formation is a formation to live—not a formation to do something in your head." Monasticism lies in the doing and being, in practice, not in explaining and speculating. In the earliest days the disciple would go to the abba in the desert and ask, "Father, what must I do?" and the abba would give him a practice, without any explanation. The disciple would be expected to follow the practice and when it was completed, return and tell the abba what had happened. Then the abba would tell him what to do next. Tom feared that we spent too much time reading about prayers, talking about prayers, and perhaps even saying prayers, instead of actually praying. "The best way to pray is: stop. Let prayer pray within you, whether you know it or not. This means a deep awareness of our true identity. . . . By grace we are Christ. Our relationship with God is that of Christ to the Father in the Holy Spirit."

One of the dangers of an institutionalized monasticism is the danger of falling into the trap of doing the right things, even praying, for the wrong reasons. In *Conjectures of a Guilty Bystander*, a book he began in 1962 only to abandon for several years because he was convinced he could not get it past the censors of the order, Father Louis issues a strong indictment against "pseudo-Christianity." His monastic writings in general indict a "pseudomonasticism"—that monasticism which cloaks selfishness and self-centeredness with cloister and enclosure; which calls relaxation, moderation; which uses separation from the world, silence and solitude—all true monastic values—to avoid the true demands of charity. Long hours are spent busily saying office and other prayers and performing the liturgy (*performing* is the right word here), avoiding the painful encounter with the living God in the darkness of our own inner depths. These dangers are perhaps more present now, as part of a strong conservative swing, than they have been at any other time since Tom's death.

The dictum, No prophet is without honor except in his own country and among his own people, was to some extent true of Father Louis at Gethsemani and in relation to the Cistercian order as a whole. The attitude of some of his fellow Cistercians caused Tom pain at times. If the cause for Tom's canonization is ever introduced, his heroic virtue can be easily established on the basis of what he suffered at the hands of the censors of the order. His surviving correspondence tells only part of the tale. The attitude at Gethsemani did provide Tom with a relatively comfortable, at-home context within which he could lay aside the prophet's mantle and just be "Uncle Louie," much loved and enjoyed by many. If he played with—and I think play is the proper word; he enjoyed the idea and the search—finding a more remote hermitage, a Shangri-la, it was never meant to separate him from Gethsemani. Gethsemani was and remained his home and family. He loved "the guys" there and they loved him. He was bound to them by a solemn vow of stability and that was written deep in the fabric of his being. The idealism that surrounded that vow when he sang it before the baroque altar in the old Gethsemani basilica was never uprooted from his heart, even if it did have to find its later place within a rich synthesis that more and more appreciated the all-inclusive simplicity of the Divine.

Tom never disowned Gethsemani and Gethsemani has never disowned their Father Louis. If for practical reasons—and they are good ones from the monastic perspective—the monks have shipped out Father Louis's literary heritage to Bellarmine College—and this was very much Tom's own choice, though a choice formed in part by the community's response and reaction to him and his activity—they have buried his relics in their midst, simply, as one of the family, one of the brethren, and have quietly tried to keep things that way.

I think it was good that during Father Louis's lifetime his community at Gethsemani did not make too much of him. It helped him keep his feet firmly on the ground. The younger monks did have a special appreciation and affection for him. In response he dedicated No Man Is an Island to them. On the whole his community gave him a sobering and solidifying support. I do not think many of the stresses and strains of his life can be blamed on the abbot or community. They were the inevitable experience of a genius and an artist who embraces the monastic life; for those with the eyes of faith, they were the divine honing of a saint in the making, of one especially loved by God and especially responsive to that all-demanding love.

I would like to see Cistercian communities fully living out of the powerful prophetic vision of Thomas Merton. I think he exceptionally fulfilled the call to religious renewal of the Second Vatican Council. With his genius and ardor he imbibed the spirit of the Gospels and of the Cistercian founders. Through his years at Gethsemani he got deeply in touch with the healthy traditions of the order. He magnificently and effectively brought them into confluence with the signs of the times. If any abbey of the order lived the fullness of the Mertonian vision, the fullest and clearest expression of the Cistercian heritage for the journey into the twenty-first century, I think that monastic community would be fulfilling all the hopes of the council for monasticism in the Church today and be making a powerful contribution to the renewal of the whole Church. It would have quality young men or women flocking to its doors as they flocked to the doors of Gethsemani in Merton's day. They would not all stay—as they didn't when he was novice master. Tom would probably be the first to endorse the value of "temporary monasticism" in today's Cistercian abbeys. Grounded and profoundly enriched by a year or two or more in a monastery, those young men and women who would go forth would be significant persons in the leavening of the Church and society. For the sake not only of the whole Church but of the whole human family, of our global village, I hope and pray that some of our Cistercian communities, if not all, have the guts, the Divine courage and the human courage, to hear and live the challenge of Vatican II with something of the fullness that Father Louis did. We could hardly find a better guide and tutor in seeking to do this than "Uncle Louie." This would involve freedom—evangelical freedom, authenticity—not in an immature, adolescent sense but in the creative sense of the author of true life, and an integrity that truly integrates.

With or without the nuns and monks, though it certainly would be easier with them as a powerful leaven, I hope (and it is a well-founded hope) to see others within the Church and beyond more and more inspired and inspirited by the dynamic vision of this twentieth-century prophet. He may not have had a "dream" but he did have deep Christian hope. It kept him going, as a faithful monk, member of the Gethsemani community, and member of the global community. Because it was a Christian hope, a very human hope, a basic hope, it is something with which we can all identify. Herein lies something of the power of Thomas Merton. In his successful quest for human (and therefore divine) freedom and integrity, he attained something of an "Everyman" quality—which his poetic and literary genius was able to communicate well—that speaks clearly to the heart and the deepest human aspirations of anyone who really hears him. This is a need—that we, especially we Cistercians, do hear Father Louis and his prophetic message. This is the purpose of this book: to give, in some small but, I hope, effective way, another voice to Thomas Merton—a voice that might perhaps reach some who have not previously "heard" him and invite them to listen again to the voice of the prophet of Gethsemani.

Before concluding I would like to point to two particular contributions that Father Louis has made to the Christian community. The first is more widely known and acknowledged than the second.

About a decade ago a simple method of prayer that comes from our oldest of Christian traditions found a new life and popularity within the American Catholic Church and especially among religious. Workshops were jointly sponsored by the Leadership Conference of Women Religious and the Conference of Major Superiors of Men in various parts of the country. Religious brought the method to prayer centers, retreat houses, campuses, and other areas of ministry. This method was first taught in the West by Saint John Cassian, who wrote of it in his *Conferences* early in the fifth century. He was reporting what he had learned from "one of the oldest and holiest Fathers" of Scete who, in his turn, had taught the young Cassian what he had learned when he was young from "one of the oldest and holiest Fathers."

This ancient Christian method, as it was taught and shared in this renewal, received a new packaging and a new name. The name given it was Centering Prayer, a name inspired by Father Louis's teaching. In speaking about this kind of prayer, he would say things such as this:

The fact is, however, that if you descend into the depths of your own spirit ... and arrive somewhere near the center of what you are, you are confronted with the inescapable truth, at the very root of your existence, you are in constant and immediate and inescapable contact with the infinite power of God.

And like this:

A man cannot enter into the deepest center of himself and pass through the center into God unless he is able to pass entirely out of himself and empty himself and give himself to other people in the purity of selfless love.

In a letter to a Sufi scholar, Aziz Ch. Abdul, Father Louis gives a long and clear description of his ordinary way of praying. It is, quite simply, Centering Prayer:

Now you ask about my method of meditation. Strictly speaking I have a very simple way of prayer. It is centered entirely on attention to the presence of God and to His will and His love. That is to say that it is centered on *faith* by which alone we can know the presence of God. One might say this gives my meditation the character described by the Prophet as "being before God as if you saw Him." Yet it does not mean imagining anything or conceiving a precise image of God, for to my mind this would be a kind of idolatry. On the contrary, it is a matter of adoring Him as all. ... There is in my heart this great thirst to recognize totally the nothingness of all that is not God.

My prayer is then a kind of praise rising up out of the center of Nothingness and Silence. If I am still present "myself" this I recognize as an obstacle. If He wills He can then make the Nothingness into a total clarity. If He does not will, then the Nothingness actually seems to itself to be an object and remains an obstacle. Such is my ordinary way of prayer, or meditation. It is not "thinking about" anything, but a direct seeking of the Face of the Invisible. Which cannot be found unless we become lost in Him who is Invisible.

Among Merton's literary legacy is a manuscript marked, "Not for publication." It is entitled "School of the Spirit." Much of it has been incorporated into later works. In this incomplete manuscript Tom tells us that "to live in the fullest sense is to know and to love God the author of life in the center of our soul." Withdrawing from the multiplicity of objects outside ourselves, rising above the level of argumentation and discourse, which can only attain to a remote reflection of God's truth, we seek by the act of living faith to find God present within ourselves.

It is a matter of faith and communion. As Tom tells us in *New Seeds of Contemplation*, if we succeed in emptying our minds of every thought and every desire, we may indeed withdraw into the center of ourselves and concentrate everything within us upon the center, where our life springs out of God. Yet we will not by this purely human effort find God. No natural exercise can bring us into personal contact with him. Unless he utters himself within us, speaks his own name in the center of our souls, we will no more know him than a stone knows the ground upon which it rests. But when we enter within in faith and love, the point of our contact with him opens and we pass through the center of our nothingness and enter into the infinite reality at the center of his Being, where we awaken as our true selves. "Draw all the powers of the soul," Tom tells us, "down from its deepest center to rest in silent expectancy for the coming of God," poised in tranquil and effortless concentration upon the point of our dependency on him.

What we are grasping for is a rediscovery of the immanence of our God. But "the immanentism of Asian religions, fixed and static in exstasis, will not quite do." We want to recover the New Testament awareness that our God has one indestructible temple here on earth: the human person, where he dwells as a living God. Although the word *center* seems to express something static, it is truly understood only when we see it dynamically. It is grace and presence.

According to "A New Christian Consciousness," it is an encounter with God "not as Being but as Freedom and Love." In *New Seeds of Contemplation*, Tom describes it dynamically: "A door opens in the center of our being and we seem to fall through it into immense depths which although they are infinite are all accessible to us; all eternity seems to have become ours in this one placid and breath-less contact." We have sunk into the center of our own poverty and there we have felt the doors fly open into infinite freedom. Then we simply abide there, rest there in the reality: "In silence, hope, expec-tation, and unknowing, the man of faith abandons himself to the divine will not as to an arbitrary and magic power whose decrees must be spelt out from cryptic ciphers but as to the stream of reality and of life itself. The sacred attitude is then one of deep and fun-damental respect for the real in whatever form it may present itself."

Centering Prayer is not an end in itself; no prayer is. Prayer is a moment in life, it is life. We want all life to be prayer, that is, to be a living communion with God and living out of that communion, a living out of our true oneness with God. That is the center that we first seek to open ourselves to through the practice of Centering Prayer. On the Sunday before Christmas in 1965 Tom came down from the hermitage to speak to the community and he spoke of this:

What matters is the freedom to be in contact with the center. It is from this center that all comes. We have to be in contact with the deep inner center; we have to face the possibility of the destruction of all else to know that this can never be destroyed. We can't get there by study, analysis, digging. Psy-chiatrists can't get to it. Not even the devil. Only God. It is the real you. This is where all freedom comes from, the source of all freedom. You can't find it by hunting for it. Leave it be and it will be. You have to school yourself to choose what lets this be; this is what the life of prayer is. Learn never to choose things that throw lots of static in this center. Choose to handle things in a way that remains open to this center.

Freedom lies, then, in our capacity to choose what really is. And this comes out of being centered, in touch with ourselves. If we are manipulating life, trying to correspond to some image or ideal or concept of ourselves, we are not open to the center, to our true self, to things being what they are. Choosing always as best we can the will of God—what is—keeps us in contact with the center.

One of Father Louis's great contributions was his insistence that the contemplative experience both as a way of praying and as a dimension of life, was meant for all: "I have not only repeated the affirmation that contemplation is real, but I have insisted on its simplicity, sobriety, humility, and its integration in *normal Christian life*. This is what needs to be stressed. . . . It is surely legitimate for anyone to desire and to seek this fulfillment, this experience of reality, this entrance into truth."

The second contribution of Thomas Merton to which I would like to point is related to this Centering Prayer, or prayer of presence, or what we might call existential prayer. As Tom wrote, "rising above the level of argumentation and discourse" we seek to be with God at the level of Being. Tom accurately described himself as a Christian existentialist. He was not content to stay with ideas and concepts, with essentialist notions and definitions; he wanted to know and be with reality where it is, in the realm of being. He appreciated the contributions of Aquinas and of Scotus. They helped give clarity to his thinking. (But he did have some difficulties with them. Glenn Hinson tells of attending four lectures Dan Walsh gave on Thomism. Tom attended the first but stayed only half an hour. The second time he persevered for twenty minutes; the third, only ten. He never got to the fourth lecture. Later he met Dan and apologized, saying nonetheless that it was just so much "manure"— actually he used a more earthy word, but my abbot won't let me use four-letter words.) Merton found himself more in the school of Gabriel Marcel.

Gabriel Marcel has never received the hearing he should from the Catholic community. The timing was off. At the moment he was claiming for Christ the valuable insights of existentialism, bringing the necessary correctives, the Church was in the midst of a Thomistic revival. Men such as Etienne Gilson and Jacques Maritain commanded the attention, building as they were on the mandate of Pope Leo XIII. As a result, Thomistic philosophy has remained the philosophy used by the American hierarchy along with the rest of the Western Catholic hierarchy to present its theological reflection and to set forth the natural law with its demands.

Perhaps the greatest contribution of the Second Vatican Council to the ongoing life of the Church was the call to be truly catholic. Our Blessed Lord gave us his divine revelation in a simple Semitic language, one that was potentially open to every language and to every valid philosophical base. Through the five or six centuries following our Lord's Ascension, the Christian community struggled to find an adequate expression of what he had taught, using Greco-Roman concepts. Once this expression was established, after much trial and error and painful and costly controversies, it became normative. This was fine as long as the Christian community was largely limited to the Greco-Roman world. But in time, in fulfillment of the Lord's departing command, the Good News was carried forth to distant lands. The peoples in these lands who embraced the faith found that in order to enter fully into the teaching, they had virtually to become Greco-Roman in their thinking. The leadership of these new churches were largely drawn from natives who had gone to Rome for studies. All who aspired to the priesthood had to study scholastic philosophy in order to pursue theological studies. It is not surprising then that the Church has never taken a strong hold in such populous nations as India, China, or Japan, in spite of heroic missionary efforts and centuries of work. There have been exceptions, such as Kerala, where Saint Thomas the Apostle brought the faith long before the norms of Western theology were established. But for the most part, to become a Christian one had to become a Westerner in one's thinking, even though our Lord and Master himself was an Asiatic!

I met a humorous but telling witness to this fact in India. In their popular faith Hindus believe in one God who manifests himself in many ways. They see Krishna and Ram and others as the manifestation of God among themselves. And they see Jesus as the manifestation for the West and Mohammed as the manifestation for the Arabs. Thus for an Indian to change allegiance from Krishna or Ram to Jesus is seen as a betrayal, a shifting of allegiance from Banaras to Rome. Nonetheless, Hindus honor Jesus as a manifestation of God and celebrate a great feast in his honor on December 24. His image, which is kept in many temples, on this day is set forth and garlanded and carried in processions. In the course of the day there is a *puja*, when offerings are made to him. But instead of the usual rice and *chupatty* that might be offered in the pujas to Krishna and Ram, they offer to Jesus Pepsi-Cola and potato chips and maybe some pizza. For he is the God of the West and therefore likes Western food.

This story highlights the need to free Christ from a Western bondage and let him be the universal Person that he is. To do this, for the Church to become the universal teacher of a universal Saviour, Jesus' message must be able to be taught and understood and plumbed to the depths not only by means of Greco-Roman philosophy, but by the valid perceptions of philosophical truth used by peoples of other nations and cultures.

Father Oshida shared an enlightening experience with me. Father had converted to Christianity when he was nineteen and then joined the Dominican order. When he began studying scholastic philosophy and theology he got such headaches that he began Zen sitting, something he had never done as a Buddhist. The great breakthrough came for him when he studied Hebrew and was able to read the Sacred Scriptures in Hebrew and read the Greek Scriptures in light of the Hebrew. Then, for the first time, he understood Jesus and his Good News as a Japanese. No longer was everything filtered through Western concepts. Father is now one of the great Christian masters of Japan, helping especially seminarians to understand and express their faith in a way that flows from the Japanese experience and philosophy. I have listened to his commentaries on Saint John's Gospel. I must confess there was little I could understand—the approach was so different; but what little I did understand was magnificent, was new, was a piercing ray of light into texts with which I had long been familiar.

I had a similar experience in India when I sat at the feet of Dom Bede at Shativanam and he used the ancient Vedic philosophy as the basic tool for opening our Scriptures for us.

The call of the Second Vatican Council was to all national and local churches to become indigenous. When this happens, not only will the Good News be brought more effectively to all the nations, but each church will be enriched by the light coming from the others. But the tendency so far on the part of a monolithic Western Catholic church has been to interpret this call to become indigenous to refer only to the churches in Asia and Africa, not to itself. This is sad. I daresay the scholastic philosophy that was so difficult for Father Oshida and for the young Indians coming to Dom Bede's ashram (which is now a part of the Camaldolese Benedictine order), is no more comprehensible or indigenous to our young Americans. It is time that the American Church, led by our bishops and theology professors, looked to making the American Church indigenous with a theology based on a philosophy that will facilitate bringing the Good News to the American people.

No one can deny that Thomas Merton speaks powerfully, effectively, and profoundly to a very broad spectrum of the American people. Perhaps no one in the American Catholic community has so effectively brought the Good News to the American people. The bishops themselves have learned from him. There would be few among them who would not acknowledge Tom's role in the creation of their Peace Pastoral, which is probably the most significant and effective document they have produced. No one has ever challenged the orthodoxy of Thomas Merton. He stands out as a man who has a great love for the fullness of the Catholic tradition, who believes in it, believes in it as something living and still going on. In him it lived and spoke to our times and was handed on to a new generation to be enriched and handed on to the future. Witnessing the power and effectiveness of Merton, who professedly based his living and dynamic theology on Christian existentialism (the original title he gave to what is his most important and profound theological work, *The New Man*, was *Existential Communion*), do not our bishops need to ask themselves, Is is not time to reconsider the philosophical basis for Catholic teaching in the United States today in order to proclaim effectively the Good News of Jesus Christ.

Many bishops bemoan the nonreception of Catholic teaching, especially that in regard to the natural law, on the part of vast numbers of the faithful, even those who are in all other regards exemplary in their Christian living and practice. Is this nonreception occurring because the teaching has not been effectively communicated to these good people? Bishops, many of whom have studied at Rome, and priests have absorbed scholastic philosophy and theology through many years of postgraduate study. For them, with their background, a presentation of the natural law based on static, essentialist, philosophical concepts established in the thirteenth century may seem crystal clear and totally cogent. But for many an American Catholic, highly educated though he or she may be, such teaching is "all Greek." In its teaching on the natural law, the Church is not bringing forth the revelation that must be accepted simply on faith, it is interpreting the law that is written in the hearts of us all. Such interpretation should be intelligible to all, not something we have to take on faith. All theology should be the fruit of "faith seeking understanding." If the tool being offered to seek this understanding is largely unintelligible, how can we hope that it will be an aid to an understanding that can effectively guide our response to God in love.

I think then that Thomas Merton stands as a clear challenge to the American Church to move ahead in the spirit of the Second Vatican Council, to seek truly to make the Church indigenous in America, and to examine honestly the need for a new philosophical base for our theological teaching and the potential of Christian existentialism to serve as that base.

A Merton Chronology

1915   January 31, born in Prades, France.

1916   Moves to the United States with his parents.

1921   October 3, his mother, Ruth Jenkins Merton, dies of cancer.

1922   October 22, goes to Bermuda with his father.

1923   Returns to Douglaston, New York to live with Ruth Merton's parents.

1925   Moves to France with his father; they settle at St. Antonin.

1926   Begins studies at Lycée Ingres, Montauban, France.

1927   Summer, lives with the Privats in Murat, France.

1928   May, moves to England and continues his studies at Ripley Court.

1929   Easter, at Canterbury with his father.
August, goes to Aberdeen, Scotland, and his father enters the hospital in London.
Fall, enters Oakham Public School in Rutland, England.

1930   June, Grandfather Jenkins gives him financial independence.
Christmas recess, goes to Strasbourg.

1931   January 18, his father, Owen Merton, dies of a brain tumor.
Easter recess, goes to Florence and Rome.
Summer, visits the United States.
Fall, editor of the *Oakhamian;* writes on Gandhi.

1932   Easter recess, visits Germany.
September, attains a higher certificate.
December, wins a scholarship to Clare College, Cambridge.

1933   February, goes across France to Rome for a prolonged visit.
Summer, visits the United States.
Fall, begins classes at Cambridge.

1934   Summer, visits the United States.
Fall, returns to England to obtain resident visa for the United States.

1935   January, begins classes at Columbia University.
Spring, joins and leaves the Communist party.

1936   October 30, his grandfather, Samuel Jenkins, dies.

1937   Editor of the Columbia *Yearbook;* art editor of the *Jester.*
        February, reads Etienne Gilson's *The Spirit of Medieval Philosophy.*
        August 16, his grandmother, Martha Jenkins, dies.

1938   Receives his Bachelor of Arts degree and begins to work for his
        Master of Arts.
        August, mass at Corpus Christi.
        Fall, moves to 114th Street apartment; studies under Daniel Walsh.
        November 16, baptized as a Roman Catholic.

1939   February 22, receives his Master of Arts degree.
        Visits Bermuda; moves to Perry Street in the Village.
        Teaches at the Columbia University Extension and writes book
        reviews for the New York newspapers.
        May 29, receives the sacrament of Confirmation.
        Summer, lives at Olean, New York, with Lax and Rice; writes *The
        Labyrinth.*
        Fall, begins teaching English at Saint Bonaventure's College.
        November, applies to join the Franciscans.

1940   April–May, visits Cuba.
        June, rejected as an applicant to the Franciscan order.
        Summer, at Olean.

1941   Easter, retreat at the Abbey of Gethsemani, Trappist, Kentucky.
        September, retreat at Our Lady of the Valley Monastery, Cumber-
        land, Rhode Island.
        December 10, enters the Abbey of Gethsemani.

1942   February 21, receives the novice's habit and his monastic name of
        Frater Louis.

1944   March 19, temporary profession.
        Thirty Poems.

1946   *A Man in the Divided Sea.*

1947   March 19, solemn profession, consecration as a monk.

1948   August 4, death of Dom Frederic Dunne.
        August 23, election of Dom James Fox.
        December 21, ordained subdeacon.
        *Exile Ends in Glory; Figures for an Apocalypse; The Seven Storey Mountain;
        The Spirit of Simplicity; What Is Contemplation?*

1949   May 26, priestly ordination.
        The Tears of the Blind Lions; Seeds of Contemplation; The Waters of Siloe.

1950   *Selected Poems; What Are These Wounds?*

1951   May, master of students.
        The Ascent to Truth.

1952   July, visit to Ohio.
        Bread in the Wilderness; The Sign of Jonas.

1954   *The Last of the Fathers.*

1955   Master of novices.
        No Man Is an Island.

1956   *The Living Bread; Praying the Psalms; Silence in Heaven.*

1957   *The Basic Principles of Monastic Spirituality; The Silent Life; The Strange
        Islands; The Tower of Bable.*

1958   March 18, the enlightenment at Fourth and Walnut.
        Monastic Peace; Nativity Kerygma; Thoughts in Solitude.

1959   *The Secular Journal of Thomas Merton; Selected Poems of Thomas Merton.*

1960   October, building of the hermitage on Mount Olivet.
        *Disputed Questions; Spiritual Direction and Meditation; The Wisdom of
        the Desert.*

1961   *The Behaviour of Titans; The New Man; New Seeds of Contemplation.*

1962   *Clement of Alexandria; Original Child Bomb; A Thomas Merton Reader.*

1963   Awarded medal for excellence by Columbia University.
        Breakthrough to Peace; Emblems of a Season of Fury; Life and Holiness.

1964   Honorary Doctorate of Letters, University of Kentucky.
        Come to the Mountain; Seeds of Destruction.

1965   August 20, formally enters the hermitage.
        Ghandi on Non-Violence; Seasons of Celebration; The Way of Chuang Tzu.

1966   *Conjectures of a Guilty Bystander; Hagia Sophia; Raids on the Unspeakable.*

1967   *Mystics and Zen Masters.*

1968   January 13, election of Father Flavian Burns as abbot of Geth-
        semani.
        May, visits California and Arizona.
        September, visits around the country and then Asia.
        December 10, dies in Bangkok, Thailand.
        Cables to the Ace; Faith and Violence; Zen and the Birds of Appetite.

1969   *Climate of Monastic Prayer* (later published as *Contemplative Prayer*);
        *The Geography of Lograire, My Argument with the Gestapo; The True
        Solitude.*

1970   *Opening the Bible.*

1971   *Contemplation in a World of Action; Early Poems: 1940–1941; Thomas Merton on Peace.*

1972   *The Asian Journal of Thomas Merton; Cistercian Life.*

1975   *He Is Risen.*

1976   *Ishi Means Man.*

1977   *The Collected Poems of Thomas Merton; A Hidden Wholeness* (with John Howard Griffin), *The Monastic Journey.*

1978   *A Catch of Anti-Letters* (with Robert Lax).

1979   *Letters from Tom; Love and Living.*

1980   *Thomas Merton on Saint Bernard.*

1981   *Day of a Stranger; Introductions East and West; The Literary Essays of Thomas Merton.*

1983   *Woods, Shore, Desert.*

1985   *The Hidden Ground of Love; Letters.*

1986   *The Alaskan Journal of Thomas Merton.*

A Bibliographic Appendix

I think everyone agrees that Thomas Merton's best and most successful writing is autobiographical. I would even go so far as to say his only successful writing is autobiographical, though significant works such as *The New Man* might elude such a classification. From what we know, his destroyed novels fell into this category, and the one surviving, *My Argument with the Gestapo*, certainly is. In fact, this novel is important for getting to know the young Merton. Although *The Seven Storey Mountain* gives us the facts, this novel reveals to us some of the deeper inner feelings that went with those factual events. Tom's best poems are autobiographical. His most successful book is his autobiography, followed in popularity by his journals.

In this, Tom may again have been a person ahead of his times, reflecting the deeply introspective period that was to come. He was influenced by the French personalist and existentialist schools, where the search for one's own identity was of great import. He certainly was an existentialist. The only thing about which he felt he could write well was what was real to him. As he once wrote, "Every book I write is a mirror of my own character and conscience." Along with this philosophical outlook, a theological intuition comes into play here. Merton had an overriding interest in his own life because he knew it to be a divine mystery. God had willed him into being for a purpose. He was living out a divine mystery; everyone is. This is something he constantly examined and reexamined and to which he bore witness as a writer. Moreover, he saw his life as in some way lived out for others, working things out for the benefit of others. In this he was like John Henry Newman. He realized profoundly, as he wrote in "The Inner Experience," that the person who lives and acts according to the grace of Christ within, acts as another Christ, as a child of God, prolonging in his or her own life the effects and the miracles of the Incarnation. The person who lives according to the grace he or she receives is a sacrament of God's presence and love in the world now. In the letter Father Louis wrote in response to

Pope Paul VI's request for a message of contemplatives, he under-lined this: "We exist solely for this, to be the place God has chosen for his presence, his manifestation in the world, his epiphany. . . . If we once began to recognize this, humbly but truly, the real value of our own self, we would see that this value was the sign of God in our being, the signature of God upon our being."

I will not say anything further here about Tom's autobiography. Let us go on to survey his other writings.

THE JOURNALS

The history of Tom's journals is rather complex. He probably began keeping a journal in his public school years at Oakham, but the earliest extant texts we have are those from the time just prior to his entering the monastic life in 1941 at the age of twenty-six. Perhaps someday some fragments of the early journals will be found, just as some fragments of his early novels, which he destroyed in 1941, have been recovered.

Beginning with the journal written in 1939 there is an almost con-tinuous accumulation, reaching to the eve of his death in December 1968. Within this collection we can distinguish four kinds of journals.

There are the private journals, those which Merton wrote for himself. The oldest of these are the Perry Street journal and then the Saint Bonaventure journal, begun on October 17, 1940. This lat-ter covers the time just prior to Tom's entry into the monastery, the period when he was teaching at St. Bonaventure's College in Alleghany, New York. On the eve of his departure for the monastery Tom sent these journals to Mark Van Doren, who in turn entrusted them to Father Irenaeus, the librarian at St. Bonaventure's, asking him to lock them away. Several years later when he was working on *The Seven Storey Mountain* Tom sent for them.

Most of the private journals rest today in the Merton Collection at Bellarmine College in Louisville. Those from 1956 on are sealed until 1993 by the provisions Tom dictated when establishing the Merton Legacy Trust. Only the trustees, and the biographer appointed by them, were to have access to them, Actually, the biographer proved to be two biographers, when the late John Howard Griffin was replaced by Michael Mott.

There are some gaps in this long collection of journals, especially during the first years in the monastery until 1945 when, in obedience to a confessor, Frater Louis again began a serious journal. There are some journalistic entries in Tom's early notebooks. These books are quite different from the journals. The journals were written in bound ledgers and in ink. Thus it is always evident where there have been erasures or pages removed, events that were more common in the earlier days—later Tom was content to allow the development of his thoughts and emotions, inconsistent as they might be, to remain on record. The notebooks are spirals, which allowed for pages to be easily removed without detection. These are essentially workbooks, used for gathering notes and ideas for his literary work. There is much repetition in the personal journals; they reflect the daily thoughts of the author, which did not necessarily alter significantly from day to day. The handwriting, too, brings us into the mood of the writer—small, cramped script reveals times of greater concentration and large, flowing letters express moods of expansiveness.

Alongside the private journals, and substantially abstracted from them, is a collection of journals prepared for publication. This collection begins with *The Secular Journal* and includes *The Sign of Jonas*, a monograph called "Conjectures of a Guilty Bystander," the book *Conjectures of a Guilty Bystander, A Vow of Conversation*, and the beginnings of a sequel to this last work.

Besides these extracted journals there are several journals that Tom wrote specifically for publication. There is the very short *Day of a Stranger*, the fascinating *Woods, Shores, Desert, The Alaskan Journal*, and *The Asian Journal*.

Finally, there are a couple of special journals of which we will speak later.

Let us look at these journals in chronological order.

The first abstracted journal, which was published under the title *The Secular Journal*, was prepared by Tom in 1940–1941. It was abstracted from three journals, the Perry Street journal, the Saint Bonaventure journal, and an earlier one, which is lost. Tom first called this edited journal *The Cuban Journal*. The central part recounts his trip to Cuba, where he had some profound experiences in faith—the *Credo* came alive for him and he came to know Nuestra Senora de Cobreces. The journal opens on Perry Street,

October 1, 1939, with much talk of poetry, literature, and war. He explores a Franciscan vocation, with sad consequences. The move to Saint Bonaventure's comes after the springtime pilgrimage to Cuba. It is from the college that Tom makes his first visit to Gethsemani, discovers Harlem, and visits Our Lady of the Valley. In the final entry he traces his spiritual itinerary as a man of literature might, through the books he has read. It is important:

I spent most of the afternoon writing a letter to Aldous Huxley and when I was finished I thought: "Who am I to be telling this guy about mysticism?" I reflect that until I read his book, *Ends and Means*, four years ago, I had never even heard of the word mysticism. The part he played in my conversion, by that book, was very great. From Gilson's *Spirit of Medieval Philosophy* I learned a healthy respect for Catholicism. Then *Ends and Means* taught me to respect mysticism. Maritain's *Art and Scholasticism* was another important influence, and Blake's poetry. Perhaps also Evelyn Underhill's *Mysticism*, though I read precious little of it. I was fascinated by the Jesuit sermons in Joyce's *A Portrait of the Artist as a Young Man*! What horrified him, began to appeal to me. It seemed to me quite sane. Finally G. F. Lahey's *Life of Gerard Manley Hopkins*; I was reading about Hopkins's conversion when I dropped the book and ran out of the house to look for Father Ford. All of this reading covered a period of a year and half or two years — during which I read almost all of Father Weiger's translations of Buddhist texts into French, without understanding them.

He goes on to write, "Today I think: should I be going to Harlem, or to the Trappists?" and concludes, "I shall speak to one of the Friars." The entry is dated November 27, 1941. Two weeks later Tom was on his way to Gethsemani.

The flavor of *The Secular Journal* is quite different from that of the surviving personal journal and from the account in *The Seven Storey Mountain*. That is perhaps because is was twice edited. Before he boarded the train for Gethsemani, Tom sent the manuscript to Catherine de Hueck Doherty. It was his hope that she might one day get it published and use the income for her Friendship House, to which he had felt so drawn. It was to make up for a car he had promised her but would now never be able to deliver. More important, it would help her to understand his decision. From this time on Tom called the manuscript *Journal for Catherine*. It was fourteen years later, when the journalist had attained worldwide fame, that Catherine approached him about publishing the journal. In 1955

Father Louis found himself subject to the censors and superiors of his order. A long and painful struggle ensued, with Father Louis writing some rather melodramatic letters about the starving poor who would be fed and housed with the royalties. At one point the abbot of Gethsemani agreed to repay the $500 advance Catherine had already collected for the journal's publication. In the end permission for publication was granted, but further editing was required and it was to be made clear that the journal was written before Tom entered the monastery. Hence the very specific name, *The Secular Journal*. Tom had offered others: *Diary of Young Thomas Merton*, *Reflections of Yesteryear*, *News of an Ancient Battle*, *Meditations of a Young Moose*, *To Hell and Back with Uncle Lou*, and *The Grass Was Greener in the Late Thirties*.

Tom's next abstracted journal has remained one of his most popular books. *The Seven Storey Mountain* allowed only about forty pages to describe Frater Louis's life as a monk. They were tantalizing. Everyone who read the best-selling autobiography wanted to know more about life inside the walls. They wanted to know how this wild young man actually fared as a monk. *The Sign of Jonas* is the nearest thing to a sequel to the autobiography. It stays close to his personal journal and therefore has a refreshing actuality, as it follows him through his monastic life from December 10, 1946, till July 4, 1952, the night of his famous "fire watch," described in the Epilogue.

This was a significant period for Tom as a monk, as a man, and as a writer. As a monk he moved on to solemn vows, his final consecration as a monk, a commitment he never was tempted to go back on, at least in regard to the essence—being a monk. But it contained an element, the vow of stability, which he perceived as the belly of Jonas's whale, the paradox, for it took this prophet—for every monk is a prophet—resolutely in the direction opposite to the one in which he wanted to go. Greater solitude in many forms constantly lured him, yet his vow carried him ever more deeply into the life of a community.

Tom felt his manhood received its crown in this period in his ordination to the priesthood. He sensed deeply that this was what he had been created to be: a priest of Jesus Christ, one with Christ in his priesthood. He would live out this priesthood very personally and very deeply.

The period also saw Tom's only prolonged period of writer's

block. In the end he broke through, but not without some serious psychosomatic problems. In completing *The Ascent to Truth* though, Tom came to realize that kind of theological writing was not for him. He found his genre and it never abandoned him from that time on.

The Sign of Jonas is rich in homey monastic details, and this is part of its attraction. Although it was not written as a spiritual journal it has some beautiful and profound insights. Above all, it reveals a very real and human man-made-monk.

Within weeks of the final entry in *The Sign of Jonas*, Father Louis began another, still unpublished, journal. It is a short one, dating from July 25, 1952, to March 3, 1953. Tom calls it the *New Journal*. It recounts in its opening pages his first significant journey outside the monastery. He went to meet Dom James Fox in Ohio to look at property that was being offered to Gethsemani for the establishment of a new monastery. Father Louis went with the idea that Dom James was going to name him superior of the new house, an idea Dom James disabused him of on the journey home. In fact, the monastery never was established. In this journal too Tom speaks about the first quasi hermitage he was given at Gethsemani, a shed in the woods just outside the enclosure walls, which he called Saint Anne's.

The next abstracted journal is a much more mature work. Tom's long-time friend and literary agent, Naomi Burton Stone, has declared this her favorite, and holds up a dog-eared copy to prove her assertion. *Conjectures of a Guilty Bystander* is worth going back to again and again.

Tom lays out the facts concerning the book in the preface:

The material is taken from notebooks I have kept since 1956 [this is being written in November 1965, though the material used leaves off at the end of 1963]. Though they are personal and conversational and represent my own version of the world, these entries are not of the intimate and introspective kind that go to make up a spiritual journal. There is certainly nothing private or confidential here.... Maybe the best way to characterize this book is to say that it consists of a series of sketches and meditations, some poetic, some literary, others historical and even theological, fitted together in a spontaneous, informal philosophic scheme in such a way that they react upon each other. The total result is a personal and monastic meditation, a testimony of Christian reflection in the mid-twentieth century, a confrontation of twentieth-century questions in the light of monastic commitment.

The journal reveals the rich variety of Father Louis's world, a cosmic person, full of tradition, poverty, and compassion. Russian mystics, space travelers, and oppressed blacks follow each other on the pages. Heisenberg and John of the Cross walk hand in hand. At times it is jolting. Tom dispatches his reactions to President John Kennedy's assassination in a couple of paragraphs (one can sense the great emotion beneath the words) and goes on with some rather abstruse albeit important theologizing with Anselm of Bec. Tom, seeing things from a vantage point shared with Saint Peter—for the monk is the latter-day upside-down martyr—turns the world right side up. Materialism is seen as "the opium of the people." The objectivity of conventual physics is as much a myth as the sun going around the earth.

Conjectures is rich, too rich to be summarized.

It was actually preceded by another "Conjectures of a Guilty Bystander." In an author's note to this eighty-three-page monograph, Tom tells the story:

The following pages are excerpts from notebooks and journals written about 1958–1961. They were typed up with a view to publication. On reflection, the idea of publication in this particular form was felt to be impractical at the present time. The book was abandoned when about half stencilled. The stencils remained on the shelf for some time. Before destroying them, I thought we might run off twenty-five copies for friends. Some of this material should eventually reappear in another form, and a book is planned with the same title. It will however be very different from this.

The author's note is dated April 1965. Most of the material that is found in this monograph is in fact found in *Conjectures*, though some exquisite pages have been left out, most notably the entry on Ernesto Cardenal, his novice and friend who has become so well known. Almost all of the forty entries have a political note about them, whether they speak of Moscow or the Congo, Central America or Kentucky, where Happy Chandler stands on the steps of the Gethsemani guesthouse and speaks of his "young friend, Thomas Merton." The tone is set in the first entry: "The real way to spiritual renewal is precisely where you would least expect it: in the field of political life. *It is here that all the crucial struggles and temptations of our time have to be faced.*"

While *Conjectures of a Guilty Bystander* was making its slow journey toward publication, Tom set about producing another abstracted journal for publication. This one he called *A Vow of Conversation*. It covers Tom's last days in the community, his last days as novice master, his gradual move toward the full eremitical life. The first entry is New Year's Eve, 1963; the last—September 9, 1965—is written a couple of weeks after he had left office and moved up to the hermitage on the Feast of Saint Bernard, August 20.

It is definitely a continuation of *Conjectures*, yet like *The Sign of Jonas*, it is closer to life. The little boy is still there: flying kites, sliding in the snow, tearing his pants on barbed wire; yet the poet catches beauty and expresses it in words that no child could ever find. The theologian hobnobs with Bultmann ("fantastically good"), Sartre, and Simone Weil, and the literary critic evaluates the contribution of Merleau-Ponty. What we see most vulnerably exposed in this journal is a hurt Tom, a misunderstood monk, a feared because powerful writer, who struggles with basic questions as to his proper stance while occasionally lashing out with masterly irony in the direction of authority, be it the Abbot General, his abbot, or Church institutionalism in general.

The polished typescript was completed not long before Merton's final journey East. Tom sent it to his agent and friend, Naomi Burton Stone, with a note acknowledging that he had been a bit strong in his reactions to Dom James, his abbot, and others and encouraging her to use her blue pencil liberally. Naomi would have, had Tom been there to OK her penciling. But Providence had it otherwise. Naomi did not feel free to change the text of the deceased monk. She thought it should be published as it stood. In the end she was outvoted by the other two members of the Merton Legacy Trust and the typescript remains unpublished. On the title page Tom had typed "for Doubleday," the publisher of *Conjectures of a Guilty Bystander*. On the copy in the Merton Center at Columbia University we find a note from Sister Therese Lentfoehr: "He *certainly meant this to be published!*" Perhaps if it had, the "revelations" in Monica Furlong's biography would have been first seen in their true context and would have been less upsetting than they were in her exaggerated presentation.

We have a final piece of abstracted journal that is still in an initial state of being abstracted. In September 1967, Tom began to dictate a manuscript drawing on his 1966 journal. In the typescript we are given more insight into Tom's way of constructing these abstracted journals for publication: "Now I am going to cheat a little bit here and insert some brand new material that I am just thinking of at the moment, that is to say October 5, 1967, which is not in the sequence of the journal, but which fits in with it, I believe. It just happens this morning that I have been reading. . . ."

In the last pages of this beginning—fifty-one pages, ending with the entry for April 2—Tom is preparing to enter the hospital and he waxes nostalgic. "Certainly the spirit of the community [at Gethsemani] is good and the place is blessed. There are good men here. It is a sincere and excellent community." Then he goes on to speak of individuals, coming to Dom James: "Dom James, with all his limitations and idiosyncrasies, has done much good in this community just by stubbornly holding everything together. He too is an extraordinary person, many-sided, baffling, often very irritating, a man of enormous, stubborn will, and who honestly in his own way really seeks to be an instrument of God. And in the end that is what he turned out to be, whether for good or for otherwise." Tom goes on to express his gratitude for his gradual entrance into a more completely eremitical life, concluding, "But there are greater gifts even than this, and God knows best what is for my good and for the good of the whole world. The best is what he wills."

It would have been most interesting if Tom had continued this editing of his journal. For it was just after this time, while he was in the hospital, that he met the young nurse with whom he shared a deeply felt experience of love. How would he have treated this personal and significant relationship and all the impact it had on his monastic life for some months and afterward in a selective and carefully edited journal?

I mentioned previously that are a couple of special journals. These are two journals Tom wrote in 1966 for this young nurse, whom I have called Marge. The *Midsummer Diary: Piece of a Small Journal. Or an account of how I once again became untouchable*, which was composed between June 15 and 25, 1966, is typed rather than handwritten and was delivered to Marge on the latter date. *Retrospect* was written for her a little later. In his personal journal Tom notes that these accounts written for Marge give "a more balanced view" of their relationship. Michael Mott handles this whole matter with delicacy and balance. I depend on him, who has studied the matter carefully, and I will add nothing further here. An inventory of Tom's journals would not be complete, though, without mention of these two significant pieces.

Finally, we must look at the journals that Tom wrote specifically in view of publication.

The first was written in May in 1965 in response to a request. Tom had a special affection for Latin America, and a growing interest in its poets and in its political affairs. When a South American editor asked him to describe a typical day in his life he responded with *Day of a Stranger*. The Spanish word *extrano* ("stranger") is not far from the English word *bystander*. This one-day journal was written in the period when Father Louis was moving more and more toward the hermitage. The piece was published two years later in English in *The Hudson Review* and in 1981 in an attractive booklet. All the threads of Tom's day from 2:15 A.M. till night are woven into a rich prose poem that makes us realize how much peace and war, ecology and desecration were a part of the fabric of the life of this concerned "stranger" whom we know as a brother.

Three years later, in the same month, under a new abbot, Tom made one of his first significant journeys. He was looking for a more remote site for his hermitage—too many were discovering the road that led up to the cinder block cottage behind Gethsemani Abbey. The journey gave him an opportunity to visit admired and admiring friends, the Trappistines of Redwoods Abbey in Northern California and the Benedictines of Christ in the Desert in New Mexico. The journal, entitled *Woods, Shore, Desert*, opens with notes for the conferences he will be giving the nuns, continues with an entry written on the first day of his trip, May 6, and goes on to May 30, a final entry written sometime after his return to Gethsemani. This journal is Tom near the end, but without the ponderous weight of Asia. It is Tom the poet and artist.

Father Louis has become an integrated mystic and conveys his cosmic and earthly contemplation in the way it can best be conveyed: through poetics and artistry. For the most part the text is poetry, prose poetry, pure poetry. We delight in it. Then suddenly we come upon seemingly bizarre passages about the comic art of Molière and we realize we are far from grasping the full scope of Tom's luxuriant and diverse personality.

The breadth of the context within which Merton experiences the creation is indicated in the prelude; it mentions the *Astavahra Gita*, a Russian Orthodox (Yelchaninov), Paschal, Saint Bernard, and Martin Luther King, among others. The text goes on to quote A. Stern, Unumuno, Theophane the Recluse, Francis Ponge, Lu T'ung, Krishna, Daumal, Poulet, Sidi Abdesalam, and Hisamatsu.

The text invites the question, At this point where is Thomas Merton in his personal journey toward freedom? We read: "Too much conformity to roles. Is it just a matter of brushing up the roles and adjusting the roles? A role is not necessarily a vocation. One can be alienated by role filling." And then: "Two daiquiris in the airport bar. Impression of relaxation. Even only in the airport, a sense of recovering something of myself that has been lost. On a little plane to Eureka, the same sense of ease, of openness."

Yet Tom remains the monk, concerned about monasticism—authentic monasticism, a monasticism of being: "Fatal emphasis [in the monastic life] on acquiring something.... Baloney!" It is a matter of being in relation. Social concern, ecological concern constantly crop up:

In our monasticism we have been content to find our way to a kind of peace, a simple undisturbed thoughtful life. And this certainly is good, but is it good enough? I, for one, realize now I need more.... There is need of effort, deepening, change and transformation.... I do have to break with an accumulation of inertia, waste, foolishness, rot, junk, a great need of clarification of mindfulness, or rather effort, need to push on to the great doubt. Need for the Spirit.

Father Louis places himself in the context of the Hindu states of life. Not *Brahmacharya*—the student in chastity; not *Grhastha*—the householder begetting; not the ultimate *Sanyasa*—total renunciation; but *Vanaprastha*—the forest life. "My present life. A life of privacy and of quasi-retirement. Is there one more stage?" In the end he finds himself and true freedom: "I am the utter poverty of God. I am his emptiness, littleness, nothingness, lostness. When this is understood, my life is His freedom, the self-emptying of God in me is the fullness of grace. A love for God that knows no reason because he is the fullness of grace. A love for God that knows no reason because He is God; a love without measure."

The *Alaskan Journal* as published is a compilation of material extracted from a journal Tom was writing in view of publication and material extracted from the private journal that was also used in editing *The Asian Journal*. It covers the brief period from September 17 to October 3, 1968. It has something of the flavor of *Woods, Shore, Desert*, but because it was not polished by Merton for publication it remains rather clipped, compressed, and impressionistic. It details his search for a site under the American flag, where he might more securely establish himself as a hermit. He loves the expansive beauty of Alaska and sees some places that might merit a second look as possible sites. His days are filled with conferences and visits — chats with barbers and bishops and contemplative nuns are recorded, yet he finds time for richly eclectic reading.

On October 15, as his plane lifts off from San Francisco, Tom begins a new journal for publication, *Asian Notes*. He will never complete it. At the same time he continues his personal journal of the period to which he has given the interesting title, *The Hawke's Dream*. And he will be keeping a pocket notebook for cryptic notes, various jottings, and poetic inspirations. From these three sources, Naomi Burton Stone, Brother Patrick Hart, and James Laughlin (the man who first published Tom's poetry and, like Naomi Stone, a member of the Merton Legacy Trust) produced the published *Asian Journal*. In *Asian Notes* Tom had put texts that interested him on one side of the notebook and his journal on the other. The editors brought this into a coherent text, used the private journal to fill in some gaps, and from the cryptic pocket notebook rescued the delightful "Kandy Express." It was a monumental labor of love.

An edited and in some part collated work, *The Asian Journal* does not have the literary perfection of *Woods, Shore, Desert*, but it does have the same staggering richness of content, blown large. And it has passages that are classic Merton. As we have seen, the conjunction of the very Catholic pilgrimage to Saint Thomas in Madras, the very-much-of-this-world pilgrimage to the bars of Colombo, and the barefoot approach to the Buddha at Polonnaruwa tells us, if we listen, to what extent this very human mystic did get it all together and experience a unity in all as coming incessantly from the one Source of all. And if this confluence tells us something of the expansiveness of his mystical sense it is the text from Polonnaruwa that tells us of the intensity, the depth, and the height of his realization. I end this brief survey of Thomas Merton's journals by inviting the reader to read again that passage, written but days before his transitus, which expresses as best poor human words can the end and goal of his journalizing and his journey.

The great smiles. Huge and yet subtle. Filled with every possibility, questioning nothing, knowing everything, rejecting nothing, the peace not of emotional resignation but of Madhyamika, of sunyata, that has seen through every question without trying to discredit anyone or anything— *without refutation*. . . . I was knocked over with a rush of relief and thankfulness at the *obvious* clarity of the figures, the clarity and fluidity of shape and line, the design of the monumental bodies composed into the rock shape and landscape, figure, rock and tree. . . . Looking at these figures I was suddenly, almost forcibly, jerked clean out of the habitual, half-tied vision of things, and an inner clearness, clarity, as if exploding from the rocks themselves, became evident and obvious. The queer *evidence* of the reclining figure, the smile, the sad smile of Ananda standing with arms folded. . . . The thing about all this is that there is no puzzle, no problem, and really no "mystery." All problems are resolved and everything is clear, simply because what matters is clear. The rock, all matter, all life, is charged with dharmakaya . . . everything is emptiness and everything is compassion. I don't know when in my life I have ever had such a sense of beauty and spiritual validity running together in one aesthetic illumination. Surely, with . . . Polonnaruwa my Asian pilgrimage has come clear and purified itself. I mean, I know and have seen what I was obscurely looking for. I don't know what else remains but I have now seen and have pierced through the surface and have got beyond the shadow and the disguise.

THE LETTERS

Tom's letters are in many ways more valuable than the journals for getting to know him, at least for the last years of his life. He was a generous correspondent, amply rewarding those who wrote to him. Evelyn Waugh, who had received a number of Merton's letters in connection with the editing of the British edition of *The Seven Storey Mountain*, had urged him "to put books aside [Waugh had done a rather savage job in editing Tom's autobiography and had even more to say in his letters to Tom], and write serious letters and to make an art of it." Unfortunately, it was only late in his life that Father Louis began regularly to make and keep carbons of his correspondence. For earlier periods we have to depend on what others have kept and have made available. Happily, this has proved to be a rich lode, although with significant lacunae, some of which we are aware. I had thrown away most of the letters I had received from Tom. The correspondence with Father Louis Bouyer, the liturgical scholar who took a lead in the days of the Second Vatican Council and before, has not yet been made available to the Merton Center. As I have noted before, Tom and Father Bouyer lived together for a brief time some years before either of them embraced the Catholic faith. Another rich collection, only a sampling of which has so far come to light, is Tom's long correspondence with Dr. Sergius Bolshakoff, the extraordinary Russian émigré. He is an Orthodox oblate of an Anglican Benedictine community who has lived much of his life in Cistercian monasteries.

The letters are the unedited, more spontaneous thinking of the author. They reveal great depth, practical spiritual wisdom, broad social concern, remarkable humor, amazing versatility. It is interesting to look at all the letters Tom writes in one particular day. Sometimes this will include as many as six long, serious epistles, each on a different subject. Tom typed rapidly (he typed most of his own letters and didn't worry too much about typos). His mind moved quickly; it was a rich and creative mind, put in motion by a compassionate heart. The negativity that arises in his letters comes out of the pain and anger caused by the violence that is being done to God's most beautiful plan for his children.

At the present time a competent and dedicated team is preparing an edition of Merton's letters. It will be extensive—five hefty volumes are presently planned—yet necessarily selective, for the store to draw from is immense. The first volume, prepared by the general editor, William Shannon, includes Tom's letters on religious experience and social concern. Robert Daggy, the curator of the Merton Collection in Louisville, is editing the second volume, which has Tom's letters to family and friends. Brother Patrick Hart is pulling together the letters of spiritual direction and those concerning renewal in the Church and in our order. This volume will include an interesting piece on his vocation, which Tom wrote for his first abbot, Dom Frederic Dunne. David Cooper, a young scholar at the University of California at Santa Barbara, will edit Tom's letters to literary figures and those that concern writing. In a final volume Monsignor Shannon will collect the notable letters that have not gotten into the first four volumes.

Although it would be impossible to survey this vast source, let us take a quick look at a particularly interesting collection, Tom's circular letters.

THE CIRCULAR LETTERS

It was in 1965 that Father Louis began to resort regularly to the use of a circular letter. As he explained to his recipients, he used it "to provide some way of answering all those I cannot answer personally." The response to his circulars was quite favorable. The recipients felt that a circular letter was better than no letter at all, and Tom's richly personal style was evident in these relatively short, newsy epistles.

His first form letter was mimeographed on a long sheet. It is candid and straightforward, with a certain sharpness creeping in as he shares with conciseness his thoughts on poetry, art, and politics. He does give an important statement in response to the question, "What does the contemplative life mean to me?" "It means finding the true significance of my life, and my right place in God's creation. It means renouncing the way of life that is led in the 'world' and which, to me, is a source of illusions, confusion and deceptions." He adds, "There are all kinds of ways to God, and ours is only one of the many." Then he goes on to say, "There are three gifts I have received, for which I can never be grateful enough: first, my Catholic faith; second, my monastic vocation; third, the calling to be a writer and share my beliefs with others. I have never had the slightest desire to be anything else but a monk, since I first came here."

At Christmas, Father Louis composed another letter, much shorter and more irenic, from his new perspective as a full-time hermit. (He does not use the label, he just says, "I am living in solitude.")

Christmas 1966, found him writing two circular letters, one dated "Christmas-New Year Letter 1966–1967" and the other, "Christmas Morning." In the first, he does call himself a hermit and uses it as one of a list of "alibis" for resorting to the mimeograph. In the opening paragraph of the second he tells us this "is my second attempt at a mimeograph letter this season. I junked the other because it was too full of alibis." The second is a much richer and more inspiring letter, but the first was not lacking in warmth:

I keep all your desires and needs in my heart, in my thoughts, in prayer, and especially in the Holy Eucharist. Let us be united in the silence of love and peace and in the deep expectation of that Spirit sent from the Father in Christ, the Spirit who cannot and will not fail us for He is ever present to those who desire Him. . . . May He bring you peace in your joy and joy even in anguish.

In the second letter he describes Christmas night in detail, speaks of the community with concern, and looks forward to an afternoon visit to Father Flavian's hermitage. Even with all this and some good spiritual advice—"Often in helping someone else we find the best way to bear with our own troubles"—a good third of the letter is devoted to the Vietnam war, "so desperately stupid and brutal." Tom concludes this letter, "Pray for freedom both for those who know they are not free and especially for those who think they are free and do not realize they are prisoners of dead ideas and prejudices."

With his recipients' encouragement, Tom went on to write thirteen more circular letters in the course of the two years that remained of his life. These letters are one and one-half to two pages long, except for the last two. A letter captioned "Fall 1968" is only a page long. The last letter, written from New Delhi and dated November 9, 1968, is a bit longer. Apart from this last one and the letter for Septuagesima Sunday (January 22) 1967, the letters have a more general dating, usually following the liturgical calendar: Lent 1967, Easter 1967, Pentecost 1967, Midsummer 1967, Advent-Christmas Letter 1967, New Year's Letter 1968, Pre-Lent Letter 1968, Easter Letter 1968, Paschal Time 1968, and Midsummer Letter 1968. These are the dates Tom assigned to them, though, as he notes in one case, the letters were sometimes written well in advance of the assigned date. Septuagesima Sunday no longer exists in the liturgical calendar of the Roman Catholic Church or of the Cistercian Order. It was the Sunday seventy days before Easter.

These letters have a particular value and importance. In them we find summed up those items Father Louis considered most significant during the last two years of his life—the things he wanted to share with his friends and companions on life's journey.

Less than two months after the two Christmas letters, Tom was again writing, opening his letter with "Several wrote that they liked my mimeographed Christmas letter and urged me to go on mimeographing more often." He hardly needed encouragement.

His Septuagesima letter is largely inspired by the event of Father Charles Davis's leaving the Catholic Church. The letter is strong and reasonable and a powerful witness to faith. Tom is sympathetic and compassionate—and urges this same response on the part of his readers—admitting candidly that "being a Catholic and being a monk have not always been easy." Noting Davis's criticisms of the abuse of authority in the Church, Tom writes strong words:

I do not think these criticisms were altogether baseless or unjust. The present institutional structure of the Church is certainly too antiquated, too baroque, and is often in practice unjust, inhuman, arbitrary and even absurd in its functioning. It sometimes imposes useless and intolerable burdens on the human person and demands outrageous sacrifices, often with no better results than to maintain a rigid system in its rigidity and to keep the same abuses established, one might think, until kingdom come.

He speaks frankly about his own reaction to all of this: "There have been bad days when I might have considered doing what Fr. Davis has done. In actual fact I have never seriously considered leaving the Church, and though the question of leaving the monastic state *has* presented itself, I was not able to take it seriously for more than five or ten minutes." It is noteworthy that Tom made this statement after his relationship with Marge.

Tom found his solution partly in Pascal: "He recognized the destructiveness of his own inner demon in time, and knew enough to be silent and to believe. And to love." And even more in a spirit of gratitude. "I owe too much to the Church and to Christ . . . the grace, love and infinite mercy of Christ in His Church. . . ." He acknowledged he could be as unreasonable and intolerant as any hierarch in the Church. He knew his need to be forgiven and the evangelical command not to judge and to forgive. "By God's grace I remain a Catholic, a monk and a hermit. I have made commitments which are unconditional and cannot be taken back."

The other element in this letter is that of friendship. "More and more I see the meaning of my relationship with all of you, and the value of the love that unites us, usually unexpressed." He talks about the difficulties of keeping up correspondence and of visits. "But there is such a thing as being united in prayer, or even thought and desire (if you can't pray) [Merton's corresponding friends included an immensely wide and varied audience, hence his parenthesis]. . . . the main thing is that we desire good for each other and seek within the limits of our power to obtain for each other what we desire."

Some homey details about life in the hermitage are included, updating his correspondents on the development of that aspect of his vocation. In the P.S. he tells of his recent and forthcoming publications.

A few weeks later Tom is again composing a letter. His supply of the last one is gone and Easter is still four weeks away. Moreover, he is about to go into the hospital for an operation on his elbow for bursitis and will have difficulty typing, so he is stocking up on a new letter. We see from this that Tom used these periodical letters to respond to mail as soon as it came in.

The burden of this Lenten letter is to respond, and respond strongly, to a couple of criticisms he had received about *Conjectures of a Guilty Bystander*. Some readers had felt he was too negative in regard to technology.

Tom makes it clear that what he was aiming at was the "myth that technology infallibly makes everything in every way better for everybody." The reality is that in our technological world we have wonderful means for keeping people alive and for killing people off, and they go together. "We rush in and save lives from tropical diseases, then we come along with napalm and burn up the people we have saved." Tom, of course, is writing at the time of the Vietnam war.

Tom sees the potential of technology and the obligation that flows from that: "Technology could indeed make a much better world for millions of human beings. . . . We have an absolute obligation to use the means at our disposal to keep people from living in utter misery and dying like flies." The fact is, Tom says, that we are not doing this. If we did use our immense technological expertise we could easily feed everyone and get the *12 percent* (Tom underlines that figure) who live in shantytowns into human habitation. Instead of creating work, labor-saving technology has left more and more unemployed and in abject poverty, enriching the few who have the capital.

The problem lies in the fact that human needs have been politicized. Tom is harsh in his judgement of President Johnson's great "War on Poverty": "It is a sheer insult to the people living in our Eastern Kentucky Mountains. All the attention and money are going . . . to enrich the big corporations that are making higher profits now than they ever did before." The answer lies in freeing technology from profit and power and using it for the people. Tom points to Church documents: *Mater et Magistra* and *Gaudium et spes*. He takes the documents very seriously. His social concern, even though he admits to his letter being a bit of a "tirade" with some "caricatures," flows from the teaching of the Church. He is a Catholic who takes the Gospel and the Church seriously and not selectively.

As he moves toward a concluding paragraph, Tom says he "thought it was worthwhile to make this point clear." I agree with him. We still need to hear today what he wrote more than fifteen years ago.

His final paragraph looks to the coming feast of Easter. Christians must not use this feast "to canonize earthly injustice and despair." The power and presence of the Resurrection is with us now to give us hope and enable us to make a difference that flows out of an "entire and total commitment to the Law of Christ which is the Law of Love."

This is a powerful letter.

Tom's Easter letter opens with the plaint, "Answering letters individually gets to be more and more of a problem." To underline the point he goes on to detail the work lying on his desk waiting to be done—it takes half a page to do this. The conclusion: carrying on an ordinary friendly correspondence is normally out of the question. "The life of a writing hermit is certainly not one of lying around in the sun or of pious navel gazing." Yet Father Louis affirms that for him meditation "is always the first thing of all because without it the rest becomes meaningless."

Tom goes on to recommend a new British publication, *Theoria to Theory*, even giving the address to subscribe. This magazine was to foster a dialogue between theologians and contemplatives on the one hand and scientists, philosophers, and humanists on the other, a dialogue that greatly interested Tom. He would, of course, make his own contribution to the journal, though he had little opportunity in the time that remained him to do much.

This shorter letter concludes with a rich meditation on the meaning of Easter, which evokes Blake's "Tyger, Tyger burning bright." Faith cannot be a response to statements or systems; it must be a response to persons and above all to the Person. We must surrender our ego mastery to His mastery. "There is no joy but in the victory of Christ over death in us: and all love that is valid has something of that victory. . . . Easter celebrates the victory of love over everything."

Tom again takes up his pen at Pentecost and joy erupts in the first sentence. The man who had first put him on the path to Gethsemani and made the priesthood possible for him, Dan Walsh, has just been ordained to the priesthood. Tom and many others see the ordaining of this elderly professor of philosophy without a lot of formalities as a sign that the Church is moving in the direction for which they have hoped—"less systematic and less rigid . . . something that leaves room for a more charismatic kind of religion." Tom went into Louisville to concelebrate with Father Walsh at the Carmelite monastery, a great celebration, "a great deal of very authentic joy."

The feast of Pentecost invited Tom to comment on the widespread desire for the *experience* of God and the Pentecostal movement. He is in support of these things, though he for his part has "always tended more toward a deepening of faith in solitude and . . . not seek special experiences."

Tom sees this spiritual awakening as part of a larger coming into fuller humanity, a liveliness that seeks greater participation in life. There will be no easing of the vocation crisis in religious orders, he feels, until the pyramid of authority gives way to more participation. His abbot, Dom James Fox, is in Citeaux for what will be his last general chapter, the first renewal chapter of the order. Tom notes that he and most around Gethsemani are doubtful whether anything special will come of the chapter. He is later proved to be right. Unfortunately, Tom did not live to see the chapter two years later, which would be a tremendous breakthrough thanks largely to his disciple and friend, the new abbot of Gethsemani, Father Flavian Burns.

Tom ends by speaking of a couple of signs of monastic renewal that are taking place outside the order: Dom Jacques Winandy's eremitical colony in Vancouver and a simplified foundation undertaken by some Cistercians on the Island of Bornholm, off Denmark. Both these endeavors continue quietly on, though Dom Winandy has had to retire to a hermitage nearer his native monastery in Belgium.

But we cannot rest on what others are doing: "As for me, the job of renewal boils down to the conversion of my own life."

In the middle of the summer Tom again writes his friends. In this letter he describes his current existence as "a marginal life in solitude." It opens with a curious account of a phone call Frank Sheed received in London at four in the morning from a man falsely claiming to be Merton. The burden of the letter is to explain his inability to write to all personally and at the same time to defend his continued production as an author in spite of his move into solitude. The reason for acting contrary to what is "favored officially by monks" are "that if you know something and do not share it, you lose your own knowledge of it" and that there are "some obligations to take up a position on this or that moral issue of general urgency."

We may or may not agree with Tom's reasons but we cannot help but be touched by the down-to-earth humility that marks this letter. In commenting on Sheed's experience he says, "There are people around who are crazy enough to think that if they pretend they are Thomas Merton it means something." Speaking of the development of his thought and insight he notes that he had been saying, "I don't know the answers, but I have some questions I'd like to share with you." He continues, "But now I am beginning to wonder if I even know the questions."

His concern for issues is very real and practical. This comes out in his request that those who would like to send him something should rather send it to the Quakers to relieve those suffering on both sides of the Arab-Israeli war. "I am trying not to appear to take either side in this senseless conflict, rooted in hate and misunderstanding and fomented by power politicians in the 'big' powers. But the refugees and homeless are refugees nevertheless, regardless of the merits and demerits of their 'side.'"

The only item of news in this letter is the announcement of the passing of Victor Hammer, who is well known because of his beautiful publications of Merton's works at the Stamperia del Santuccio. The brief, moving eulogy notes that Victor was painting the Resurrection when he fell ill.

There would be a considerable lapse of time before Tom again composed a missive for his friends. "This year has gone by fast."

It had had its sorrows. Two Columbia friends had died, Ad Reinhardt and John Slate. We would remember them from *The Seven Storey Mountain*. They are touchingly eulogized with the concluding thought, "Both died of heart attacks, and both were about my age. So if I suddenly follow their example I will be the last one to be surprised." Prophetic words!

His community has moved into their renovated church and

Father Louis is happy with it: "The Church of Gethsemani is an inspiring place to worship."

But he is not happy about everything. He goes on to explain again the need of these circular letters. He then speaks about the many invitations he receives for lectures, all of which he has had to refuse. "For me it would be a waste of time. I have better ways of communicating with the outside world." I think we are inclined to agree with the judgment but are suspicious as to whether Tom really holds it. The fact is that at this time he must refuse all invitations; Dom James will not allow any such exits. But a few months later when he has a new abbot, he is soon moving about and giving lectures.

Tom gives a shrewd appraisal of monastic renewal. In the long run he is hopeful. The renewal is going to move slowly. He likes what he sees among the young, the older ones "have had it," and as for the middle group, "They have a fifty-fifty chance, maybe." In fact, things have not worked out all that well for them. As he goes on, Tom sounds almost callous in the way he endorses what might be God's pruning plans.

He then whirls through a series of opinions on hippies, President Johnson, the Beatles, LSD, and the peace movement, ending with his sharpest words on the Vietnam war: "It is one of the greatest and most stupid blunders in American history, and the results are a disgrace." The letter ends with a call to live out of faith and love, a real struggle—but that, this Advent-Christmas letter says, is what Christmas is all about.

Shortly after, there is a New Year's letter—for the year Tom would not finish on earth. Besides the need to answer many letters, Tom has a special reason to write this one, and two special matters with which to deal. The first matter and the reason, is a *National Catholic Reporter* article by Coleman McCarthy, a former member of the Gethsemani daughterhouse in Conyers, Georgia. McCarthy had quoted Tom in ways that gave misleading impressions. The second matter is the forthcoming abbatial election.

Announcing Dom James's retirement, Tom acknowledges the abbot's contribution, especially in regard to the acceptance of the eremitic life into the order, the life the abbot was soon to embrace, but also for "all the other ways he built up our community and provided for it over more than eighteen years as Abbot."

In speaking of both of these matters Tom gives us his criteria for true monastic revival, a concern that looms large for him at that time. It "must focus on the reality of the monastic vocation to inner freedom, to creativity, to dialogue with other contemplative traditions." The new abbot was to be one who would "help us find creative solutions," who would lead the monks "fully in line with the charism of the monastic life and . . . enable us to fulfill our real function in the Church and the world today." For Father Louis, the monastic life, even though apart, is not a fully enclosed thing that is divorced from the Church and the world. He recognizes the difficulties, the challenges, the need for creativity. He agrees with McCarthy in many ways, but has a fuller, deeper, richer perspective.

A deep current of traditionalism flowed in this monk who underwent a rigorous Trappist formation in the 1940s. It crops out here in a promise to offer mass on the Epiphany for the recipients of this letter, "my dear friends, near and far [At the opening he speaks of receiving letters from Argentina, Pakistan, Brooklyn, India, and Japan—Brooklyn should be flattered by the company!], new and old, including all of you whom I have never met except through the courtesy of the U.S. mail—and the monastery mail room."

As he opens his Pre-Lent Letter, he speaks at greater length of his correspondents: students, those in the peace movement, men in service in Vietnam, fans, critics, inquirers, and those asking favors: "I am tempted to follow the example of Edmund Wilson with his famous printed card, on which he simply checks off the item he cannot supply." He is happy about the abbatial election of Father Flavian, "a young monk who, I would say, represents a middle position between conservatism and wild innovation."

Tom then turns his attention to those who have left the monasteries—their numbers are growing—especially those who are seeking to continue their basic monastic calling in some new and simpler way. He wants a real dialogue between them and the communities. He also wants to have an opportunity to live the eremitical life.

In this letter Tom marks the passing of another friend, "one of my oldest and best friends from Columbia," Sy Freedgood. It was Sy who had brought Bramachari into Tom's life, an important influence.

A new abbot—has the scene changed? Tom again rejects the idea of going on lecture tours. Again we wonder if he protests too much.

He does not yet know the freedom and responsibility he is to find under Father Flavian in regard to such matters. He speaks of two forthcoming books, which he sees will be misunderstood: *Cables to the Ace*—"may baffle a lot of readers ... obscure and indirect ... perhaps some of the younger ones will intuitively pick up some of the short-hand"—and *Faith and Violence*—"It will make a lot of people very mad." He concludes, "I have already said more than I intended."

The Easter letter of 1968 is written early, in fact a couple of weeks early, as the next letter indicates. There is snow on the ground. Requests are pouring in for him to come and talk (No wonder, after all the hints in his previous letters!) but all "have to be refused."

The bulk of this letter is taken up with a heavy, yet compassionate consideration of the question of the validity of the religious life. Tom speaks of his coming to Gethsemani. He found a life that had "something warped and inhuman about it ... hard, even unreasonably hard ... with a theology that is in some ways pathological." "We carry deep wounds that will prevent us from ever forgetting it." This is a statement that should be kept in mind when looking at the later Merton. It should not be forgotten when dealing with older monks who find it hard to move with some of the changes.

This negative side, though, has its counterbalance. For one thing, the basic values of medieval monasticism retain their validity. And one has to admit that "the injustices, the distortions, the inhumanities of secular life are incomparably worse (so we feel)." But most important, there is a sense of being really called by God. Gethsemani is for Tom a "sign of Christ." "Though we may have shed one illusion after another and gone deeper and deeper into the radical questioning of our life and our vocation, we have nevertheless elected to stay with it because we have continued to believe that this was what God asked of us." Tom admits he would be slow at this point to write extolling the monastic vocation as it then was, or to encourage anyone to enter. He rather points to the eschatological life proclaimed by Saint Paul. Sometimes when we have grown we forget that others are not where we are and still need and can profit by the things that helped us get where we are, even though now we can see the flaws in those things and can no longer be helped by them.

Before concluding the letter Tom lists (with addresses) some of the less accessible journals where his writings can be found: *The*

Catholic Worker, Monastic Studies, Unicorn Journal, Poetry, and the
Sewanee Review.

The next letter, dated Paschal Time 1968, again marks a personal
loss for Tom. This time it is his nearest living relative, his father's sister, who visited him at Gethsemani in 1964. She has died in a ship-
wreck, losing her own life after giving heroic help to others.

This personal loss is accompanied by another loss that was both
personal and national, if not universal—the tragic martyrdom of
Martin Luther King, Jr. King had been scheduled to visit Tom at
Gethsemani for a retreat. In spite of his passionate feelings about
the oppression of blacks in this country, Tom keeps to sober and
measured tones here. It is the measure of his grief and sense of loss
for a people and a nation. It is perhaps tempered by the fact that
President Johnson has decided not to run for another term.

Tom devotes a long paragraph to speaking about the importance
of dialogue between Christianity and Asian religions. He has just
been asked to write the introduction for an important book on Zen
Buddhism. He has been lecturing to the monks on Sufism. There is
depth to be found in these religions, the kind of depth Tom had
sought in coming to Catholicism. The renewal would be sadly mis-
taken if it sought to be relevant rather than deep. With Pentecost
approaching, Tom summons the Church to be "in every sense
prophetic and eschatological: a sign of Christ which is at once a sign
of supreme hope and a sign of contradiction."

The next letter, which is dated Midsummer 1968, again features
an assassination. Tom reflects on the murder of Robert Kennedy on
June 5 in the context of the sickness of a society, our society with its
growing tendency to harm and to destroy the very things we need
and admire.

In the face of this, Tom feels it necessary to defend or at least
explain the act of Dan and Phil Berrigan in their "extreme" and
"shocking" destruction of draft cards. At this distance it seems ludi-
crous that some people could be more upset about the destruction
of draft cards than they were about the destruction of the lives of the
draftees, sent to die in a meaningless war. For some people law and
order are more important than life itself. For his part, Tom opposes
the draft as needless and in fact being used for aggression. But he
thinks it should be abolished "by the normal political means."

These circular letters were the only way Tom could respond to the mounting volume of mail. In them, as he says at the beginning of this Midsummer Letter, he tries to answer some of the questions that have been addressed to him, though he feels he has "expressed too many opinions about everything and I wish I could really be silent on controversial events." He is tired of "clarifying." His stance is clear: "I am against war, against violence, against violent revolution, for peaceful settlement of differences, for non-violence but nevertheless radical change." The Gospel commitment has political implications. One cannot be for Christ and espouse a political cause that implies indifference to the needs of millions of human beings and even cooperates in their destruction.

In the opening paragraph of this letter Father Louis again speaks of refusing invitations. This is a bit less than candid. He speaks of being "quite busy during May" but says nothing of his trip to California and Arizona. No mention is made of the plans underway for the long and final journey East.

He comes clean in the Fall Letter: "I'd better make the whole thing clear." He outlines the plans that have been made: meetings to attend, monasteries to visit. And he expects more invitations. The reasons for all this, in spite of previous statements, are "the crucial importance of the time, the need for monastic renewal, the isolation and helplessness of our Asian monasteries, their constant appeals for help." Certainly, very valid reasons. Add to them his personal hope "to get in contact with Buddhist monasticism and see something of it first hand." He expresses a couple of times his concern about rumors and adds, "Needless to say, this [trip] is not anything unusual in the monastic life." In his monastic life? After the years of refusals?

The trip is to be "absolutely non-political." He will not go to Vietnam in spite of earlier hopes and plans. Tom questions whether the time for protests and petitions has now passed. For him it has. There is a certain completing about this September letter. There will be another from Asia, a much longer letter than any of these, and more formal—not quite the same friendly missive these have been.

The final circular was penned by Merton in New Delhi on November 9, a month before his death, two months into his journey. Unlike the others it is not a reply to mail, for he has not been getting much as he has moved along.

There were concerns and rumors that he would stay in Asia, that he would become a Buddhist. There is no indication of that in this letter. Indeed, it gives witness to the opposite: "I also hope I can bring back to my monastery something of the Asian wisdom with which I am fortunate to be in contact.... In my contact with these new friends I also feel consolation in my own faith in Christ and His indwelling presence."

The letter includes many colorful vignettes from India and Bangkok, though it is principally a report on his visit with the Dalai Lama, a monk who evidently made a strong impression on him. On the whole he found his "contacts with Asian monks have been very fruitful and rewarding." He had met a Cambodian Buddhist monk, an English Buddhist monk (Phra Khantipalo), and a Tibetan Buddhist, Chogyam Trungpa Rimpoche, who is now located in Colorado. "It is invaluable to have direct contact with people who have really put in a lifetime of hard work in training their minds and liberating themselves from passion and illusion." The Dalai Lama had asked Tom if there were possibilities of deep mystical life in our monasteries. Tom had replied "Well, that is what they are supposed to be for, but many seem to be interested in something else." It is with this sobering thought and challenge that Father Louis leaves us.

This brief survey of seventeen rich letters hardly gives a summary view of their varied contents. I think the letters demonstrate the extent and the depth of Tom's concerns, as well as the way he integrated them all into the fundamental stance of his monastic vocation—an understanding and sense of monasticism that is fuller than that of most monks. The many homey details found in the letters express the human dimension of his monastic living. Merton was a good letter writer. There is a warmth of friendship that is beautiful. Many friends are mentioned by name. The closings are oftentimes touching.

So let me close this section with one of his:

I appreciate the loyalty of so many old friends and the interest of the new ones. I shall continue to feel bound to all of you in the silence of prayer. Our real journey in life is interior: it is a matter of growth, deepening, and of an ever greater surrender to the creative action of love and grace in our hearts. Never was it more necessary for us to respond to that action. I pray that we may all do so. God bless you. With all affection in Christ.
                                                                —Thomas Merton

THE POETRY

There is another important source to which I confessedly cannot do justice, and that is Tom's poetry. It is fully available now in an ample volume put together by James Laughlin. In the poems we can get in touch with the deeper feelings and intuitions of faith that underlie his actions and his prose writings.

In the form letter Father Louis sent out in 1965 in response to the many letters he could not answer he speaks candidly about himself as a poet:

For those who ask what I think about poetry (I write poetry), there is an essay published in my *Selected Poems* which deals with poetry and the contemplative life. At one time I thought I ought to give up writing poetry because it might not be compatible with the life of a monk, but I don't think this anymore. People ask me how I write poetry. I just write it. I get an idea and I put it down, and add to it, and take away what is useless, and try to end up with some kind of a poem. A poem is for me the expression of an inner poetic experience, and what matters is the experience, more than the poem itself.

There are poems about his everyday life, beginning with the first prayer service of the day: "The Trappist Abbey: Matins" and then "After the Night Office—Gethsemani Abbey" (the night office is another name for matins). Then there is "Early Mass." "Hagia Sophia" takes us through the offices of the day and "The Blessed Virgin Mary Compared to a Window" brings us to the *Salve* after the final office. "Trappist, Working," complemented by the delightful "Cheese," tells us of his monastic labor and "The Trappist Cemetery—Gethsemani," of his leisure, for it was there that Tom spent much of his free time in his early days, when he could not yet go beyond the confines of the enclosure walls. Humor wins out again in "A Practical Program for Monks," and the monastic ideal glows in the long poem "Clairvaux." Later Tom would write of "Clairvaux Prison." And still later "Psalm 132: A Modern Monastic Revision":

> Ah! What a thrill it is for us all,
> descendents of Adam—
> by way of Cain and the Marquis de Sade—
> to dwell together
> and kick each other into heaven.

The free man could see the other side of things and the humor in it.

His poems take us through the annual cycle of feasts and seasons: "Advent," "A Christmas Card" and the later "Christmas as to People," "A Prelude: For the Feast of Saint Agnes" (January 21), "The Candlemas Procession" (February 2), "Lent," "The Annunciation" (March 25), "A Whitsun Canticle," "St. John's Night" (June 24), and so on.

Significant events receive their poetic commemoration. He chooses an anniversary to speak about his rebirth through Baptism: "On the Anniversary of My Baptism." Another commemorates his "second Baptism", entering upon the monastic way of life: "A Letter to My Friends." Perhaps his best-known poem is "For My Brother: Reported Missing in Action, 1943."

Father Louis's sense of closeness, even oneness, with those who have gone before, the saints in the Kingdom, is brought out in the many poems about the saints. There are poems for Saints Agnes, Paul, Lucy, Thomas Aquinas, Alberic, John the Baptist, Jerome, Paul the Hermit, Clement, Ailred, Clair, Malachy, Macarius the Younger, Maedoc, and, of course, several for the Blessed Virgin Mary. He has poems for others too, who are perhaps not so saintly, such as Dylan Thomas, Ernest Hemingway, James Thurber, Rilke, Seneca, Origen, Miguel Henandez, Edward Dahlberg, Machiavelli, and Adolf Eichmann. There is a beautiful poem on the death of Martin Luther King, Jr., and another for his friend Victor Hammer. We are brought into many movements of the great and compassionate heart of a monk who truly loves people and loves to be connected.

The meanings of the Scriptures for Tom are often revealed in his poetry, both the Old Testament (in poems such as "Rahab's House" and "Elias—Variations on a Theme") and the New Testament (in poems such as "Cana," "The Widow of Naim," the appropriately extravagant "Figures for an Apocalypse," and the more central "The Betrayal"). The confluence of the Christ mystery with his own life is brought out in "The Biography." But the poem by far the most revealing of himself is the epic completed on the eve of his final journey, "The Geography of Lograire." This is not an easy poem to read, but the time spent on it is amply rewarded with the insights it gives in regard to the mature monk, mystic, and humanist.

THE TAPES

In April 1962 the regular practice of taping Father Louis's conferences to the novices began. The reason for this was a pragmatic one. At that time the community of Gethsemani, as all Cistercian communities, was divided into two groups: the choir monks and the lay brothers. These latter lived out their dedication to God largely through labor, while retaining the basic monastic ideal of constant prayer. The brothers labored long hours each day for the good of the community. As late as 1951 the general chapter passed a law that the brothers were to be given at least one hour a day for spiritual reading. Besides their particular assigned roles in the monastic economy, there were a number of chores that fell into the generous hands of the brothers. One of these was the task of preparing the vegetables needed each day to feed the community. After their simple morning office or communal prayer of *Paters* and *Aves* (Our Fathers and Hail Marys), a period of mental or silent prayer, and a Communion mass and thanksgiving, the brothers would go to the scullery to prepare the vegetables. While they did this, they would recite the Rosary and then listen to some edifying reading. Understandably, in a situation where the brothers each had their own particular duties to perform in the community, often with pressing things to be done, there was a tendency to skip the vegetable peeling in order to get on with their own work, especially if the edifying reading was not that attractive.

Father Louis was popular, especially among the younger brothers. So Father Gerard Majella, the father master of the professed lay brothers, hit upon the idea of taping the conferences Tom was giving to the novices—at this time he was master of the choir novices and giving them usually four conferences a week—and playing the tapes at the vegetable peeling session in place of the reading. Of course there was more to it than this pragmatism. Father Gerard, who had been a novice under Father Louis, was eager for the brothers to share in the formation that Tom was giving the novices. In fact, at the end of that year, the separate novitiate for the lay brothers was abolished and the lay novices joined the choir novices to fully benefit by Tom's ministry as a spiritual master.

There is at Gethsemani a collection of 192 open reels of magnetic tape, each one usually recording four talks. The collection includes, besides the novitiate talks, the conferences that Tom gave on Sunday afternoon for all those in the community who wished to attend. The novitiate talks present an organized treatment of the topics basic to initial monastic formation—the vows, monastic history and spirituality, an introduction to Scripture and the Fathers, and so on, and the Sunday talks reflect Tom's current reading and embrace a wide spectrum of subjects. When Father Flavian was elected abbot in January 1968, Tom was talking about Sufism. Father Flavian asked him to continue the talks, urging him, though, to give talks on specifically Christian mysticism. Other topics that come up are racial justice, nuclear disarmament, world population, the computer revolution, Marxism, the death of Martin Luther King, Jr., Cardinal Suenens's controversial book on religious renewal, the Shakers, T. S. Eliot, Rilke, Greek tragedy, Epictetus and the Stoics, Faulkner, Joyce, Camus, and so on, in no particular order.

The series also contains a couple of the sermons Father Louis preached to the community in chapter on feast days. It was not the practice in those days to have homilies or sermons at mass in Cistercian monasteries, except on the occasion of monastic professions. The priests of the community, however, took turns giving sermons in the chapterhouse on the more important feasts, which were called feasts of sermon.

About three dozen of Merton's talks, organized into several series according to topic, have been edited and published by Electronic Paperbacks. Some of the tapes, in unedited form, have been distributed by a community of nuns to whom Tom had sent the tapes. Usually Tom's talk is preceded by informal remarks about things going on in the monastery. In the case of the talks to the novices these can be earthy homemaking details. At times Tom also relays to the monks news events that he has heard about from his correspondents (newspapers and news magazines were not yet available to the community) and comments on them. These off-the-record remarks (all of which have been edited from the published tapes) are perhaps the most interesting and revealing part of the tapes. They certainly demonstrate Father Louis's freedom to take a stand on issues both within the community and in regard to world affairs.

MERTON'S NOTES

It is unfortunate that the taping of Father Louis's conferences was started so late in his career. Even before he became master of the scholastics in 1952, he was giving some conferences to the novices. With his appointment to oversee the monastic formation of the young professed choir monks, he began to lecture regularly, his first course being on the Epistles of Saint Paul. For these courses he produced some lecture notes. These notes were largely outlines, complemented by a great many quotations from sources and significant authors. Tom's method, especially after he became more sure of himself and lost some of his early concern about covering all the matter he had prepared, was Socratic. He sought to coax out of his young men some of the wisdom that they themselves were not aware of possessing. This was the style of teaching his good friend Mark Van Doren used to such effect at Columbia, leaving a powerful and lasting impression on Tom. Tom was never too successful at it, but he was such a fascinating and humorous lecturer that he had little difficulty attracting and holding an audience.

These notes, besides the ones for the Pauline course, include volumes for "Monastic Orientations" and "An Introduction to Cistercian Theology." There are also notes from a course he gave for the priests of the monastery in 1961–1962, "An Introduction to Christian Mysticism." In the biographical writings on Merton I have never seen his notes used as source. Yet in this last set, the notes on Christian mysticism, there is found, as we have seen, a key to an important step in the evolution of Thomas Merton as a true contemplative and a spiritual master.

Bibliography of Selected Works by Thomas Merton

The following list of books by Thomas Merton contains the major and most readily obtainable works. For those who require a more complete list, see the comprehensive bibliography prepared by Marquita Breit and Robert Daggy (New York: Garland Publishers, 1986.)

The Ascent to Truth. New York: Harcourt Brace, 1981.
The Asian Journal of Thomas Merton. Edited by Naomi Burton Stone, Patrick Hart, and James Laughlin. New York: New Directions, 1973.
A Catch of Anti-Letters. By Thomas Merton and Robert Lax. Kansas City, MO: Sheed, Andrews & McMeel, 1978.
The Climate of Monastic Prayer. Kalamazoo, Mich.: Cistercian Publications, 1973.
The Collected Poems of Thomas Merton. New York: New Directions, 1980.
Conjectures of a Guilty Bystander. New York: Doubleday, 1966.
Contemplation in a World of Action. New York: Doubleday, 1973.
Contemplative Prayer. New York: Doubleday, 1971.
Disputed Questions. New York: Farrar, Straus & Giroux, 1960.
Eighteen Poems. New York: New Directions, 1985.
Faith & Violence: Christian Teaching & Christian Practice. Notre Dame, Ind.: University of Notre Dame Press, 1968.
The Hidden Ground of Love Letters. Edited by William H. Shannon. New York: Farrar, Straus & Giroux, 1985.
"The Inner Experience" in *Cistercian Studies*, 18–19. Trappist, Kentucky: Gethsemani, 1983–1984.
Introductions East & West: The Foreign Prefaces of Thomas Merton. Edited by Robert E. Daggy. Greensoro, N.C.: Unicorn Press, 1981.
The Last of the Fathers: Saint Bernard of Clairvaux & the Encyclical Letter, Doctor Mellifluus. New York: Harcourt Brace, 1981.
Life & Holiness. New York: Doubleday, 1963.
The Literary Essays of Thomas Merton. Edited by Patrick Hart. New York: New Directions. 1981.
The Living Bread. New York: Farrar, Straus & Giroux, 1956.
Love & Living. Edited by Naomi Burton Stone and Patrick Hart. New York: Farrar, Straus & Giroux, 1979.
The Monastic Journey. Edited by Patrick Hart. New York: Doubleday, 1978.

My Argument with the Gestapo: A Macronic Journal. New York: New Directions, 1975.

The New Man. New York: Bantam Books, 1981.

New Seeds of Contemplation. New York: New Directions, 1972.

No Man Is an Island. New York: Harcourt Brace, 1978.

The Nonviolent Alternative. New York: Farrar, Straus & Giroux, 1980.

Original Child Bomb. Greensboro, N.C.: Unicorn Press, 1983.

Raids on the Unspeakable. New York: New Directions, 1970.

Seasons of Celebration. New York: Farrar, Straus & Giroux, 1978.

The Secular Journal. New York: Farrar, Straus & Giroux, 1959.

Seeds of Destruction. New York: Farrar, Straus & Giroux, 1964.

"St. Aelred of Rievaulx and the Cistercians" in *Cistercian Studies* 20–21. Trappist, Kentucky: Gethsemani, 1985–1986.

Selected Poems. New York: New Directions, 1967.

The Seven Storey Mountain. New York: Harcourt Brace, 1978.

The Sign of Jonas. New York: Harcourt Brace, 1979.

The Silent Life. New York: Farrar, Straus & Giroux, 1975.

Six Letters with Boris Pasternak. Lexington, KY: The King Library Press, 1973.

The Spirit of Simplicity. Trappist, KY: Gethsemani, 1948.

Thomas Merton on St. Bernard. Kalamazoo, MI: Cistercian Publications, 1980.

A Thomas Merton Reader. Ed. by Thomas McDonnell. New York: Doubleday, 1974.

Thoughts in Solitude. New York: Farrar, Straus & Giroux, 1976.

The Waters of Siloe. New York: Harcourt Brace, 1979.

The Way of Chuang Tzu. New York: New Directions, 1969.

What is Contemplation? Springfield, IL: Templegate, 1981.

Wisdom of the Desert. New York: New Directions, 1970.

Woods, Shore, Desert: A Notebook, May 1968. Albuquerque: University of New Mexico Press, 1983.

Zen & the Birds of Appetite. New York: New Directions, 1968.

Also published by Continuum

M. Basil Pennington
ON RETREAT WITH THOMAS MERTON
"This is a challenging book. We are led to see God in all and through all with Merton as our guide."
—Sister Felicity

Thomas Keating
CRISIS OF FAITH, CRISIS OF LOVE
"Under the influence of Christian mystics such as St. John of the Cross, Keating weaves a narrative account of spiritual development that will be of interest to spiritual directors and seekers."
—*Booklist*

Henri J. M. Nouwen
MINISTRY AND SPIRITUALITY
REACHING OUT, THE WOUNDED HEALER, CREATIVE MINISTRY
Three classic works brought together in a beautiful gift edition.

William A. Meninger
THE LOVING SEARCH FOR GOD
CONTEMPLATIVE PRAYER AND *THE CLOUD OF UNKNOWING*
"A powerful, even stunning job of explaining contemplative prayer...an excellent guide for anyone interested in deepening his or her Christian prayer life." —*Publishers Weekly*

William A. Simpson
FROM IMAGE TO LIKENESS
THE CHRISTIAN JOURNEY TO GOD
"This down-to-earth book is an invitation to the delight of love of God and creation. With deceptive simplicity, humor, and clarity, the author translates a traditional approach of the mystical path into available, user-friendly language."
—Jean Dalby Clift

David G. Hackett
THE SILENT DIALOGUE
ZEN LETTERS TO A TRAPPIST ABBOT
"A clearly written and important book for anyone interested in Zen and Catholicism." —*Library Journal*

Brian C. Taylor
SETTING THE GOSPEL FREE
EXPERIENTIAL FAITH AND CONTEMPLATIVE PRACTICE
"An ideal example of the new, but very old synthesis that always renews Christianity from the bottom up and from the inside out. Brian Taylor's reaching is clear, faith-filled, and grounded in centuries of experience." —Richard Rohr, O.F.M.

Nan C. Merrill
PSALMS FOR PRAYING
AN INVITATION TO WHOLENESS
"[Merrill] has reworked the *Book of Psalms* in a loving, contemplative manner....Merrill's psalms evoke that deep sense of reverence and soul-stirring dialogue with the divine." —*Library Journal*

THE COMPLETE BOOK
OF CHRISTIAN PRAYER
A beautifully arranged treasury of 1200 classic and contemporary prayers from over 560 authors and sources, more than half of whom are from this century.